NATIVE FOODS

FOOD AND FOODWAYS

SERIES EDITORS:
JENNIFER JENSEN WALLACH
AND MICHAEL WISE

OTHER TITLES IN THIS SERIES

Race and Repast: Foodscapes in Twentieth-Century Southern Literature

Food Studies in Latin America Literature: Perspectives on the Gastronarrative

The Provisions of War: Expanding the Boundaries of Food and Conflict, 1840–1990

Rooted Resistance: Agrarian Myth in Modern America

A Rich and Tantalizing Brew: A History of How Coffee Connected the World

To Feast on Us as Their Prey: Cannibalism and the Early Modern Atlantic

Forging Communities: Food and Representation in Medieval and Early Modern Southwestern Europe

Inventing Authenticity: How Cookbook Writers Redefine Southern Identity

Chop Suey and Sushi from Sea to Shining Sea: Chinese and Japanese Restaurants in the United States

Aunt Sammy's Radio Recipes: The Original 1927 Cookbook and Housekeeper's Chat

Mexican-Origin Foods, Foodways, and Social Movements: Decolonial Perspectives

Meanings of Maple: An Ethnography of Sugaring

The Taste of Art: Food, Cooking, and Counterculture in Contemporary Practices

Devouring Cultures: Perspectives on Food, Power, and Identity from the Zombie Apocalypse to Downton Abbey

Latin@s' Presence in the Food Industry: Changing How We Think about Food

Dethroning the Deceitful Pork Chop: Rethinking African American Foodways from Slavery to Obama

American Appetites: A Documentary Reader

Native Foods

AGRICULTURE, INDIGENEITY, AND SETTLER COLONIALISM IN AMERICAN HISTORY

MICHAEL D. WISE

The University of Arkansas Press
Fayetteville
2023

978-1-68226-238-2 (paper)
978-1-61075-803-1 (electronic)

27 26 25 24 23 5 4 3 2 1

Manufactured in the United States of America

∞ The paper used in this publication meets the minimum requirements of the American National Standard for Permanence of Paper for Printed Library Materials Z39.48–1984.

Library of Congress Cataloging-in-Publication Data

Names: Wise, Michael D., author.
Title: Native foods: agriculture, indigeneity, and settler colonialism in American history / Michael D. Wise.
Other titles: Agriculture, indigeneity, and settler colonialism in American history
Description: Fayetteville: The University of Arkansas Press, 2023. | Series: Food and foodways | Includes bibliographical references and index. | Summary: "Native foods are ubiquitous in America, but they often go unrecognized and unidentified. So too do the countless farms, gardens, and other places created by Native American people to feed and nourish their families and communities over generations. Over the last five centuries of settler colonialism, this inconspicuousness of Native American food and agriculture has helped configure Americans' imaginations of food and agriculture in ways that require critical identification. Drawing attention to this issue, Native Foods brings to bear approaches from the fields of food studies and Indigenous studies to explore how biophysical patterns of settler-colonial land use have worked as narrative frames for structuring historical views of Native agriculture. Following the lead of Indigenous food sovereignty advocates and activists, the book emphasizes the presence and persistence of Native American cuisine and documents how Native foods and agricultural techniques were never "lost" but only obscured by the peregrinations of colonialism, capitalism, and various other historical transformations"—Provided by publisher.
Identifiers: LCCN 2023013579 (print) | LCCN 2023013580 (ebook) |
ISBN 9781682262382 (paperback) | ISBN 9781610758031 (ebook)
Subjects: LCSH: Indians of North America—Food—History. |
Indians of North America—Agriculture—History. | Food sovereignty—United States. |
Settler colonialism—United States.
Classification: LCC E98.F7 W57 2023 (print) | LCC E98.F7 (ebook) |
DDC 970.004/97—dc23/eng/20230425
LC record available at https://lccn.loc.gov/2023013579
LC ebook record available at https://lccn.loc.gov/2023013580

FOR MOM AND DAD

CONTENTS

ACKNOWLEDGMENTS

During the years it took to write this book I relied on the patient support of many friends, family members, and colleagues, but only Jennifer Jensen Wallach stepped into all of those roles at once, so it seems appropriate to acknowledge her first. A decade ago, when she invited me to contribute a volume to her new Food and Foodways series, I had no idea that we would soon become best friends, nor that we would start a family together, nor that I would eventually become coeditor of this book series. I am grateful to Jen for her love, her hard work, her generosity, and her intellectual companionship. I can't think of anyone from whom I've learned more. My sincerest admiration and thanks also go to D. S. Cunningham, editor-in-chief of the University of Arkansas Press, who navigated this manuscript through peer review and revision with rigor and professional elegance. Others at the press deserve acknowledgement for their friendship and support, including Mike Bieker, David Cajías Calvet, Jenny Vos, and the late Larry Malley. I owe a large debt of gratitude to Carol J. Adams, who kept me motivated to finish this project, in part, by modeling for me her own writerly practices. My colleagues at the University of North Texas, past and present, also inspired my work through informal conversations, especially Chelsea Ball, Katy Beebe, Guy Chet, Danielle Dumaine, Connie Hilliard, Sandra Mendiola Garcia, Kerry Goldmann, Manny Grajales, Harland Hagler, Mike Leggiere, Vojin Majstorovic, Rick McCaslin, Alex Mendoza, Keith Mitchener, Al Mierzejewski, Rachel Moran, Todd Moye, Chad Pearson, Wesley Phelps, Diana Reinhardt, Walt Roberts, Robert Smith, Todd Smith, Nancy Stockdale, Harold Tanner, Audrey Thorstad, Chris Todd, J. L. Tomlin, Andrew Torget, Olga Velikanova, Geoff Wawro, Courtney Welch, Kelly Wisecup, Steve Wolverton, and Priscilla Ybarra. I would like to thank Tracey Deutsch and Psyche Williams-Forson for inviting me to share some of my early work at the Intersectionality and Food Studies symposium hosted at the University of Minnesota in 2019 as well as the symposium's many participants who provided me with helpful and supportive feedback. Ruth Ann Elmore, Neil Foley, Andy Graybill, and Sherry Smith also deserve thanks for welcoming me to the Clements Center when I arrived in Dallas ten years ago. The Food Across Borders symposium that Melanie DuPuis, Matt Garcia, and Don Mitchell hosted in 2014 also helped equip my work with some important critical approaches for which I am grateful.

One of the things that I viscerally came to learn as I wrote this this book is the importance of family, not only in terms of the love and nourishment that a family can provide but also in terms of the deep influences that the quotidian practices of family life can have on one's scholarship. Becoming a parent has reconfigured my worldview in many ways, but among them, living, learning, and playing with my son, Augie, has enriched my work with more curiosity, more analytical empathy, and more sympathy. The stakes seem higher. So, thank you, Augie, for helping me grow. And thanks also to Carolyn S. Briggs, David Briggs, Gaby Gollub, Aaron Jensen, David Jensen, Sara Jensen, Jamie Jensen, Tristan Mehlin, Iris Mehlin, and Brighid Wise. Debbie and Don Wise, my mom and dad, grew up on farms separated by a country mile. Although I grew up in the city, they still taught me how to grow my own food and encouraged me to ask hard questions about the everyday sacrifices that agricultural workers make so that many of us can live. For their own love and sacrifices, I dedicate this book to them.

NATIVE FOODS

INTRODUCTION

Maxidiwiac's Farm

Native foods are ubiquitous in America, but they often go unrecognized and unidentified. So too do the countless farms, gardens, and other places created by Native American people, both in the past and in the present, to feed and nourish their families and communities over generations and centuries. To a certain extent, the inconspicuousness of Native American food and agriculture is discursive, explained by patterns of language that first emerged with the colonial appropriation of North America by Europeans more than five centuries ago. The word *corn*, for instance—a generic English term for any type of edible grain that could be harvested and stored—leapt from the lips of colonists who were too impatient to consider more precise distinctions for the novel vegetable grown by Native farmers in an array of colors and cultivars. The linguistic act of encoding corn as *corn* reduced those complexities and helped to make it recognizable as an English possession. Language, though, is not the only domain in which expressions about Native food and its milieu of activities have been voiced or silenced. Because names become embodied in the places and substances to which they refer, renamings are accompanied by reworkings of the biophysical world, of the ecological mechanisms that sustain human life, the laws and customs that provide and deny sustenance, and the habits that convey taste and disgust. Over time, dominant patterns of food and agriculture become ways of seeing the landscape, determining what gets altered, what gets preserved, what gets forgotten. Embodied in our guts as well as in our sensations of place—and of self and of other—food and agriculture exist as narrative frames that structure the stories historians write about the past. These stories, in turn, help shape the range of culinary and agricultural futures that can be envisioned and enacted. Five centuries of settler colonialism have configured Americans' imaginations of food and agriculture in ways that require critical identification, and that is the task with which this book is concerned.

A good starting place is Maxidiwiac's farm, a now invisible monument of Native food history. Submerged beneath the waves of Lake Sakakawea, inundated since 1950 by the floodwaters of the Garrison Dam, Maxidiwiac's farm once rested in a bottomland field at the center of Hidatsa and Mandan agriculture on the Northern Plains. Maxidiwiac was sixty-seven years old when her son, Edward Goodbird, introduced her to a graduate student from the University of Minnesota named Gilbert L. Wilson. Over the next several years, Maxidiwiac described her lifetime's worth of knowledge about Hidatsa agriculture and culinary practices for Wilson's dissertation research. Goodbird worked as Wilson's interpreter, translating his mother's ethnography from Hidatsa into English. In 1910, their work earned Wilson his doctorate in anthropology, the first ever awarded by the University of Minnesota. Today, a revised version of Wilson's dissertation is a classic work of ethnographic literature commonly published with the title *Buffalo Bird Woman's Garden*.[1]

Contrary to popular expectations of so-called Plains Indians, Maxidiwiac's life revolved around farming—not hunting. She and her Native neighbors depended for their livelihoods on raising crops of beans, corn, squash, sunflower, and tobacco on alluvial soils that could be easily worked by hand and that were annually enriched with organic matter deposited by the river. They were well fed and traded their agricultural surpluses with neighboring Native communities to acquire other food items to suit their individual preferences and tastes. This work had gone on for generations before Maxidiwiac's birth in 1839. After her mother died of smallpox when Maxidiwiac was four years old, Maxidiwiac was raised by her grandmothers, and they taught her how to cultivate, plant, harvest, cook, and keep seeds. Lovingly translated by her son, Maxidiwiac's detailed descriptions of these practices convey a world of Hidatsa food and agriculture that thrived on the Missouri River bottomlands. Part gardening memoir and part gardening guidebook, *Buffalo Bird Woman's Garden* is a remarkable document relied upon by many people today who wish to learn more about the history of Native seed-keeping and other food and agricultural practices.

Before her emergence as a famed ethnographic subject, however, Maxidiwiac's agricultural labor also provided the seeds of global agribusiness in ways that go unremembered in Wilson's dissertation. In 1883, Maxidiwiac's husband, Son of Star, gave a pouch of Hidatsa white beans she had grown to the founder of the Pioneer Seed Company, a recent migrant to the Dakota Territory named Oscar H. Will.[2] The result of centuries of Hidatsa seed saving and seed selection, these beans were tuned for taste, uniformity, and horticultural productivity. Will grew his own seed stock from the beans on his company's farm near present-day Bismarck, North Dakota, and marketed the legume worldwide as the great northern bean. He had similar commercial triumphs with several Hidatsa varieties of corn, including some of the original parent stocks for the corn hybridization experiments conducted by his friend, Henry A. Wallace, in the 1920s. Wallace went on to serve Franklin Delano Roosevelt's administration, first as FDR's secretary of agriculture then as his third-term vice president, and spent a long political career in close communication with world leaders and emerging global business opportunities. After the Second World War, Wallace's and Will's heirs merged their seed businesses into the Pioneer Hi-Bred Seed Company, which led the development of corn and bean seeds engineered for industrial production for the rest of the twentieth century, producing the first soybeans transgenically modified for resistance to the Monsanto Corporation's glyphosate-based herbicide, Roundup. The company that used Maxidiwiac's beans and seed corn to revolutionize modern agriculture is now a wholly owned subsidiary of Corteva Agriscience, the world's largest agribusiness firm.

If decades of merger and acquisition have served to somewhat obscure these Hidatsa contributions to agricultural bioscience, then so too have the opaque waters of Lake Sakakawea, the second-largest man-made lake in the United States. At 480 square miles in area, but averaging only two miles in width, Sakakawea drowned Hidatsa bottomland farms all along the Missouri River, from just north of Bismarck to the river's confluence with the Yellowstone River near the Montana border. Downstream, the lake's immediate neighbor, Lake Oahe, is another federal impoundment marginally larger by area than Sakakawea, covering an additional 580 square miles of river bottomlands. And downstream from Oahe, three smaller but still enormous reservoirs bring the total extent of flooded bottomland fields to more than eight hundred thousand acres.

Authorized by Congress in 1944, during Wallace's tenure in the Roosevelt administration, these dam projects on the upper Missouri River submerged a heartland of Native American agriculture, flooding out the farms and commercial centers of several major Native communities and forcing the relocation of thousands of Assiniboine, Arikara, Dakota, Hidatsa, Lakota, Mandan, and other Native people. The dams were built to control seasonal flooding in Omaha, Nebraska; Sioux City, Iowa; and Kansas City, Missouri. But floods cannot really be controlled, only diverted, and along a river the sole solution for preventing flooding in some places is to permanently flood others. In spite of intense political and legal opposition, the plan approved by Congress was one that permanently flooded Indian land. Carried out in a rare episode of cooperation between the US Bureau of Reclamation and the US Army Corps of Engineers, the Pick-Sloan plan—named after the regional directors of these rival agencies—transformed more than a thousand square miles of some of America's most ancient and fertile farmland into a series of flood-control reservoirs. The effects were profound.[3] Discussing these dams' effects on the Sioux, for instance, in 1982 Lakota scholar and activist Vine Deloria Jr. described Pick-Sloan as the "single most destructive act perpetrated against an Indian tribe in this century."[4]

On a smaller scale, similar hydrological projects affected Native communities across the United States during the mid-twentieth-century peak of dam building.[5] Turning rivers into lakes recast entire flows of energy away from Native people and the diverse bottomland agricultural systems that they had built and invested in over centuries. It reoriented those flows toward a global agricultural system that prioritized the production and export of livestock and commodity crops. The river water that once nourished Maxidiwiac's farm on its meandering descent down the continent is now piped up from lakeside pump stations to the prairies, where it irrigates hay crops of imported alfalfa for feeder cattle.

The inundation of Maxidiwiac's farm serves as a metaphor for Native foods in America, which form the ubiquitous core of modern American food and agriculture and yet have been mostly erased, made invisible, or at least obscured, by historical processes that have occurred over the last five centuries. In my role as a university history professor, I find that my students—as well as my scholarly colleagues—often do not know much at all about Native American food history. For many of us, this unfamiliarity stems in part from our own limited opportunities for hands-on engagement with agriculture in our daily lives. At least for myself and for many of my students and colleagues residing in the suburbs of the Dallas-Fort Worth metroplex, we can eat food and study food history without substantially immersing ourselves in any agricultural processes. In my classes I try to amend this—to the extent that I can, at least—by sharing seeds and plants from my own garden and encouraging students to see what new historical insights they might glean from trying to grow something for themselves to eat. A few years ago, for instance, while teaching a three-hundred-seat section of the introductory course on early American history, I passed around a large paper grocery bag of I'itoi onion starts that I had dug and divided from an onion bed in my backyard.[6] This shallot-like heirloom multiplier onion from the Tohono O'odham Nation has been cultivated and propagated for more than four hundred years. My students were eager to take home and plant some of these unique, peppery-flavored onions after enduring a long lecture about the history of Native southwestern agriculture. I had been saving these onions for my students for a few months, and, sitting around in the bag, the bulbs had begun to sprout, their green shoots arching skyward. All the same, over the next few days and weeks I responded to emails from students asking me to clarify which side of the onion should be planted up.

While certainly meaningful, confusion about how to sprout and grow vegetables is not the only, or even primary, impediment for understanding the history of Native foods. On a much deeper level, many of us have been socialized, in the United States at least, into a particular way of seeing the landscape that frames agriculture as a possession of settler colonialism and not of Native peoples. In fact, food and agriculture are two of the primary lenses through which Americans have long been trained to see the world from a settler-colonial perspective, a logic of erasure and replacement that seeks to confine Native lives to the past in order to legitimize the dispossession of Native land and labor in the present. The effect of this logic has been to continually render Indians as people "*in* America, but not *of* America," as the Ojibwe novelist and literary critic David Treuer has recently put it.[7] To a large extent, this alienation emerged through—and is sustained by—legal structures dating to the early colonial era that identified white, able-bodied, heterosexual men as the globe's fundamental property-owning subjects.[8] As the legal scholar Cheryl I. Harris argued three decades ago, the emergence of property ownership in the American colonies not only relied on the seizure and dispossession of Native lands but also rested on a legal system in which "possession—the act necessary to lay the basis for rights in property—was defined to include only the cultural practices of whites."[9] Throughout American history, white identity—as well as notions of white property ownership—has been deeply invested in cultural practices that link the

American landscape with white proprietorship, "the farm" serving as one particularly potent, primordial site. In this respect, both conversations about food and agriculture and the biophysical transformations that have altered America's food and agricultural systems function, as they have from the moment of colonial encounter onward, as powerful forces for affirming Native dispossession today.

Focusing on Native food as category of critical analysis reveals its significance as a site of affective tensions that have long framed settler-colonial history. These tensions work as "structures of feeling," as Raymond Williams once called them, reinforcing the sensibilities of settler colonialism by obscuring Native food and agriculture in ways that resist systematic interpretation.[10] As literary critics and cultural anthropologists have demonstrated time and again, historical narratives play a major role in sustaining these structures of feeling by portraying progress and transformation as inherent features of settler colonialism, while at the same time marking the Native American past as unknowable—as a "prehistory" akin to a state of nature.[11] These narrative operations do not only occur in the discursive realm, however. They happen also through unscripted practices that punctuate daily life, the "excruciating workings of business as usual," as Jean O'Brien pithily described them.[12] The historical assumptions of settler colonialism are enacted in physical practices, and through the transformations wrought by those practices, they become embodied in the biophysical world in ways that suggest their timelessness and universality. Agricultural activities assert this naturalness as they transform nature on the landscape scale. And, in the public and private spaces where we cook, chew, and metabolize these flows of energy, our culinary activities and our processes of digestion harness this nature of settler colonialism to the nature of our own bodies. For all these reasons, Native foods have long presented a compelling medium of expression for stories about land, labor, ownership, interconnection, and justice; and histories of Native foods have served as narrative forces bearing pressure in ongoing struggles for the recognition of Native sovereignty, both in the United States and elsewhere throughout the colonized world.

Native activists have long recognized these connections between food and community self-determination, and a growing body of scholarship has highlighted the necessity of approaching Native foods from Indigenous-centered perspectives of food sovereignty rather than from the perspective of food security that have driven settler-colonial public policy for centuries.[13] A multitude of critical voices have debated the appropriateness of using the colonial concept of sovereignty to articulate Native self-determination.[14] However, one common insight to emerge from these conversations is that a focus on Native people and communities as food producers—and not just food consumers—is necessary for decolonizing discussions about Native food security.[15] For instance, for generations, the colonial solutions for alleviating "Indian hunger" and other issues of unequal food access have served to further subordinate Indigenous communities as the recipients of American agriculture and worked to disavow the Native origins of American agriculture in the process. The result is that when it comes to the mainstream narratives of Native foods in America, centuries of colonial inertia have embedded a set of myths into the American historical imagination that reference Native people as the recipients of agriculture, rather than its providers. Following the lead of the activists, scholars, and allies aligned with the movement for Indigenous food sovereignty, my approach in this book is to crack these myths apart by reframing Native food history from the standpoint of production, starting with agriculture in the field and, whenever possible, carrying the stories through to the kitchen table.

Over the course of my career as a historian of food and agriculture in America, I have encountered four primary myths that have buttressed, for centuries, the imperatives of settler colonialism and white supremacy. The first myth is that most Native communities did not practice agriculture. The second is that Native people were primarily hunters. The third is that Native people were usually hungry, leading to the fourth myth that Native people, because of this persistent hunger, did not care about flavor and therefore never developed taste or cuisine.

To even call these *myths* in the first place is a little imprecise, since their power does not really exist so much in the form of fables or folk stories but in their structural support as largely invisible pillars of settler colonialism and white supremacy. They are assumptions that even many scholars in the humanities and social sciences often take for granted, despite our critical training. In fact, the university—bound up from the beginning in logics of settler colonialism and Native dispossession—has been one of the institutions most responsible for perpetuating these myths about Native food and agriculture. Despite the pretense of the university as transcendent repository of objective, universal knowledge, these institutions are beholden to history and power. For instance, many American public research universities owe their existence to Congress's Morrill Act of 1862, which granted tens of millions of acres of unceded Native land to fund state universities designed, as the law stated, "to teach such branches of learning as are related to agriculture."[16] Over the last 160 years, these land-grant universities have played powerful institutional roles as expert witnesses in global biopolitical governance, which is a form of authority premised, as Michel Foucault famously put it, on the power to "*foster* life or *disallow* it to the point of death."[17] As our entire human world faces the existential threats of climate change, pandemic disease, and other challenges inextricable from global systems of food and agriculture, confronting these myths about Native food history not only enables more honest assessments of the past but also helps us reframe our visions of food and agriculture in ways that may help us imagine more just and sustainable futures.

Each chapter in this book refutes these four myths about Native foods by retelling an episode of American history that is commonly used to give force to colonial assumptions that Native Americans lacked agriculture, lived only by hunting, usually went hungry, and had no sense of taste. In selecting the historical topics for each chapter, I prioritize events and periods that are recognizable to many students of American history—such as seventeenth-century New England, the Cherokee Removal, and the history of American Indian boarding schools—in order to prompt reflection on how reconsidering Native food and agriculture help us disrupt familiar historical narratives that have undergirded settler colonialism for centuries. Additionally, in several chapters I dive more deeply into lesser-told histories that are closely related to my own subject matter expertise as an environmental historian of the American West. In fact, I first envisioned this project ten years ago while working at the Newberry Library as a research fellow, investigating the history of slaughterhouses on the Blackfeet Reservation in northern Montana.[18] In the intervening years I have also worked on this project at the Archive Center of the National Museum of the American Indian, at the Huntington Library, and in the Manuscripts Division of the Library of Congress. This book, then, pulls together published literature from history, anthropology, American Indian studies, and other fields in order to make larger claims about Native food history through an exploration of selected topics using an original interpretation of primary sources that range from archival manuscripts to memoirs and conversations among Native farmers, chefs, and seed savers. My goal is not to provide a comprehensive history of Native American food and agriculture, but instead to offer a starting point for understanding how stories about food and agriculture, as well as people's lived experiences of food and agriculture, have played critical roles in framing, illuminating, and obscuring the histories of Native foods in America. And I have chosen to do this both by paying critical attention to narratives that may be familiar to many readers as well as some less-familiar circumstances I have encountered over the course of my career working as a historian.

The first myth of Native food history—that Native Americans did not really practice agriculture—is rooted in a longstanding, settler-colonial vision of America's agricultural landscape that has been formed and reformed around an aesthetic of nature that frames land as a basic commodity of capitalist production and that scales the farm as a fundamental space for patriarchal social reproduction. In settler-colonial America, any form of cultivation or other human intervention in land-based biophysical processes became unrecognizable as agriculture if it did not fundamentally address the challenge of maximizing production on the farm—an arena of work bounded by private property and market forces. As a lens for seeing the agricultural landscape, the farm also signified a heteronormative set of expectations that identified white, land-owning men (and their able-bodied and virile sons) as the land's primary economic actors, a way of seeing that pushed the visibility of other labor—waged, unwaged, or enslaved—into the background.[19]

This colonial gendering of the farm as a male space is reflected in the gendering of the garden as a female space. Women not only performed agricultural labor in many Native communities, but their agricultural roles frequently provided them with political and sexual empowerment.[20] These facts threatened the sensibilities of European colonists in America from the early colonial era well into the twentieth century, compelling offhand denials of the existence of Indian agriculture both to justify the seizure of Native land as well as to reaffirm the patriarchal foundations of settler-colonial society. Instead of taking seriously the expertise of Native women as farmers, for instance, colonial observers condemned the laziness of their Native husbands, a sexual scripting that marked the fertile American landscape as a virgin land primed for colonial possession. When colonists did recognize the agricultural work of Native women, they typically identified it not as farming, but as gardening—idiomatically associating it with the domain of leisure rather than productive labor, as the popular title of *Buffalo Bird Woman's Garden* attests.

Because Native food and agricultural practices rarely, if ever, conformed to the gendered expectations and capitalist aesthetics of what counted as agriculture in the settler-colonial landscape, ethnographers and other historical observers—as well as many present-day historians relying on the documents they produced as their sources—have often denied the existence of Native agricultural places simply because they could not see them.[21] The significance that these geographical framings of American agriculture have had in settler-colonial narrations of American history cannot be overstated. We cannot just trust our superficial vision of a place when we look at a map or gaze across a rural vista. History does not just "play out" in places. The setting itself requires critical attention, and one of the central tenets of my approach in this book is to assess geography not as an inert stage upon which historical actors perform their roles but as a stage curtain that itself structures our historical view.

This stage curtain has long obscured our view of Native agricultural history in ways that have condoned not only the seizure of Native land but also its conversion into parcels of private property possessed by non-Native owners. The curtain descended almost immediately upon the mass arrival of European colonists to what is now the United States in the early seventeenth century. These colonists idealized landownership as a precondition of their labor, and their governments responded with evolving schemes to finance and extend colonial authority by selling and exchanging land titles. Despite other differences separating European colonists in early America, within just a few years nearly all of them, from tobacco planters in colonial Virginia to subsistence farmers in the Plymouth Colony, shared an emerging, capitalistic vision of land as a commodity. They also shared a specific set of spatial and aesthetic ideals that delimited agriculture as an activity confined to plowed and harrowed fields where farmers intensively cultivated a single crop.[22] After the founding of the United States, geometric rows of grain spaced with furrows came to more fully idealize this agricultural space as a certain commodity—as "improved" land—and the square-mile survey was developed as the basic geographical principle in order to facilitate both row crops and land sales. By the end of the nineteenth century, this agricultural lattice had transformed much of the North American continent. With each crop, plows inverted prairies and drain tiles poured water into ditches trellised to the cardinal directions. Mechanization further defined the grid's lines and ruts, producing a countryside of farms just as vendible as a city block.

By general comparison, Native agricultural practices across much of North America differed from those of the capitalist, colonial farm by taking advantage of extensive—rather than intensive—cultivation strategies that prioritized low-input and long-term yields over maximum yields per acre, per season. Unlike the straight rows of grain characterizing the ideal fields of enclosure-era England, Native agriculture from the Northeast, to the Gulf, to the bottomland farms of the Great Plains was dominated by the interplanting of corn, beans, and squash on small hills of soil, generally in clearings that had been produced using fire rather than plows or blades. Relying on community labor, rather than just the labor subordinated within the private household, and investing that agricultural labor on projects spanning time scales of a few months to a few centuries, Native farmers created "fields" that comprised entire ecological systems and that were tended on seasonal rounds. With ongoing human assistance, these ecological systems produced food to meet human nutritional and social needs on an intergenerational basis, serving the function of what might be called permaculture in the twenty-first century.[23] However, colonial observers, along with many anthropologists and historians who follow in their terminology, have commonly reduced these agricultural activities as *foraging* or *gathering*, in the process misidentifying Native people as beneficiaries of "the spontaneous fruits of the earth," as Thomas Jefferson put it, or "merely the reapers of this abundance, not the sowers," as the ethnobotanist Kat Anderson has powerfully critiqued.[24] As I joke sometimes with my students, these errors of agricultural comprehension are tantamount to saying that a backyard tomato gardener goes out once or twice each summer to "forage" for the tomatoes that they planted four months earlier.

The net result of these colonial misapprehensions is that the historical extent of Native agriculture has long been denied even in moments when it has stared colonial observers in the face. In 1827, for instance, a French ethnographer extolled how Osage communities on the lower Missouri River grew "wheat, tobacco, pumpkins, and corn," and that "they weed and water their fields in dry seasons," yet, in the same sentence also concluded that "they have made up to the present very little progress in agriculture."[25] And even in our own century, I frequently encounter examples of scholarship that reify these colonial assumptions about agriculture, serving not only to preclude the possibility of a Native agricultural past but also foreclosing discussions of how changing our agricultural assumptions might lead us toward new understandings of how food systems could work in our own present and future. The myth that Native Americans did not practice agriculture has long pervaded American history and persists to the present.

The second myth that this book confronts—that Native people were primarily hunters—has played a similar role in justifying past and present dispossessions of Native land and labor, and it is equally pervasive as a baseline assumption that has guided much of American history and historiography. If Native Americans did not have agriculture, as the first myth posits, then they must have gotten their food from killing and eating animals; a presumption that not only reflects a deep uneasiness about the place of meat in settler-colonial food cultures but that also sets colonial expectations of Native people as blood-thirsty predators. As Philip Deloria has observed, the supposedly violent proclivities of Native hunters "breaking out" of their reservations and threatening colonists' animal property—or worse—enabled the settler-colonial imagination to justify violence against Native people as an act of defense rather than aggression.[26] In recent years, these colonial expectations of Native hunting have also framed contentious debates over the fishing and hunting rights preserved for Native communities across the continent under many federal treaties dating back to the eighteenth century.

In general, the ownership of animals as private property marked one of the central distinctions between colonial and Native understandings of the differences between hunting and herding. As Virginia DeJohn Anderson, William Cronon, and Andrea Smalley have all pointed out, an ethos of ownership pervaded colonial relationships with animals from the very moment settlers stepped foot on the North American continent.[27] Domesticated animals imported from Europe, such as cows, pigs, and horses, were all subject to the possession of an individual owner whose responsibility it was to husband the animal according to a variety of customs that changed dramatically as meat, milk, and fiber transformed into global, industrial commodities. Wild animals too existed as property in the colonial imagination. Unlike in England, where wild animals during the age of enclosure lived at the mercy of a Lord or King, North American wildlife supposedly belonged to all as a kind of property owned by public trust, an ethic of ownership that structures American wildlife law to the present day.[28]

By contrast, most Native people did not interact with animals as property, or at least not in the same ways. Although a wide diversity of practices makes generalization difficult, in the main, principles of reciprocity, rather than principles of possession, governed Native interactions with animals whose flesh was consumed as food. Of course, it was not uncommon for parties of Native hunters to avoid one another to avoid competition and conflict—a kind of mutual recognition of others' usufruct rights to different spaces at different moments. But instead of owning animals to which they were abstractly entitled, many Native communities instead incorporated hunting as a part of a seasonal round in which the work of killing and butchering animals was mediated by ritual practices that justified the taking of an animal's life with reciprocal sacrifice as payment—a negotiation with the animal directly rather than a court of title litigation.[29]

Moreover, Native practices often blurred colonial distinctions between hunting and husbandry by revealing ambiguities between what colonists considered as the distinct categories of wild and domesticated animals. For instance, the unenclosed pigs and cattle rooting wildly through the woods and meadows of New England and Virginia unsupervised, but presumably owned by colonists, strained the credulity of the English concept of domestication. Likewise, open-range cattle grazing on the Great Plains and rounded up once or twice a year to be separated based on cattle brand skidded across the blurry boundary that demarcated the wild from the domesticated. Conversely, the bison that Blackfeet hunters managed through centuries of the judicious use of controlled burns and drive lanes also, in their own way, crossed from wild to domesticated. Even the deer that Wendat hunters regenerated by burying their bones in the forest were, in a sense, domesticated—bred and managed through generational cycles that were no more mysterious to Wendats than the function of bull semen was to English stock raisers. Then and now, these Native relationships with animals exposed colonial fictions of animal ownership in ways that threatened the stability of a colonial society premised on the reduction of living organisms to chattel.[30]

By denigrating Native people as hunters, rather than recognizing them as farmers or herders, colonial authorities also sought to justify the colonial dispossession of Native land and labor on the basis that Native communities used both wastefully and inefficiently. In fact, a similar set of arguments framed the criminalization of customary subsistence hunting throughout Europe during the enclosure era of the seventeenth and eighteenth centuries, when manorial landowners evicted their villagers and tenants to maximize the efficiency of their estates to produce capital, casting off their feudal obligations to the peasantry as an unaffordable expense. Hunting became predominantly a leisure activity performed only by landowners who held private ownership rights to all the wildlife found on their estates. Subsistence hunters became poachers, forced to trespass secretly on enclosed manorial lands, a crime that by the middle of the eighteenth century had become punishable by death in England.[31] Although the punishment for poaching was generally less excessive in America, by the end of the nineteenth century a similar series of state and local game laws sought to circumscribe subsistence hunting throughout North America in ways that affected both Native and non-Native hunters. These laws privileged the emerging affluent sport hunters (such as Theodore Roosevelt, who founded the Boone & Crockett Club in 1887) with permits and hunting seasons and discouraged traditional subsistence hunters and fishers with fines and imprisonment.[32] All in all, these historical transitions toward a colonial ownership society premised on capital accumulation and private property—and wage labor and rent—meant that settler society approached hunting not as a legitimate form of labor but as an extravagant leisure activity.[33] Because they were cast as subsistence hunters according to this set of colonial imaginations, the challenging and sophisticated work of Native herding and husbandry often went unrecognized.

The third myth, that Indians typically went hungry, also reflects colonial assumptions of wastefulness and inefficiency that had emerged at least by the end of the seventeenth century to serve as justifications for American efforts to assimilate Native people into colonial society as colonial subjects. Ironically, much of the hunger that colonial observers perceived among Native communities was a direct result of colonial practices that disrupted Native agriculture. For instance, the various wars of the seventeenth and eighteenth centuries devastated thousands of Native farms and forced the relocation of entire communities. King Philip's War in New England, the Anglo-Cherokee wars of the southern Appalachian Mountains and the Piedmont, and the backcountry campaigns of the American Revolution all shared aspects of what one historian called, in describing the infamous Sullivan Expedition against the Haudenosaunee, a "war against vegetables."[34] In an era of unwieldy muskets and blades, Spanish, French, British, American, and Native troops waged war by shooting livestock, setting fire to stores of grain, cutting down orchards and crops in the field, and destroying homes, barns, and fences—seeking to destroy their enemies through impoverishment and starvation at least as much as through military prowess. This approach to colonial warfare persisted into the nineteenth century as the American nation-state expanded its dominion westward and utilized the scorched-earth military tactics perfected by officers like William Sherman and Philip Sheridan during the final, desperate years of the American Civil War. Under these circumstances, the resiliency and adaptability of Native food and agricultural systems were continually stress-tested over a period of more than three centuries. Rather than remarking on the extraordinary capacity of Native communities to withstand and respond to these assaults on their lives and livelihoods, colonial observers more frequently cited temporary moments in the aftermath of wartime death and disarray as indicators that Native hunger was a permanent condition.

The presuppositions of Native hunger that followed in the wake of war and devastation became pretexts for colonial policies aimed at the further subordination of Native land and labor. One of the most significant examples was the forced removal of Native children from their homes and their placement into mandatory residential boarding schools during the late nineteenth and twentieth centuries. In 1891, an act of Congress authorized the commissioner of Indian affairs to enforce "such rules and regulations as will secure the attendance of Indian children of suitable age and health at schools established and maintained for their benefit," an administrative power that persisted eighty years until it was revoked by Congress in the late 1970s.[35] Despite evidence of rampant disease and malnutrition throughout the federal boarding school system, Indian office personnel seized children from their homes on allegations that Native families were not equipped to provide sufficient food for their children. In practice, this administrative force was most often wielded by agents of the Indian Office on a local scale. These agents often supervised reservation food rations that were provided to tribes under the provisions of treaty agreements with the federal government. But because these federal agents—and not tribal authorities—controlled the actual distribution of these rations and other treaty annuity goods and monies, relatively low-ranking members of the Indian office held immense power over reservation economies. When politically expedient, they manufactured hunger by withholding treaty goods from particular individuals or families. When boarding school superintendents needed new classes of students, reservation agents could "secure the attendance" of Indian children through organized kidnappings justified by reservation hunger and ill health caused by such withholding.[36] In short, the immense hunger that did exist across Indian country was not only largely caused and exacerbated by colonial forces but also subsequently used as justification for new policies that produced even greater hunger.

As a result of these colonial experiences, presumptions of Native hunger became so commonplace that even well-meaning allies of Native communities often came to understand hunger as a characteristic misfortune of Native people dating back to time immemorial. What, in actuality, were political, economic, and ecological problems related to the historical enactment of settler-colonial policies were instead understood as timeless afflictions associated with Native ways of food and livelihood that needed reform. As a result, colonial efforts to address food security in Indian country achieved mixed results at best and, at worst, took on a kind of malign benevolence that further eroded Native food sovereignty by proceeding as if Native communities were merely recipients of the colonial welfare state. For example, as the final chapter of this book explores, federal efforts in the 1970s to replace the treaty-secured distribution of commodity foods on reservations across the American West with the federal food stamps program pitted Native activists against federal officials who misunderstood commodity foods in Indian country as a matter of welfare provisioning rather than of treaty rights. The eventual success of these Native activists in wresting control over reservation food security from the US Department of Agriculture was fundamental both for reasserting American Indian self-determination and for articulating a vision of food sovereignty that prioritized Native-led solutions to problems of hunger and health.

These histories of the colonial struggle to recognize, interpret, and address Native hunger also reveal other facets of food and settler colonialism that often go overlooked. Like any sensation, hunger is a physiological phenomenon inseparable from the specific environmental and cultural contexts that shape its meaning and experience. Historically, expectations of regular, reliable, and immediate access to food only emerged unevenly over the last several centuries, accompanying the rise of settler colonialism and capitalism as global phenomena. And, in many moments throughout the nineteenth and twentieth centuries, these new forces of colonial capitalism were just as responsible for producing mass hunger as they were for alleviating it.[37]

For most of human history, regardless of their location or social status, people periodically went hungry according to twenty-first-century American expectations of what it means to be well fed. In fact, the consequences of overeating were commonly perceived to be just as threatening as those of a more parsimonious diet, not only in terms of an individual's bodily health but also in relation to social expectations of moderation and gluttony. In the communal world of the Haudenosaunee, for instance, customs of generosity dictated that anyone—Haudenosaunee or otherwise—should be offered food while visiting a longhouse. Yet, visitors were also responsible for respecting this hospitality by not wasting food or by eating more food than needed to satiate pangs of hunger. In 1910, the Seneca archaeologist Arthur C. Parker recorded that one of his Haudenosaunee research partners was shocked to discover that white people "[were] not even familiar with the common rules of civility which our mothers teach us in infancy." Among those lessons was the tale of "a monster known as Sago'dakwus who would humiliate [children] in a most terrible manner if he found out they were gourmands," an apocryphal anecdote attesting to the fact that hunger is a trained cultural response as well as a physiological one.[38]

Moreover, to simply equate historical sensations of hunger with typical twenty-first-century ones overlooks the fact that human bodies can thrive on a wide variety of diets, not only in terms of nutrient sources but also in terms of the digestive tempos in which those nutrients are metabolized. Eating three meals a day, every day of the year—with some snacks thrown in—may be the general expectation of many Americans in the twenty-first century, but it is not, in and of itself, a physiological necessity or even a healthy practice. As the nutrition plans of modern endurance athletes attest, our bodies can also be trained over time to store and metabolize macronutrients in a fasted state, accruing enormous caloric deficits over weeks or months that are only replenished by long-term recovery diets in the off season. The point here is that the physiological adaptability of the human body to different dietary conditions requires assessments of hunger to grapple with the various environmental and cultural factors that play key roles in structuring expectations of nourishment. When colonial observers remarked on Native hunger, they were reflecting on far more than just calories. They were asserting colonial visions of food and health that reinforced their claims to Native land and labor by pathologizing the bodies of Native people.[39]

Likewise, the fourth common myth of Native food and agriculture—

that Indians had no taste—even more clearly reveals the colonial assumptions that have long accompanied American conversations about Native cuisine. To many European colonists, the dietary selections of Native people could only be explained as foods of necessity. For instance, in 1597 the English botanist John Gerarde famously described corn as a "more convenient food for swine than for men," and added that "the barbarous Indians are constrained to make virtue of necessitie, and think it a good food."[40] Of course, corn became a favored colonial possession within the span of a generation, and English colonists quickly acquired their own fondness for hominy, succotash, and other Native preparations. Nevertheless, presumptions of disgust pervaded colonial accounts of Native cuisine for centuries onward, typically informed by a colonial point of view that assumed that the only reason Native people chose to eat a particular dish or ingredient was because otherwise they would starve.

Like hunger, sensations of taste embody a milieu of cultural, physiological, and environmental stimuli, and when both Native and colonial travelers left their homes for unfamiliar destinations, they embarked on boundary-crossing culinary journeys that forced them to confront and adapt their expectations. For instance, though first introduced to roasted dog meat while spending the winter of 1804 and 1805 with the Mandan along the Upper Missouri River, the men and women of the Lewis and Clark expedition eventually ate a total of 190 dogs over the course of their journey, and Meriwether Lewis himself remarked that dog had become "a favorite food."[41] (Miraculously Seaman, Lewis's own 150-pound Newfoundland, somehow survived this voyage of discovery.) After crossing the continental divide and descending the tributaries of the Columbia River by boat, however, the expedition encountered the Nez Perce and other Native communities that were quite appalled at the Corps of Discovery's habit of eating dog meat. They quickly refused to sell any more dogs to the expedition after learning of their fate. Despite the clarity with which Native people expressed their own divergent tastes and culinary desires, however, most colonists seemed unable to acknowledge the richness and diversity of Native cuisine, denigrating it instead as a food of necessity borne only from hunger.

This settler-colonial myth of Indian tastelessness persists to the present day in complicated ways. On the one hand, Native American foods in the twenty-first century are becoming more visible and fashionable across a broad swath of American food culture. Popular desires to abandon industrial food systems in favor of locally grown, heirloom, or heritage ingredients prepared and consumed according to traditional practices have elevated Native food knowledges to prominence. Many people who care about their own health, as well as the health of their neighbors and the ecological communities they inhabit, commonly understand Native food history as a practical, if somewhat mystifying, reservoir of solutions for eating right in an America that values environmental sustainability and nutritional responsibility as key parameters of ethical eating. And yet, despite a proliferation of interest in ancient Native American staple ingredients such as amaranth, quinoa, tepary beans, flint corn, and wild rice, there is far less acknowledgement of Native *cuisine*—the recipes, preparations, and, above all, the *tastes*—that has come to constitute so much of global food and agriculture over the last half millennium and especially over the last century as the seeds saved by Maxidiwiac and other Native American farmers revolutionized the entire way our world eats.

The goal of this book is to open new conversations about the historical roles of Native American cuisines in American history, as well as to emphasize the significance of ongoing colonial processes in present-day conversations about the place of Native foods and Native history in our evolving worlds of taste, justice, and politics. The five chapters that follow are not intended to tell these stories comprehensively but to exemplify a critical historical approach toward decoding and interrogating the settler-colonial visions that structure global understandings of Native food and agriculture. This critical approach can help us uncover—rather than "rediscover"—the persistence of Native American foods and cuisines, revealing how Native foods were never lost, but only obscured by the peregrinations of colonialism, capitalism, and other historical transformations to agriculture and livelihood that have altered all of our lives over the last several centuries.

1.

Food and Possession in Colonial New England

For many Americans, Thanksgiving marks the time of the year when considerations of Native food and agriculture are most prevalent. This holiday, perhaps more than any other, reflects the settler-colonial food mythologies that accompany the history of the British North American colonies and the founding of the United States. As popularly remembered, the "first Thanksgiving," which occurred in present-day Massachusetts in the autumn of 1621, commemorated the survival and success of the Pilgrims, a group of religious exiles who arrived in the New World on their ship, the *Mayflower*, the preceding year. As the story goes, the Pilgrims invited their Wampanoag neighbors to join them in a feast and celebration after bringing in their first corn harvest. However, even here at the outset, the historical details are blurry. From the Pilgrims' perspective, for instance, only two manuscript sources recorded the event, and neither indicated that the Wampanoags were "invited."[1] Nor did they specify the Thanksgiving table fare commonly associated with the American holiday today, such as turkey. Wampanoag oral traditions claim that the Indians reluctantly joined the Pilgrims at the feast only because they had been alarmed by musket fire when the Pilgrims were conducting militia drills as part of their festivities, an aspect of the Pilgrims' celebration that Edward Winslow's account emphasized.[2] The tale of the first Thanksgiving is just that—a tale. It is an apocryphal fable of settler colonialism that, in its annual repetition, establishes colonizers as hosts and Native people as guests. In the days and weeks surrounding the holiday, caricatured turkeys, Pilgrims, and Indians constitute a pageantry that obscures the historical realities of food, agriculture, and colonialism in the estuaries, river valleys, and uplands of what became southern New England in the seventeenth century.[3]

At least this much of the Thanksgiving tale seems accurate: corn was a crop indigenous to the Americas that the Pilgrims' Wampanoag neighbors had taught them to grow during the spring and summer of 1621. Corn was also the food most responsible for keeping the Pilgrims alive after roughly half of them starved to death during the previous winter. Many other elements of the Pilgrims' Thanksgiving fable have been discarded over the last several decades as a variety of Native critics, historians, and others have exposed the tale's inaccuracies and its racist and patriarchal assumptions.[4] The overturning of one tradition, however, always allows for the invention of new ones. Among the diverse and dynamic routines of Thanksgiving in the twenty-first century, it seems that a recognition of Native contributions to American food history is emerging as a common shared theme.

On the one hand, it is wonderful for Native contributions to the history of food and agriculture to be recognized after years of denigration and neglect. But on the other hand, the heightened visibility of these contributions in association with the Thanksgiving holiday can sometimes obscure our vision of the deeper complexities of Native food history by restricting our appreciation of Native foodways to the moment of colonial contact. Take, for instance, the celebration of the month of November as National Native American Heritage Month, which helps bring discussions of Native issues to the forefront of public attention at the same time of year that many Americans are planning their Thanksgiving feasts. First designated by Congress in 1986 after years of proposals by the National Congress of American Indians and other Native organizations and activists, this month (which was originally limited to just the week of Thanksgiving) was intended to recognize the Native origins of "many of the foods we eat," as well as to acknowledge "the assistance American Indians provided to the Founding Fathers of our Nation."[5] These declarations were well intended, but their framing of Native food history within the story of American national origins is quite limiting. What about Native foods that most Americans today don't eat? What about Native foods and practices that did not "assist" in the origins of the American nation, but did the opposite—that worked to actively support the sovereignty of Native political communities and to resist colonial subordination? To answer these questions requires us to stop beginning (and ending) with the Pilgrims' first corn harvest as the primal scene of this history, and to instead describe the complex agricultural and culinary experiences of Native New Englanders during and beyond the early colonial period.

***

The diets and food practices of the Wampanoag and other Native communities in what is now New England varied dramatically in the centuries before the Pilgrims arrived in 1620 to remark upon them. No one really knows when, on the Gregorian calendar, corn cultivation arrived in the region, but it had likely been present since around the year 1000 CE and had provided a staple food for many generations prior to the arrival of the English colonists. Native farmers also planted a variety of annual beans and squash and tended a wide range of perennial fruit, nut, and seed crops including acorns, blueberries, elderberries, grapes, sunflower seeds, and walnuts. The region's geographic and climatic variations provided access to wide selection of edible plants and animals within a relatively small area. Fish, clams, oysters, and the eggs of nesting shorebirds offered year-round sources of protein. Deer constituted a significant source of meat, as did the moose and caribou in the cooler, forested mountains to the north. Although these animals were not fenced in like livestock, their numbers and locations were carefully managed through the application of controlled fires that removed woody undergrowth and encouraged the presence of tender grasses and forbs. These fires also returned nutrients to the soil and made fertile plots for the later cultivation of corn and other crops.[6]

Rather than only focusing their horticultural efforts on the fields where corn and other annual crops were grown, the agricultural work of Native communities in New England encompassed the entire landscape in ways that also maximized the productivity of perennial sources of food. Native people across the North American continent used fire as an agricultural tool to create and maintain forests and meadows that supported a variety of plant and animal species. Much evidence suggests that Native agriculture in New England relied on a complex set of agroforestry practices, rooted in fire and selective harvesting, that united fields and forests into a patchwork of agricultural units with plantings that provided both annual and perennial crops. Unlike the Pilgrims, who viewed the region's forests as the home of Satan,[7] Native people relied on forests as vital sources of plant-based foods and as habitat for deer and other game animals.

The words *agroforesty* and *permaculture* both come from the lexicon of twenty-first century agronomy, but both seem appropriate for describing the management strategies that Native communities adopted to maximize the production of fruit and nut crops in the forests of New England. By regularly burning New England's woodlands over thousands of years, Native people prevented the emergence of a dense, shade-tolerant forest comprised of beech, fern, spruce, and other species with little value for human nutrition. By burning the forest to remove seedlings of these fire-sensitive species, Native people produced and maintained an open woodland dominated by a deciduous canopy of mature oak and walnut trees that were less susceptible to fire and that produced crops of nuts that were an immense source of protein and fat in alternating years. Burning the forest floor also encouraged the growth of sun-loving, fruit-bearing shrubs and vines in openings below.[8]

Using these methods, Native communities in New England did not just "live in nature," hunting and gathering food willy-nilly across the forest; they actively managed the forest and engineered it to provide a predictable, sustainable, and diverse array of foods. Their work could not permanently alter the forest, so maintaining it in this preferred state required continual labor and the continual application of agroforesty principles. In this respect, their approach toward forest management was centuries ahead of their European counterparts, who did not even begin to appreciate the concepts of deforestation or forest succession until the end of the eighteenth century and late nineteenth century, respectively.[9] Historical and biogeographical evidence suggests that over the seventeenth century, shade-tolerant species of beech, fir, and spruce trees began to colonize the northeastern forest alongside English settlements. For instance, researchers mapping the spatial distribution of "witness trees"—the mature trees at the borders of farms that were used to demarcate the boundary lines of the metes-and-bounds surveys that colonists used to the record their land titles—have indicated that the dominance of oak and walnut trees in these seventeenth-century surveys declined over the colonial period.[10] And according to archaeoforestry studies spanning thousands of years, the rapid rate at which these nut-bearing hardwood species expanded northward from their small range near the Gulf of Mexico at the end of the last Ice Age suggests that Native people must have been instrumental in the creation of North American forests, not only by burning spruce forests to encourage the spread of oak and other nut-bearing trees but also by planting these trees directly.[11] There is nothing timeless about forests. As the Osage forestry scientist Thomas Bonnicksen has observed, "what we call forests come together for a short time; then each species goes its separate way when conditions change."[12] Native people across the continent used a suite of agroforesty techniques to modulate these forest transformations in ways that would maximize their usefulness and reliability for human subsistence. Thus, what the Pilgrims encountered as the "wilderness" of New England in 1620 was not a primeval forest, but an intentional forest that had been designed and maintained as a perennial food source by Native communities using fire and other selective techniques for centuries, if not millennia.

These Native agroforestry practices, as well as other Native agricultural practices, were largely invisible to English colonists because noticing them required a different way of seeing the landscape. For one thing, the weight of the Pilgrims' religious suspicions of the forest as the home of Satan obscured their ability to recognize patterns of Native agriculture that occurred in the woods. Their specific beliefs in the supernatural forces animating the wild world beyond their own domesticated gardens blinded them to the possibility that Native people had actually been gardening America on a continental scale, the "wilderness" included.[13] The colonists' desires for private property also framed their vision of the agricultural landscape in a way that left them near-sighted, focusing their gaze primarily on the spaces within and around their immediate farms and households.[14] These perspectives not only framed the colonists' vision of New England's agricultural environments but also helped determine the characteristics of much of the historical information that historians today have regarding seventeenth-century New England. As people today read the colonial accounts of William Bradford, Edward Winslow, and others as primary sources for the reconstruction of historical New England, it is important to remember that these accounts often tell us more about the authors' own internal perspectives than the subjects that they are purporting to describe.[15]

What was very visible to the colonists was corn. In fact, nearly all Europeans who visited the Americas during the fifteenth through the seventeenth centuries could not help commenting on it.[16] Initially, the vegetable elicited strong feelings and presumptions that it "was of hard and evil digestion."[17] Despite widespread anxieties over its healthfulness, however, in the eyes of the Pilgrims and the other Europeans who visited

New England during the early colonial period, corn was still Native America's most intriguing agricultural product. The fact that the English called it *corn* at all is evidence of the significant impression that the plant made on them. In the seventeenth-century English dialect, the word *corn* referred to any grain that could be grown and harvested and then eaten—either whole, ground into flour, or else made into a beverage. The word was especially used for barley, the grain that most English people consumed on a daily basis. Barley was a hardier plant than wheat, rye, or oats, and it grew in a wider variety of soil conditions. In the late 1400s, as England's medieval system of feudal tribute gave way to an emergent capitalist market based on the international exchange of more delicate and desired grains like wheat and oats, the English diet shifted ever-more heavily toward barley—a crop that was rarely exported and almost always available locally. Barley remained the backstop crop of English eaters as late as the nineteenth century.[18] During the early colonial period, corn served a similar purpose for European colonists across the Americas.

Although corn predominated in the diets of the region's Native inhabitants, its cultivation quickly faded to the north and west as it reached its climatic limits.[19] Attention to the technical details of corn can help illustrate how the plant's biophysical characteristics worked in conjunction with Native efforts to structure the region's agricultural geography. To produce mature kernels that can be saved for a subsequent crop, corn typically requires a growing season of approximately one hundred frost-free days. Plymouth, Massachusetts, has on average 180 frost-free days, while Deerfield, Massachusetts, has just 140. Further inland, the frost-free growing season shrinks precipitously. Hanover, New Hampshire, for instance, on the Connecticut River above Deerfield, has barely one hundred frost-free days, substantially increasing the amount of risk involved in the investment of planting and harvesting an annual crop.

This ambling edge of corn cultivation structured patterns of trade across Native New England. North of the line, Wabanaki communities grew relatively less corn and hunted and processed moose and caribou, exchanging the meat for corn with the peoples of the south.[20] Pocumtuck and Nipmuc communities in the region's interior heart presided over this trade. Dried moose tongue, for instance, was an expensive delicacy on the coastal plain of southeastern New England, where substantial Massachusett, Mohegan, Narragansett, Niantic, Pequot, and Wampanoag surpluses of corn, beans, and squash facilitated its acquisition, along with the purchase of other exotic provisions from the interior, such as maple sugar. European fishermen and other seafarers who increasingly turned up offshore during the sixteenth and seventeenth centuries also purchased a share of these staple grains and vegetables.[21]

The geographic and social circumstances that shaped Native foodways ensured that the diets of Native communities in New England were never uniform or static. The region's Indigenous communities were not starving on the eve of the English colonists' arrival; rather they had substantial and long-lasting agricultural food surpluses—particularly on the coastal plains and river valleys—along with seasonal sources of food that gave them a broad selection of options when it came time to prepare a meal. New England's Indians had developed an expansive cuisine that perhaps eclipsed the narrow dietary horizons constraining the average English eater in the seventeenth century. Corn was indeed the staple ingredient that provided the basis for many Indigenous dishes. However, it was quickly and easily eschewed from the menu when Native people grew tired of eating it. Roger Williams, for instance, observed that even when corn and other stores were plentiful, the Indians, "by much boyling," ate "Acornes for a Novelty." For dessert, Williams described an Indian dish made from "currants" (probably blueberries) and other dried fruits that he called "strawberry bread": "as sweet to them as plum or spice cake to the English."[22] On the savory side, John Josselyn reported that fish boiled with wild leeks, or ramps, was a popular dish. Striped bass, sturgeon, and salmon were generally favored; eel, lobster, or lamprey were still enjoyed; herring, mackerel, and shad were generally accepted.[23]

Corn itself was prepared in a seemingly endless number of ways. When picked green, whole ears might be roasted over an open fire, baked in hot ashes, or simply boiled. It might also be cut from the cob and boiled with fresh beans to make succotash—a word with Narragansett origins—or stewed with meat or other vegetable accompaniments.[24] Fresh corn was also parched in hot ashes and then pounded into a powder called *nocake* that constituted the standard Native provision for overland travel during the hunting season.[25] Most corn, however, was dried on the cob for several weeks in the hot, late-summer sun, and then shelled into kernels for long-term storage in cache baskets, which sometimes held other staple provisions as well, such as dried beans, dried squashes, nuts, nut flours, and even bottles of oil produced from nuts, bear fat, or fish. Whole ears of corn from the season's finest plants were also buried in special baskets to serve as seed for the next year's planting. Unmistakably heirloom vegetables, these were the reliable kernels whose characteristics Native farmers learned to identify over many years of cultivation. In this respect, Native corn plantings were hardly standardized, but encompassed a wide medley of species and varieties that were cultivated according to individual tastes. The corn that Indians and colonists consumed was a staple food, but the crops that they ate were hardly uniform.

For those of us unaccustomed to growing corn in our daily lives, a consideration of the material realities of corn cultivation is helpful not only for comprehending the meaning of this diversity of corn varieties in Native New England but also for understanding the immense time, labor, technical skill, and advance planning that was required to grow corn successfully in one place over long periods. Archaeologists, for instance, have been fond of arguing over the exact date when corn "arrived" in New England ever since the technique of radiocarbon dating revolutionized their discipline by enabling answers to these kinds of narrow questions. But this question largely misses the point. The presence or non-presence of carbon-dated corn kernels says little about the conditions in which corn was cultivated or about the crop's cultural significance. Rather than speak of adoption, a more appropriate way to describe corn's emergence in New England is adaptation. As corn spread northward to more temperate climates, Native farmers needed to adapt the plant to produce reliably within their own local climates. Although improving the earliness of the crop (lowering its days to maturity) was a major factor across almost all of North America, other climatic and geological variables, such as aridity and soil conditions, would have required adaptation as well. Given that corn is a wind-pollinated plant that can be easily (if not always predictably) transformed from one generation of plants to the next, Native communities in New England engineered different varieties to work for them under certain agronomic conditions and for specific cultural uses.

Foremost of the biophysical challenges that Native corn breeders in New England sought to overcome was their region's relatively short growing season and the plant's susceptibility to frost. Corn is a tropical plant. The archaeological consensus is that Native people in present-day Mexico created modern corn around seven thousand years ago, the result of a long-term effort to select, save, and replant the seed pods of a grass named teosinte in order to encourage starchier and more prolific kernels. Like teosinte, the first corn to emerge from these efforts grew over a long season, producing mature kernels after a growth cycle of more than two hundred days. According to Penobscot agronomist Paul Sesup in 1895, Native communities in New England increased the earliness of their corn varieties by saving seed kernels from the lowest ears of corn on the stalks.[26] These ears were the first to emerge during the plant's vegetative growth cycle, and they would have been pollinated by any nearby plants that were also the first to reach the reproductive growth cycle by putting out a corn tassel. Since ears pollinated by these early parent plants at the bottom of the stalk would ripen several weeks earlier than those at the top, saving seed kernels from ears produced at the bottom of the plant helped to breed earliness into particular lines of corn, most likely resulting in varieties that could reliably produce fresh corn within sixty or seventy days of planting.[27]

The same wind-pollinated profligacy that made corn a pliant plant for horticultural improvement also required that Native farmers devise methods for preventing the wayward pollen of different corn varieties from mixing with one another. The way that corn sets fruit is that every corn silk on the top of an ear of corn turns into a kernel of corn after pollination. The silks are pollinated from the tassels on the top of the plants, which disgorge millions of pollen grains per tassel whenever the wind blows. On a still day, the pollen will usually flutter down and land on the silks of ears located within just a few feet, but on a breezy day, viable pollen can travel as far as half a mile within just a few minutes. Then as now, controlling the pollination of different varieties of corn required significant planning and labor. Those familiar, today, with the production of in-field hybrid corns know firsthand the labor required to manually detassel of all the male plants in stands of corn that can encompass hundreds of acres. Growers of specific, open-pollinated varieties of seed corn know the necessity of isolating their fields from other stands of corn by a mile or more, especially given the prevalence of patented, transgenic corn cultivated since the 1990s. Native farmers in New England utilized other methods of protecting their corn cultivars, however, that did not require the same scale of physical labor or spatial isolation. Wampanoag farmers, for instance, interplanted their corn varieties in the same field, but timed the planting of each variety to occur in intervals so that that no more than one variety would be pollinating at once. When the French colonist Samuel de Champlain visited Cape Cod in 1605, he observed that the Nauset farmers were following this practice.[28] Using a variety of archaeological and ethnographic sources, Frederica R. Dimmick has also speculated that color-coded varieties of red, blue, yellow, and white corn aided in this sequential planting as well as ensuring—since color is one of the most susceptible traits affected by the cross-pollination—"an ear of pure color indicated an unmixed stock that was carefully maintained."[29] Fifteen years after Champlain's visit, when the *Mayflower* landed briefly on Cape Cod in November of 1620, the Pilgrims dug up (and stole) a cache of this Nauset seed corn. Edward Winslow remarked that it contained "some 36 goodly eares of corne, some yellow, and some red, and others mixt with blew, which was a very goodly sight."[30]

When at home, most Indigenous people in southern New England ate three regular meals each day, each family cooking for themselves within their wigwam (a shelter constructed from the bent trunks of ten- to fifteen-foot-tall sapling trees and covered with bark, animal pelts, or woven grass). The main challenge of meal preparation was fire management. Not only was the proper amount of fuel necessary for maintaining a cooking fire within the wigwam, but it took considerable skill and attention to cook complicated dishes over the open fire—a set of proficiencies that Native cooks shared with their colonial counterparts in the seventeenth century. To ease the difficulties of cooking over the flames, water boiling in earthen pots was used as the daily cooking medium. Adding dried corn to the boiling water provided a substantial base for most Indian and English meals of the period, as this standing dish of boiled grain could be held on a simmer and other vegetables, such as squash and beans, or meats, added according to taste. Colonists called such food pottage. Indian pottage was usually served in bowls and eaten with spoons, both made commonly from maple wood, and the dish probably constituted the basis for many daily meals.[31]

In addition to the simplicity of boiling corn in this fashion, Native cooks developed other methods of using the open fire to transform their staple provisions into cuisine. By inverting the everyday earthen pot, for instance, a number of different configurations transformed the flames into a baking-ready oven. A large, heated stone could provide the base for the oven, and hot coals could be heaped upon the top of the pot to bury the oven in order to achieve an even convection. Corn husks and other foliage were also used to wrap ingredients into a kind of *tamal* that could be baked or steamed inside such a vessel. Bear flesh was boiled down, the fat skimmed and saved as oil for frying dishes like corn cakes, which were consumed by Indians and colonists alike in the seventeenth century. The increasing availability of both metal cookware and English-owned pigs that foraged far from home made frying more convenient as the century progressed. Rather than curing the meat into bacon or ham as was the colonial habit, Indians used pork to produce grease using the same technique they had perfected on bear meat, rendering it into "pummy" that was utilized as cooking oil.[32]

Still, the diets of Native communities in southern New England in the seventeenth century were sustained mainly by plants, despite the frequent inclusion of fish, venison, and other animal fats and proteins. According to one study, it is possible that corn alone accounted for approximately 65 percent of their average daily calories; meat constituted only about 10 percent.[33] The amount of corn produced by Native communities in New England reflected their conscious decisions to devote enormous effort to large-scale grain farming. Early English accounts of Native villages frequently considered Native agricultural practices using English agricultural terminology, a factor that necessarily complicates our historical picture since so many details may have been lost in translation. For instance, Indians did not typically plant fields of separate row crops, as was the English practice, but integrated mounds of corn, beans, and squash into the same field. Called the three sisters, these crops formed a symbiotic relationships as they matured over the course of a growing season. Beans contributed nitrogen into the soil that corn and squash required to grow, and corn stalks provided a sturdy structure that the budding legumes could climb to propagate. Squash vines below crowded out unwanted weeds. Some communities also kept trained hawks to kill or dissuade small birds from eating the corn kernels, beans, and squash seeds before they germinated.[34] Using these methods, one seventeenth-century colonist reported that Nipmuc farmers in northeastern Connecticut harvested about forty bushels of corn per acre that they planted, a figure that would have marked them as competitive agronomists two centuries into the future.[35] Given harvests on this scale, Nipmucs and other Indians of southern New England could have annually produced around three hundred pounds of dried and shelled corn per person.[36]

These substantial harvests grabbed the attention of New England's colonists from nearly the very moment they set foot on the beaches of Massachusetts Bay. Soon after stealing the Nauset corn caches in November of 1620, Winslow and the other Pilgrims narrowly escaped a violent confrontation with the enraged community. Fearing further retaliation, they fled to the opposite side of the bay, where they stumbled upon another fortunate product of Native labor. They founded their Plymouth colony on the site of a farming village that had been cleared, but abandoned, by the Patuxets, its Wampanoag residents. It seems likely that a series of epidemic diseases—most likely smallpox—had ravaged this community and others along the coast just a year or two before the Pilgrims' arrival. Unlike their visit to Cape Cod, the Pilgrims here found no sign of recent Indian habitation, but they did find many acres of land that had been cleared and previously cultivated. They also reported finding the weather-bleached bones and skulls of men and women whose remains, according to William Bradford, sat scattered in "many places lying still above the ground," a dramatic observation resonating with the overall tone of Bradford's account of the Plymouth colony as a miracle of divine intervention.[37]

Aside from the basic understanding that an epidemic disease wreaked havoc upon Patuxet between 1617 and 1619, exactly what else happened to the Wampanoag community and its members remains unknown. Certainly, there were some survivors who moved to nearby Wampanoag communities. A consideration of Native agriculture practices suggests a strong possibility that factors other than the mysterious disease were at play in Patuxet's supposed abandonment. For one thing, Native communities living along the New England's southern coastal plain regularly left their farming villages for winter residences in the forested bottomlands of coastal rivers, where they found shelter from the winter wind as well as abundant wood. It also seems possible that the Native agricultural strategy of fallowing heavily used agricultural lands for periods of ten or more years might also have contributed to the decision to leave Patuxet. In any event, though it is clear that there were no Wampanoags present in Patuxet when the Pilgrims landed, that they had not disappeared, and that they were most likely planning to return.

In the decades that followed, the Pilgrims' selection of their Plymouth town site near the "abandoned" Wampanoag fields set the standard practice for colonial town-building all up and down the coastal plains and the river valleys of southern New England. Locating English towns on the remains of Indian ones was not a curious coincidence, but a colonial model repeated time and again across the New England interior. Between 1636 and 1673, for instance, the Massachusetts Bay Colony towns of the middle Connecticut River valley—Springfield, Northampton, Deerfield, and Northfield—were all sited atop prime agricultural lands that had been cleared by the Native communities of Agawam, Norottuck, Peskeompscut, and Squakheag.[38] These Puritan towns were chartered on models, such as the one authored by William Pynchon for Springfield, to house an ideal population of "between forty and fifty families" each, requiring a minimum of about three thousand acres for home sites and agricultural use, plus perhaps a few thousand more acres to accommodate the colonists' wide-ranging pigs and cattle.[39]

The growth of these hungry English villages in Connecticut during the 1630s brought Puritans into conflict with the Native communities they displaced. While farther east, the Wampanoag and other coastal people had mostly tolerated the first colonists of the 1620s as a means of developing the English as military allies, the colonists' expansion into the Connecticut River valley triggered the outbreak of war in 1636. For more than a decade, the Pequot had successfully battled Narragansett and Mohegan forces for control over the Connecticut River valley's rich agricultural lands and had maintained control over the substantial trade that flowed through the river corridor, which enriched Pequot communities with Dutch and English trade items as well as a variety of Native trade goods from the north. The establishment of the colonial river towns of Windsor, Wethersfield, and Hartford, however, altered the region's political balance. Narragansett and Mohegan traders allied themselves with the Puritan newcomers, driving the Pequot to lay siege to the Connecticut colony towns in the winter of 1636. The following spring, English colonists from the Plymouth and Massachusetts Bay colonies, along with hundreds of allied Mohegan and Narragansett soldiers, brought the war to a brutal conclusion when they surrounded and burned the Pequot's village on the Mystic River. Some of the Pequot who lived through the war were taken as captives by the Mohegan and Narragansett; the Puritans also enslaved 319, selling some to English enslavers in the Caribbean.[40] The following year, a treaty signed at Hartford by representatives of the Mohegan, Narragansett, and the three Puritan colonies outlawed the use of the Pequot name by any of the massacre's survivors. Still, the Pequot survive to this day in New England and across the world.[41] But the Pequot War of 1636 was a startling indication of the violence that would accompany English colonization in the coming generations.

Indians and colonists regarded one another with increasing suspicion in the aftermath of the Pequot War, and food took on greater importance as a complex medium of diplomatic exchange, structuring ceremonial acts premised around offering (or sometimes rejecting) food. Both Native and English conceptions of dining etiquette held specific expectations about food and political status that hinged on implicit understandings of the diplomatic role of hospitality. According to English customs, the positions of individuals around the dining room represented a microcosm of their broader social station. In the aristocratic courts of seventeenth-century England, lords would sit only among other lords. Though their knights and vassals would eat within the same hall, the lesser men and their families would be seated at separate tables, and eating the food provided by their lord—perhaps even passed down from his table—confirmed their subservient status.[42] Despite initial Puritan desires to dispense with these kinds of secular distinctions in the name of radical religious equality, their dining tables nevertheless reflected some stubborn cultural traditions of the mother country. The classic Thanksgiving image of Plymouth governor William Bradford sharing a table with Massasoit, leader of the Wampanoag, ended nearly as soon as it had begun. When Bradford married in 1623, Massassoit attended the wedding feast, marking the last time a colonial official sat beside an Indian at a ceremonial meal (at least voluntarily). Bradford's successors halted such egalitarian displays, seating Native dignitaries at subordinate tables in order to assert their gubernatorial authority over Indians and Pilgrims alike.[43]

This custom resonated among common Native understandings of dining etiquette in seventeenth-century New England that recognized the acceptance of food from a friend or rival as a declaration of submission. The decision to either accept or decline dinner invitations was therefore a delicate political act, a dilemma that could neither be ignored nor "emptied of its symbolic weight," as the historian Michael LaCombe has described. For instance, at the Treaty of Hartford, signed by the Puritans and their Native allies following the Pequot War, the Mohegan and Narragansett leaders, Uncas and Miantonomi, shook hands to formalize the agreement dispossessing the Pequot, but Uncas flatly refused Miantonomi's invitation to share a meal of venison procured by Narragansett hunters. Offering Narragansett food to Uncas, in this case, was not just a demonstration of Miantonomi's liberality; it was also an attempt to display his own power and authority over Uncas in an aggressive gesture that the Mohegan leader rejected. Their erstwhile alliance deteriorated over the following five years. In 1643, Miantonomi led a Narragansett army in a failed invasion of the Mohegan communities west of the Connecticut River and was killed by Uncas's brother.[44]

In the wake of these wars and conflicts, English colonists began to lay claim to New England's agricultural spaces more aggressively, removing the physical evidence of Native activities and presences. The desecration of Miantonomi's grave offers an example of how the transformation of southern New England from a Native agricultural space to a colonial one entailed the removal of monuments that marked the region's deep and dynamic Native history in order to facilitate the "erase and replace" imperatives of marking New England as a Puritan possession. After Miantonomi's death, his family and friends built a large cairn—or stone mound—to mark the site, a form of grave commemoration common throughout much of the Native northeast. Just as the English preferred to plant their own crops on fields cleared by past Indian labor, however, they also helped themselves to any convenient stacks of building materials left by Native families mourning their dead. In 1659, colonists from Saybrook founded the town of Norwich, Connecticut, along the trail where Miantonomi had been murdered sixteen years earlier. With "despicable cupidity," according to one of the town's earliest historians, the colonists removed the monument of his gravesite and used its stones to construct their barnyard walls.[45]

In addition to the agricultural labor that the English performed in their acts of colonial dispossession, their process for taking the lands of New England also entailed the willful forgetting of its Native histories. This activity hinged on eliminating any physical traces of Indian permanence—such as Miantonomi's grave. The myth also gained traction from the fabrication and propagation of narratives that depicted Native people not as farmers at all, but as misogynistic and bloodthirsty hunters.

The transformation of Native fields into Puritan farms was a jarring cultural transition that required a complete regendering and resexualization of the agricultural landscape. Whereas Puritan farms were generally, outside of the kitchen garden, the responsibility of men, Native agricultural production had long been the responsibility of women. Thus, from the colonial perspective, the transformation of New England's agricultural landscapes into a patriarchal universe of towns and farms was accompanied by the male possession of the land itself. If the land was not "virginal" in the strict sense that it had never before been farmed—as it had, in fact, been farmed for many generations by Native women—it was nevertheless virginal, in the colonial rendering, in that it had remained unplowed by white men. Sexual imaginations of Native New England's fields and farms animated many of the excitements and anxieties of Puritan life in the seventeenth century.[46]

Puritan men commonly asserted that the polygyny of Native family structure, as well as the fact that Native women were typically responsible for agricultural labor while men attended to the "leisure" of hunting, marked Native women as the slaves of their lazy Native husbands. The

Plymouth poet William Morrell set such condemnations to verse. His "Poem on New-England," for instance, after some long-winded assessments of the physical attractiveness of Native women, concluded with a judgment of their drudgery: "Thus all worke—women doe, whilst men play / In hunting, armes, and plesures, end the day."[47] For Morrell and other Puritan men, these perceptions of Native women's bondage fueled sexual fantasies that extended not only to the bodies of Native women but also to the fertile lands they occupied. Purporting to rescue Native women from these unmanned fields, English men asserted a masculine conquest of New England's agriculture landscape.

Much more so than revealing any truths about the relationships between Native men and women, these colonial assessments of Native women's drudgery reflected anxieties about the realities of marriage in colonial society. Marriage in colonial New England was an expectation, especially for women. And while the relative demographic shortage of women to men in early colonial New England meant that women were in high demand as brides, the misogynistic circumstances of the Puritan institution of marriage also ensured, paradoxically, that women held low social value. In the event that Puritan women complained about this plight, the Puritan imagination of Native women's drudgery served as counterpoint. In *New-England's Prospect*, for instance, William Wood made this misogynistic lesson plain in his discussion of Native women's agricultural work. "To satisfie the curious eyes of women-readers, who otherwise might think their sex forgotten, or not worthy a record," he scorned, "they may see their own happinesse if weighed in the womans ballance of these ruder Indians."[48] Denigrating the labor of Native women farmers served the dual purpose of justifying the colonists' patriarchal claims to Native lands as well as the mistreatment of Puritan women.

Life was difficult for most women in colonial New England, who were pressured by social convention, religious ordination, and legal decree to subordinate themselves to a man's authority. The English principle of coverture stripped married women of their legal identities, a suppression of basic civil rights with wide-ranging consequences. In a colonial world where the accumulation of wealth relied upon access to other people's labor, the key to a Puritan patriarch's success was a large family, and so Puritan men kept strict political control over women's bodies in order to maintain their command over reproduction. The need for the agricultural labor of sons to grow food and the household labor of daughters to cook it, according to James Voto and Dorothy Denneen Voto, gave children an "economic value that could not be dismissed simply due to the inconvenience of pregnancy and childbirth."[49] In the seventeenth century, an average woman in New England gave birth seven times, a figure that actually underestimates the experiences of those women who survived their first several pregnancies and typically went on to birth ten or more children over their lifetimes—approximately two-thirds of whom survived to adulthood.[50] Wives who did die in childbirth—a common occurrence—were replaced by their widowers, who, with their successive wives, lived to father many more children than one woman alone could ever be expected to bear. To a certain extent, then, Puritan families often encompassed a kind of monogamous polygyny that mainly differed from the polygyny of Native societies in that only one wife at a time bore the entire matronly burden.

The charge that Native women toiled away in the fields elided the reality that Puritan women also contributed substantial agricultural labor, especially during the critical months of spring planting and fall harvesting. As the research of Laurel Thatcher Ulrich has demonstrated, colonial women played diverse roles in New England's agricultural economy. While men were generally expected to oversee the fields of row crops, women were responsible for nearly all of the work maintaining the vegetable gardens, which provided colonial families with many staple foods such as dried beans and peas, root crops like parsnips, turnips, and onions, and seasonal greens including cabbage.[51] Condemning Native men for sending their women to the fields reflected the anxieties of Puritan men whose own labors could not, on their own, provide for their families.

Puritan assessments of Native men "playing" in the forest chasing wild animals also said more about their own misconceptions regarding hunting than about the actual specificities of Native hunting practices. Most English colonists had little or no experience as hunters before their arrival in North America, and as the seventeenth century proceeded, fewer and fewer would. Alongside the enclosure and privatization of Britain's late-medieval manorial common lands, royal authorities had imposed a property qualification on hunting—and gun ownership—that effectively removed hunting as a staple of the peasantry's food subsistence strategy, establishing it instead as a leisurely diversion for the landed aristocracy. The colonists had no idea how to hunt, nor did most of them know what flesh such as venison even tasted like until a Wamponoag or Powhatan put some on their table. During the infamous

Starving Time at Jamestown, for instance, even the veteran officers of the Virginia Company were unable to kill much in the way of wildlife to eat. As Captain John Smith admitted: "Though there be fish in the Sea, foules in the Ayre, and Beasts in the woods, their bounds are so large, they so wilde, and we so weake, and ignorant, we cannot much trouble them."[52] During his travels to the Massachusetts Bay Colony in the early 1630s, William Wood mocked the Puritans' useless hunting efforts: "Many goe blurting away their pouder and shot, that have no more skill to kill, or winne a Goose, than many in England that have rustie Muskets in their houses."[53] Powerless to feed themselves from what Wood and Smith both observed to be an immense natural bounty, colonists in both Virginia and New England relied primarily on provisions imported from England and the Caribbean during their first decades of existence. Only after these communities had established substantial herds of cattle and pigs could they make any claim of self-sufficient food security—a project that dawdled at least through the end of the 1630s across most of New England.[54]

Once these English herds of cattle and pigs had become established, the Puritans' dependence on the animals' bodies for their own nourishment was astonishing. "Colonists," observed colonial historian Virginia DeJohn Anderson, "took literally God's promise to Noah that 'every moving thing that liveth shall be meat for you,' rejecting only insects and reptiles."[55] Although it became a colonial commonplace to depict Native people as bloodthirsty hunters and slayers of animals—rendering them even as animalistic "beasts of the forests"—the true daily butchers of seventeenth-century New England were Puritans, who sustained their families on the meat, milk, and eggs of the cows, pigs, chickens, goats, and sheep that wandered in and out of their pastures and surrounding woods. Hunting and killing wild animals might have been beyond the typical skillset of a seventeenth-century colonist, but slaughtering tame animals was a mundane affair. Colonists, even those of modest means who could barely afford to purchase bread baked from wheat flour (an even scarcer commodity in New England than in England itself), usually ate meat, whether salted or fresh, several times a day and nearly always from the bodies of domestic livestock—an experience that differed enormously from the nearly meatless diet of working-class England.

These so-called domestic animals, however, ran amok across the fictitious borders between private land and public land, pasture and forest, wild and domesticated. Puritans such as John Winthrop, Robert Cushman, and Frances Higginson prided themselves on their cleared fields and tidy plantings, arguing that such small "improvements" to the agricultural landscape of New England justified their expropriation of Native lands and their own claims of ownership. But, in reality, the lives of their domestic animals trampled across their pastoral fantasies. Raising cattle in colonial New England, for instance, required an extensive amount of agricultural land on the order of five to six acres per animal.[56]

The ways that colonists relied on the bodies of domestic animals to feed themselves is perhaps best illustrated through their intimate relationships with milk cows. Until recently, historians have largely overlooked the significance of dairying in the colonial economy, an art—or "ticklish business," according to one Puritan farmer—that fell more often within the province of women's labor than men's. But dairying in colonial New England was far from an incidental byproduct of raising cattle for beef.[57] Colonists relied more regularly on milk, butter, and cheese for their daily sustenance than any other animal product, and each consumed an average of fifteen pounds of butter and up to forty pounds of cheese per annum.[58] These homemade staples were also useful for clearing out colonial families' mercantile accounts. As the historian James McWilliams has demonstrated, Massachusetts Bay Colony merchants took payment in dairy products from more than one quarter of their customers, who managed, on average, to pay 45 percent of their aggregate bill in milk, butter, and cheese, much of which was exported to markets in the British Caribbean.[59]

The daily chores of colonial women tasked with producing milk, butter, and cheese from the bodies of cattle reprised the broader ways that colonial society shackled motherhood to economic production. Dairying required the management of a ceaseless reproductive cycle. As is the case with all mammalian species, milk cows produce milk only after giving birth. This milk nourishes calves through infancy, providing a temporary liquid food source before their digestive systems have matured enough to eat grass, hay, and other solid foods. Colonists, however, separated dairy cows from their calves at the earliest possible moment in order to insert themselves under the teats of the nursing mother. If consistently milked three times a day, a calf-less cow could be expected to produce milk for about another nine months, after which she would be impregnated by a bull and repeat the progression anew.

Dairying was not only labor intensive; it also required a considerable amount of other inputs. Milk cows required many extra calories in order to produce milk. Thomas Jefferson's milk cows, for instance, famously ate an average of forty pounds of hay each day, in addition to garden refuse.[60] For the Puritan diet, the importance of dairying extended well beyond the consumption of fresh milk. The calves themselves were most often slaughtered at the age of about two days old, not to put veal on the table, but to help produce two other significant ingredients of colonial foodways: rennet and gelatin. Cheesemakers produced rennet from the linings of the calves' unweaned stomachs, disemboweling them, salting them, and stretching them on hoops. Once cured, cheesemakers could use pieces of this rennet as needed to separate out the unwanted whey from milk.[61] Women also boiled down the calves' tender bones, joints, and connective tissues to make calf's-foot jelly, a gelatinous staple ingredient in colonial pies, puddings, and other desserts.[62] In this way, the widespread significance of dairy cattle to multiple areas of the Puritan diet meant that domesticated animals comprised one of the essential components of the colonial food system.

Colonialism in seventeenth-century New England entailed nothing less than the reworking of Native foods and agricultural spaces to suit the desires and expectations of the English. The environmental historian Alfred Crosby has famously defined this global colonial process as the effort to transform much of the world into a "neo-Europe."[63] The importation of domesticated pigs and cattle helped to serve this purpose in New England and elsewhere. But the English did not arrive with everything they needed to become "self-sufficient." In order to accomplish that, they needed to take Native crops, like corn, and Native fields, like those at Patuxet and along the Connecticut River valley. They occupied Native agricultural spaces, refashioned them as white possessions, and then worked to erase or obscure the history of their Native American agricultural past.

The increasing violence with which the colonists took possession of New England sparked another war in 1675. Known as King Philip's War, the conflict pitted a coalition of Native people, led by a Wampanoag man named Metacom (or Philip) and a Narragansett man named Canonchet, in an anti-colonial war of resistance against the English. Food provided the single most important strategic element of the war, and hunger drove the military decisions made by both sides. For instance, the vulnerability of the colonists' livestock drove colonial officials to order those in outlying towns to "kill and salt up what of their cattell were fit to kill, and secure it in the best places they can from their enemie."[64] As the most distinctive of all English livestock, cattle were targeted by Native soldiers not just to starve the colonists but also to terrify them. In addition to the nearly three thousand English colonists left dead by the war's end, more than eight thousand head of English cattle had also been slain.[65]

For their part, the English also targeted Native foods in order to starve and terrify their enemies. At the battle of Turner's Falls, widely noted by military historians as the turning point of the war, the English turned their attention to the Indians' food stores and other possessions and dumped into the Connecticut River any item that they could neither immediately eat nor light on fire. When news of the massacre reached Boston, fellow Puritans rejoiced to hear that "several Hundreds" of Wampanoag, Narragansett, and Nipmuck people had been slaughtered, but they heralded the destruction of Indian food and property as a strategic accomplishment "more considerable than their Lives," since in their analysis, food, unlike men, could "hardly be soon and easily recruited."[66] It was in response to this news that the governing council of Charlestown, Massachusetts, proclaimed the first officially recorded Day of Thanksgiving, to be held on June 29, 1676, in commemoration of what the proclamation declared as a victory over the "Heathen Natives of this land."[67]

The massacre at Turner's Falls was one of the last mass killings of King Philip's War, a conflict that the esteemed colonial historian Frances Jennings called the "Puritan War of Conquest."[68] By waging war against both Indian people and against all manifestations of Native food and agriculture, the colonists' campaign of scorched earth and genocide shattered the Native military alliance. Canonchet, the Narragansett leader, analyzed the situation and foresaw disaster if his forces could not plant a crop of corn to sustain themselves for the coming year. Risking torture and death, he traveled through enemy territory to his former fields near Providence, Rhode Island, to salvage seed corn, hoping to bring it back to plant in the abandoned English farms of the upper Connecticut River valley where his embattled troops resided; a last-ditch effort to ensure that his soldiers and their families might subsist on more substantial foods than fish, lean game, and whatever roots and fruits could be foraged from the woods. The colony of Rhode Island was officially neutral during the conflict, but that did not stop the armies of the Plymouth, Connecticut, and Massachusetts Bay colonies, along with their Mohegan, Niantic, and Pequot allies, from ruthlessly stalking its fields and forests in search of their enemies. A company of Pequot and Connecticut soldiers captured

Canonchet near his home, with seed corn in hand, and marched him in chains to the colonial town of Stonington, where he was beheaded and quartered.[69]

Canonchet's fate was soon repeated as Metacom's hungry and bereaved army melted away. Many of his troops returned to their devastated homes in the south only to be murdered by colonists, their families wrenched apart and sold into slavery in the West Indies. Others attempted to carve out new lives for themselves in the foreign lands of the north and west, preferring to take their chances with their old enemies, the Abenaki and the Mohawk peoples, over the ruthless English. Instead of fleeing, Metacom, like Canonchet, returned to his former home near Bristol, where, in early August, he was discovered and shot by a Christian "praying Indian" named John Alderman. Puritan authorities allowed Alderman to keep one of Metacom's hands as a trophy, but took the rest of his body to Plymouth, where they beheaded and quartered his remains, then parboiled them to resist spoilage. Thus cooked, Metacom's weathered head lasted for twenty years, displayed on the end of a pike near the entrance to Plymouth's fort.[70]

This horrific brutality was more than just a technical step in the process of embalmment—it was an expression of the colonists' supposed dominance over what they understood as New England's strange and profligate wilderness, a mastery demonstrated through this metabolic act that was part taxidermy and part cannibalism. Displayed like the bust of a moose, Metacom's severed head did the cultural work of elevating the colonists' expanding agricultural society by memorializing its human foe as a vanquished wild beast. The mounted spectacle swept aside the fact that Metacom and his fellow Wampanoag brethren were farmers and rendered them instead as animalistic creatures of the forest. The grisly artifact illuminated the colonists' powers of consumption, representing their ability to harness and devour the countryside that lay beyond the gates of their towns and villages. This they had accomplished over the course of the war, laying waste to the abundant Indian farming communities that peppered their colonies and with whom they had once grudgingly shared New England as neighbors. Metacom's head was more than just a warning or a war trophy—it symbolized Plymouth's claim to Wampanoag lands based on their uprooting of the cultural, social, and economic foundations of the Indians' agricultural lives.

In this manner, food not only provided the single most important strategic element of King Philip's War but also emerged at the center of a new colonial logic that structured ideas about cultural difference through an agricultural prism that cast Englishmen as civilized farmers and Indians as savage hunters. According to this logic, colonists could lay rightful claim to Indian lands because colonization would domesticate and improve it; they would carve their farms and settlements from an unruly and forested wilderness, not from a world that was already populated with the ordered farms and settlements of Native people. During and after King Philip's War, the colonists of New England sought to erase southern New England's Native agricultural history both by destroying its physical traces in the landscape and by creating false narratives of its absence, particularly in their accounts of how Indians ate. Although colonists did eat in ways that substantially borrowed from Native foodways during their first decades in New England, by the 1640s their diets had diverged. King Philip's War tore apart the interspersed agricultural terrain of Native and colonial New England. In the shared world that emerged after 1676, where Native communities in New England acclimated to new lives under the constant threat of violence, ideas about food and agricultural largely demarcated colonial boundaries between settler and Indian, domestic and wild. These colonial misconceptions of Native food history remain and need to be untangled.

2.

Food and Diplomacy in Iroquoia

In the century after King Philip's War, food and agriculture began to take on even greater importance in shaping diplomatic relationships between Native communities and British colonists, particularly in Iroquoia, the homeland of the Haudenosaunee (or Iroquois) people. Spanning the uplands of the Atlantic coastal plain to the lower Great Lakes, Iroquoia constituted a sovereign Native geography that separated the British colonies along the seaboard from the French colonies of the continental interior. The region held immense strategic significance as a middle ground between European empires. Even more consequentially, however, Iroquoia served as the agricultural center of the Haudenosaunee. Organized into enormous, interplanted fields of corn, beans, and squash; orchards of fruits, nuts, and other perennial crops; and forest parkland for deer and other game, Iroquoia provided an agricultural basis for Haudenosaunee sovereignty and self-sufficiency. One of the most powerful Native polities in North America, the Iroquois Confederacy, interacted with English and French colonists on their own terms; treaty-making processes required European colonists to participate in Haudenosaunee rituals of food and diplomacy that not only centered their own customs but also acknowledged and preserved Haudenosaunee possession of Iroquoia.

Food played a vital role in the diplomatic engagements of the Haudenosaunee in ways that highlight the significance of food and agriculture in expressions of political identity and sovereignty. The multiday performance of Haudenosaunee treaty rituals required participants to merge their pursuit of political ambitions with the quotidian necessities of eating in ways that fundamentally reordered the imperatives of empire. Success did not just entail a final tally of diplomatic compromises; it also involved a fuller set of shared experiences that built a common ground of understanding between participants. By bundling up the business of diplomacy with the household routines of cooking, eating, and celebrating, these multiday rituals established bonds of intimacy that helped authenticate promises made by all sides. The domestic setting of these rituals and the presence of the fruits of Haudenosaunee agriculture throughout not only expressed the legitimacy of Haudenosaunee sovereignty over Iroquoia, their homeland, but also contextualized this sovereignty within an ancient territorial ancestry that tied their lives to the land through farming.

These aspects of Haudenosaunee diplomacy were unmistakable to both Native and European negotiators who were tasked with establishing terms of war and peace with the Haudenosaunee. Agreements over such life-affirming (or -denying) relationships could not be procured solely by the stroke of the pen, but through full participation in robust Haudenosaunee protocols intended to establish and ensure the earnestness of all participants. Food provided a foundation for these holistic treaty-making experiences, both in terms of its physical necessity for fueling bodies and minds during deliberations that could take months and in terms of the quotidian, diplomatic symbolism of preparing and sharing meal after meal. Over the course of the eighteenth century, British and Haudenosaunee diplomats strengthened their nations' ties through these gastronomic and diplomatic rituals, establishing a series of alliances that served not only to maintain Haudenosaunee power and possession over Iroquoia but also to expand this power westward into the upper Great Lakes and southward toward the Ohio River. Likewise, the alliances benefitted the British, who relied on the Haudenosaunee to help prosecute a series of wars against the French that culminated in the surrender of New France to the British in 1763.

In 1768, five years after the Treaty of Paris transformed Canada into a British possession, however, a much different kind of treaty proceeding was taking place in Iroquoia. That fall, more than three-thousand representatives of the six nations of the Iroquois Confederacy converged upon Fort Stanwix, one of the westernmost outposts of imperial British power in North America. Built by the British in the heart of the historic Haudenosaunee homeland in 1754, at the beginning of the French and Indian War, Fort Stanwix presided atop a small rise that separated the tributary waters of the Hudson River from those of Lake Ontario. This height of land, known to the British as the Oneida Carry, had served for generations as a direct connection between Iroquoia and the city of New York, providing a relatively short and flat canoe portage of one to six miles—depending on seasonal river flows—across a grassy plain that divided the waters of New York Harbor from the Great Lakes. By muscling their boats from the North American interior across this portage, traders and other travelers had the most direct access to the Atlantic seaboard, floating their goods down the Mohawk River—the only river carving a course through the Adirondack and Catskill Mountains—and then down the Hudson. During the seventeenth and eighteenth centuries this strategic location came to prominence as a premier trading site for the Haudenosaunee's commerce in food, furs, and firearms with the British. A variety of semi-permanent trading posts and camps emerged along the carry tracks where the Haudenosaunee moved their longboats between the Wood Creek and the Mohawk River on either end of the portage. The location retained its geographic importance into the nineteenth century, serving as the site for the city of Rome, New York, the functional halfway point between Buffalo and Manhattan on the Erie Canal route across upstate New York.

The Haudenosaunee who arrived at Fort Stanwix in 1768 trickled into the fort over the course of three or four weeks, in groups both small and large, to enter into a peace treaty with the British that would firmly establish sovereign Haudenosaunee title to thousands of square miles of land west of the Royal Proclamation Line of 1763, land that had been occupied by British colonists and land speculators in the years both during and after the French and Indian War. This war, perhaps more appropriately termed from an Indigenous perspective as the French and English War, had raged for more than a decade in North America. Unlike the seven years of fighting in Europe that were resolved with Treaty of Paris in 1763, the course of the North American conflict smoldered well into the 1760s in a series of battles fought between shifting factions of British colonists and Native communities across the vast, forested mountains and valleys of the entire Appalachian crest. The Treaty of Paris, in short, had left peace between Native Americans, the British, and British colonists unresolved. In agreeing to turn all of their North American colonies over to the British, the French, following their defeat, had effectively given the British an enormous amount of territory that had never really been French to begin with, but remained unceded Native land. Immediately after the French withdrawal, their former Indian allies organized a new offensive against British forces, striking colonial settlements and military outposts in Michigan, Ohio, and all the way down the Mississippi Valley. Named Pontiac's War after a prominent Ottawa leader who fought the British, this bloody backcountry conflict ended in a stalemate after years of back-and-forth invasions. The Haudenosaunee who traveled to Fort Stanwix had done so to meet with the British in order to figure out how to move forward after ending a war—one not acknowledged in the royal map halls of Europe—but that had nevertheless taken the British and their Haudenosaunee allies more than a decade to finish.

Greeting the thousands of Haudenosaunee guests was William Johnson, the British representative of King George who, along with a handful of subordinates, who were tasked with hosting one of the largest treaty ceremonies ever executed by British colonial agents. Johnson himself a longtime veteran of British colonial affairs, having served for nearly thirty years in varying capacities as a royal representative to the Haudenosaunee. Central to Johnson's conception of diplomacy was a pragmatic tailoring of treaty proceedings toward Native expectations. He was considered by the British to be their preeminent expert on Haudenosaunee diplomacy, and he was a valued agent and source of information for other British diplomats in Europe and elsewhere.[1] Many among the Haudenosaunee also felt that Johnson had proved his value as a go-between during his years working as a diplomat. The Mohawk chief Theyanoguin, for instance, remarked that Johnson's "knowledge of our affairs made us think him one of us (an Indian)."[2] The foremost lesson of Johnson's career was that in order to effectively negotiate with the Haudenosaunee, the British needed to do so largely on Haudenosaunee terms, which required weeks of advanced planning in order to solve the logistical challenges of feeding thousands of people for possibly weeks on end.

The scale and substance of Haudenosaunee treaty negotiations differed dramatically from what most European diplomats were accustomed to in the European courts of the eighteenth century. Unlike European diplomatic exchanges, which customarily occurred in private settings, the Haudenosaunee treaty proceedings at Fort Stanwix required entire communities to be present; decisions would not be made by a few representatives behind closed doors but with the unanimous assent of all the participants. Furthermore, the meeting was not solely, or even mostly, about the specific business of diplomacy. While everyone present would care about the specific business of where to fix the British's revised Proclamation Line of 1763 and determine how that would affect the Haudenosaunee, the ceremonies of the treaty process themselves were also an integral performance of the British-Haudenosaunee relationship that would recommit the two parties to friendship. The meeting would last for days. With this in mind, Johnson had begun making preparations for how to feed everyone before doing practically anything else, writing to his superiors in London for permission to purchase a recurring supply of thousands of pounds of pork and flour that would be delivered weekly over a period of six months while the treaty negotiations took place. He also secured a stockpile of corn, rum, and whatever other provisions were available.[3] These provisions would not only fuel the negotiations but would also be vital for rekindling the earnestness of the Haudenosaunee's relationship with the British.

The meals shared by participants throughout the treaty proceedings reflected Haudenosaunee conceptions of the democratic process. Unlike the rectangular English dining tables that structured formal events in British settings with hierarchical seating arrangements, Haudenosaunee customs dictated that all participants eat together, either seated on the floor or leaning against a wall, facing each other across the center of a room where eaters were served from a common pot.[4] The pot itself also recapitulated the circular, democratic theme, its lip separated into sections along the circumference, each portion decorated with icons representing the different nations and parties present at the proceeding. According to Arthur C. Parker, members from each nation would dip their ladles into their section of this central feast bowl before taking their seats at the perimeter.[5]

The rhythm of Haudenosaunee mealtimes also differed from British expectations. Instead of sitting for two or three distinct daily meals, typical Haudenosaunee custom was to prepare a single meal in the late morning that would simmer on heat for the remainder of the day, refreshed with ingredients as needed, and eaters served themselves additional helpings as they became hungry.[6] This Haudenosaunee habit of eating throughout the day persisted well into the nineteenth century. The anthropologist Lewis Henry Morgan, for instance, described the practice as a central pattern of longhouse life that altered only after Haudenosaunee families began to transition toward living in single-family households.[7] The custom facilitated conversations and created opportunities for participants at long treaty proceedings to talk outside of the channels of authority that structured formal meals in the English tradition.

For nearly a century the Haudenosaunee had been aligned with the British in a relationship called the Covenant Chain.[8] The Covenant Chain represented more than just a diplomatic treaty in the usual sense understood by Europeans; it was an expression of political kinship that required ongoing efforts to perform and maintain. British and Haudenosaunee diplomats, as well as their friends and families, converged often for treaty rituals that not only dealt with the immediate diplomatic negotiations of planning for war or arranging boundary lines but also reestablished and strengthened bonds of peace, symbolized visually by the Haudenosaunee with the image of interlocking arms.[9] The Covenant Chain also existed as a specific narration of Haudenosaunee-British intercultural diplomacy. An oral recitation of the history of British and Haudenosaunee kinship that was expressed by the Covenant Chain was an integral part of diplomatic meetings between the two nations and served to remind participants of the historical obligations that the two groups had toward one another while also emphasizing Haudenosaunee independence and political sovereignty by tracing the Covenant Chain back to the arrival of the English.[10]

The easternmost of Haudenosaunee nations, the Mohawk Nation, first entered into the Covenant Chain relationship with the English in 1676, when the Haudenosaunee came to the aid of the New England colonies during their war against the Wampanoags, Narragansetts, and other Native communities mobilized by Metacom (also known as King Philip). Time and again, from the end of the seventeenth century through the middle of the eighteenth, the Haudenosaunee helped the English during times of war, most usually fighting the French and their Native allies, including the Wendats (Hurons), Ojibwas, and other Algonquian-speaking peoples to the west.

Food framed many steps of this diplomatic performance, and the roots of this treaty-making process reached deep into precolonial Haudenosaunee history. Eighteenth-century practices reflected longstanding Haudenosaunee diplomatic traditions, many which remain in use today.[11] In short, before any treaties or land cessions commenced, the British had to meet the Haudenosaunee on Native ground and provide them with food and other ceremonial gifts that represented British goodwill as much as they expressed British wealth and power. Moreover, the British had to meet with what must have seemed to them to be a bewildering and heterogeneous array of Haudenosaunee leaders. The hundreds of sachems and headmen that arrived at Fort Stanwix, for instance, represented the uneven distribution of authority that accompanied the Haudenosaunee's noncoercive cultures of government and power. These considerations traced their origins to the Haudenosaunee's diplomatic traditions rather than those of the British, who would have been far more comfortable to discuss treaty terms among a small handful of monarchical representatives as was the European style. Johnson's success in aligning the varied agents of Iroquoia and Britain resulted from a long career of learning to how negotiate colonial politics on Native terms. Introducing these heterogenous spokespeople to one another took time, and formalizing these conversations to occur within the setting of a meal provided a patient and comfortable venue for representatives to acquaint themselves. Haudenosaunee custom also dictated that negotiators from one party wait for a day before responding to another party's orators, and these structured pauses built additional time for representatives to meet with each other in casual moments outside the realm of official discussion. Long after representatives had forgotten the specific details of the diplomatic agreements they had worked out, they still remembered these quotidian experiences of food and socializing at the weeks-long treaty proceedings that bonded them with their allies in ways that ink alone could not secure.

Food and the multidimensional political bonds that these treaty proceedings helped established had been central to Haudenosaunee diplomacy ever since the emergence of the original Five Nations as an affiliated bloc, a process that most likely began around the fifteenth century and had solidified by the end of the seventeenth. Agriculture was one of the foundational elements of Haudenosaunee life that united Haudenosaunee clans and nations. As the historian Thomas Wessel remarks, "farming not only provided a stable food supply, it permeated the whole of Haudenosaunee social and political structure."[12] In a matrifocal society structured by the importance of women's agricultural knowledge and labor, decisions of social and political significance were commonly made in the setting of a feast.

The feasts that accompanied the Haudenosaunee treaty-making process with the British emerged through the evolution of peacekeeping practices that were designed to curb bloodshed between Haudenosaunee clans. Like some other Native communities in precolonial northeastern North America, the Haudenosaunee participated in what historians and anthropologists have described as "mourning wars," a type of reciprocal violence driven by ritualized grieving. Whenever a Haudenosaunee clan or extended family suffered the death of one or more of its members during war, the clan would raid enemy clans with the goal of kidnapping captives to replace their dead. Once home, the family matriarchs would decide the fate of these captives: either they would be adopted as literal substitutes for recently deceased family members (as sons, daughters, husbands, or wives), or else they would be tortured and put to death according to rituals intended to comfort the families of the aggrieved. Whether a captive ended up being executed or adopted, their fate was invariably accompanied by ceremonial feasts that brought together the entire community to participate in the impending ceremony and decision-making process.

The captives themselves were invited and expected to enjoy this feast as well. After being rested and fed, those selected for adoption undertook a requickening ceremony that brought them back from the brink of death into the world as Haudenosaunees. Those condemned to death were tied to stakes and methodically burned with firebrands wielded by members of the deceased's family. Following the victim's death, their seared flesh was ripped from their bones and boiled in a cooking kettle. Whether or not the Haudenosaunee actually ate the bodies of captives slain in this manner is not known. Given the broader cultural histories of cannibalism and colonial ethnography, it is likely that the Jesuit and other colonial accounts of Haudenosaunee anthropophagy reveal more about the fears and anxieties of the European chroniclers than the Native subjects they describe. However, a large body of evidence demonstrates that the Haudenosaunee participated in significant mourning feasts centered around the mutilation and dissolution of captive bodies by fire, water, and other elements of cookery. Native sources on the grieving feasts are ambiguous, and the colonial ethnographies are also unclear and exaggerated—as Daniel Richter has put it, "most European observers were too shocked to probe its implications."[13] Whether or not the Haudenosaunee literally ate the bodies of slain captives is beside the point—the grieving climax of the mourning war represented in all cases the absorption of the enemy into the clan's body politic.[14]

For many historians, perhaps the most significant set of seventeenth-century sources documenting the ritual practices of these feasts and mourning wars, as well as other major ceremonies involving food, death, and the digestion of souls, are the Jesuit *Relations*, a series of newsletters published annually in France from 1632 until 1673 that collected written reports of the Jesuit missionaries working among the Native peoples of New France and circulated them to French readers. The *Relations*, according to historian of French colonialism Erik R. Seeman, were essentially "a fundraising tool" in that the goal of their publication was to realistically narrate "both triumphs and disappointments" in order to encourage wealthy French subscribers to continue supporting the Jesuit's missionary endeavors.[15] Although they inherently reflected the French perspectives of their authors, the *Relations* nevertheless portrayed Native ceremonies with interest, detail, and candor. The Jesuits, in fact, expressed that they held much spiritual common ground with the Haudenosaunee peoples despite the wide sacramental gulfs between them. The similarities extended especially to the shared Catholic and Haudenosaunee curiosity about death and reverence for the remains of the dead. In 1636, for instance, the Jesuit father Jean de Brebeuf witnessed with much sympathy the Wendat "Feast of the Dead," a ceremony in which two thousand villagers reburied the bones of seven hundred friends and family members after moving their town to a new location. The proximity between foodways and deathways demonstrated a Native understanding of life itself as a type of metabolism that resonated with Jesuit sensibilities. Not unlike the Catholic sacrament of communion, in which priests administer the transubstantiated body and blood of Christ to their parishioners to help ensure rebirth in the afterlife, the Haudenosaunee and Wendat customs surrounding death and interment also revolve around feasting. In this way, the spiritual links between food, life, and belonging structured Haudenosaunee sensibilities toward diplomacy in ways that many Europeans intrinsically understood.

These considerations about death and life structured Native agriculture in Iroquoia as well as neighboring areas of the Great Lakes region. For instance, the Wendats, an Iroquoian people that left Iroquoia sometime during the fourteenth century and migrated northwestward into present-day Ontario, understood that person had two souls, one of which remained in the bones after death. At death, the first soul was released to an afterlife in the village of the dead, where people lived forever with the magnificent abundance of continual good harvests. Simultaneously, the other soul remained locked in the dead person's bones until it eventually left to inhabit the body of a nearby newborn baby. Thus, keeping the bones of a dead friend or family member in close proximity was of paramount importance to ensuring this cycle of rebirth and reanimation.

Likewise, the bones of animals slain for food and fur also contained souls, so they were returned to the forest, buried, and treated with care and respect.[16]

These cycles of rebirth characterized farm work in Iroquoia, which was focused on the annual cultivation of corn and other crops, but without the use of plows or the intensive removal or tilling of the earth. Like the Native communities of southern New England, the Wendats and the Haudenosaunee lived near the northern climatic edge of corn cultivation, establishing the region as a major center for agriculture and trade. Algonquins from the north, west, and east traded furs and meat to both groups in exchange for corn. And, in turn, the Haudenosaunee and Wendats traded furs to Susquehannocks, Delawares, Shawnees, Cherokees, and other Native peoples to the south in exchange for tobacco, seashells, and other items. Both communities thrived. Archaeological evidence suggests that the populations of Iroquoia and Wendake (the Wendat homeland) numbered about twenty thousand individuals each by the end of the sixteenth century, spread among dozens of villages that ranged in population from several hundred to over one thousand people. The overall healthfulness of these communities was also astounding relative to global comparisons during the preindustrial era. Archaeologists have estimated that the average Wendat person could expect to live about fifty years and that 70 percent of Wendats survived childhood (i.e., reached the age of fifteen years) while only around 50 percent of European children did likewise. This difference can likely be attributed to the relative absence of infectious diseases in the Great Lakes region before European contact. The fact that the Wendats and Haudenosaunees kept no domesticated animals except for dogs meant that they did not suffer and die, at least until European contact, from the debilitating zoonotic diseases of the Old World such as small pox, the bubonic plague, and various influenzas.[17]

By the seventeenth century, Haudenosaunee farms south of Lake Ontario had been perfected into a largely sustainable agricultural system based on the three-sisters method of cultivating corn, beans, and squash in the fertile soils of what is now western New York state. Ethnographic sources as well as agronomic evidence suggest that the productivity of Haudenosaunee corn cultivation was double or even triple the average grain yields harvested on farms in Britain and in continental Europe.[18] Haudenosaunee farmers had the advantage of working with some of the most fertile soils in eastern North America, but the key to their success rested on paying close attention to maintaining this fertility by eliminating weeds, minimizing agricultural runoff, and returning organic matter to the soil. Unlike the Wendats and others who periodically relocated their farms and villages due to fertility constraints and the need for fallowing, Haudenosaunee fields were far more permanent. In all likelihood, chronic infestations of insects in Haudenosaunee grain storage, rather than soil fertility, prompted occasional shifts in village location.[19]

The biochemistry of corn itself also contributed to the enormous productivity of Haudenosaunee agriculture in North America. By being able to concentrate carbon dioxide and convert it more efficiently into sugar than other plants, corn offers inherent advantage over other grain crops. The cell structure of the corn plant's leaf blades enable an efficient and somewhat unique form of photosynthesis that reduces the amount of water and oxygen lost by the plant throughout its respiratory process. Called C4 photosynthesis because it relies on the creation of four-carbon molecules rather than three-carbon molecules like most other plants, the process draws carbon dioxide from the atmosphere into the corn plant through small holes, called stomata, in the bottom of each leaf blade. Special cells inside the leaf blade then convert the carbon dioxide into a four-carbon molecule that can be transformed into sugar without having to release additional oxygen. Most other major grain plants—including barley, oats, rye, and wheat—are C3 plants, meaning that they photosynthesize carbon dioxide into three-carbon molecules. The transformation of these three-carbon molecules into sugars requires the plants to vent additional oxygen and hydrogen molecules back out through the stomata, slowing down the metabolic process and drying out the plants much faster on hot and humid days. The net result is that corn and other C4 plants convert air, water, and nutrients into calories comestible by humans and animals to a far more efficient degree than C3 plants, especially in the warm, humid growing season associated with continental climates.

Aside from the biochemical advantages that corn has over wheat and other grains, it also has physical advantages. Its large seeds, or kernels, allow corn to germinate successfully more compact soils. At planting time, this provides a major advantage over wheat and other smaller-seeded grains that require looser, more intensively prepared soil in order to ensure reliable germination. The small seeds of wheat and other plants also held fewer of their own nutrients so were susceptible to being outcompeted for water and nutrients by weeds while in their seedling stage. Corn, on the other hand, contained enough nutrients in its large kernel to quickly produce a robust seedling that was far less vulnerable to physiological setbacks. Until the nineteenth-century invention of seed drills, small grains also had to be sown broadcast—thrown by the handful across a prepared field. This meant that their seeding pattern was relatively inconsistent and some areas of a wheat field would be filled more thickly with plants than others, resulting in variable growth rates and uneven yields. Corn, on the other hand, could be easily planted by hand in planned and regularly spaced rows or blocks that did not require fields to be plowed, which had other advantages for conserving long-term soil fertility.

For European colonists, the plow was a symbol of agricultural improvement. However, agronomic studies in the twenty-first century have challenged the presumption that plowing—or tilling at all—is necessary or even beneficial for successful agriculture. At worst, plowing can severely disrupt the complex soil ecologies that farmers rely upon to nourish their crops. As the Tuscarora scientist Jane Mt. Pleasant—a professor of agronomy at Cornell University—has observed, plowing was not only a labor-intensive element of European grain farming but also led to decreased soil fertility over the course of several seasons.[20] During the 1990s, Mt. Pleasant and her colleagues conducted a number of experiments concerning the effects of plowing on long-term soil productivity in western New York state. When a field is plowed for the first time, the large amount of organic material in the soil that is lifted and exposed to air will oxidize and transform into a form of nitrogen available for plants to consume as a nutrient for fueling growth. Each year after that, however, as the field is continuously plowed, less and less organic matter will be available for transformation into nitrogen. It wasn't until the nineteenth century, when the English began to adopt a three-year crop rotation scheme that alternated wheat crops with alfalfa and other nitrate-fixing legumes in order help replenish organic matter to the soil, that nitrogen ceased to be the limiting factor for agricultural productivity according to conventional European models. Eventually, these rotational strategies led to the adoption of no-till, no-plowing agricultural methods by the middle of the twentieth century that remain widely used in conventional agriculture today. Until late in the nineteenth century, however, colonists in North America did their best to get by using the European methods developed in the late medieval era: plowing their fields at the beginning of every growing season and then fertilizing the soil with manure from their livestock. This system was effective, but inefficient, as it required at least as much land devoted to hay meadows and cattle pasture as actual crop land for grain production.[21]

Moreover, by growing corn and other crops without plowing, Haudenosaunee farmers avoided disturbing the soil structure in ways that would have contributed to the depletion of organic matter and long-term soil erosion. Every time a field is plowed, the roots of plants holding the soil together are broken up and brought to the surface, leaving the soil itself vulnerable to the effects of wind and water. In the spring, thunderstorms and other large rain events can literally wash plowed soils away, and in the fall and winter, winds can do the same under the dry conditions that follow the harvest of grain crops. Even today, the long-term effects of plowing are visible on landscapes across North America and Europe. In New England, for instance, plow troughs indicate the presence of colonial-era agricultural fields where soils have run downhill or downwind over years to collect in mounds against stone walls or forest edges.[22] The gradual removal of soil from plowing accelerates the loss of organic material in fields and decreases soil fertility. In fact, following the forced removal of the Haudenosaunee from parts of New York state following the American Revolution and their replacement with colonists who farmed using animal-drawn plows, the productivity of western New York's fields actually decreased over the nineteenth century.[23]

Another benefit of the plowless Haudenosaunee agricultural system is that it helped to minimize the introduction of weeds in crop fields. In plowed fields, the annual soil disturbance of the plow cutting through the field inevitably pulls weed seeds to the surface from deeper layers in the soil. These seeds are seemingly ancient, but still viable, having evolved over thousands of years to lay dormant in the earth until a disturbance brings them to the surface to germinate. The environmental historian Alfred Crosby once remarked that weeds are the "ecological Red Cross," a vegetative first responder pulled to surface to stabilize and heal the earth whenever and wherever it is punctured.[24] Moreover, the livestock pulling the plows also spread weeds whenever and wherever they defecated. By the time of the American Revolution, English farmers—through the guts and rectums of their livestock—had imported dozens of weeds that are common today in North American farms, lawns, ditches, and gardens, but were never present in the Haudenosaunee fields of the seventeenth century. Dandelions, purslane, chickweed, and field bindweeds, for instance, were all European importations, as was the much maligned "Canada" thistle, which came from England.[25] Weeds flourished in the wake of the plows cutting apart the fields of North America, serving as veritable indicator species for European colonialism.[26]

The Haudenosaunee method of no-till, no-plow planting thus had many advantages over the more mechanized system of annual tillage that accompanied European colonists and their plows: it was less labor-intensive, more sustainable, and more productive over long periods of time. Yet, because it did not conform to European expectations of what agriculture should look like—it did not require the investment of animal labor and it did not require the breaking of the ground with a plow—noticing the advantages of Haudenosaunee methods proved to be a task that required a different way of seeing the agricultural landscape. And this vision was one that most Americans did not develop until later in the twentieth century when agronomists at land-grant universities realized the distinct advantages of no-till agriculture under most conditions and were able, over decades, to pass the message along to farmers.[27]

In the early seventeenth century, the Haudenosaunee and their neighbors began to encounter not only the weeds brought by French, Dutch, and British colonists but also their diseases, each of which would transform their foods, livelihoods, and political organizations over the following two centuries. The French were the first colonial force to enter the region, penetrating the Great Lakes interior of North America from the St. Lawrence River beginning in the mid-sixteenth century. By 1608, the French royal government had established the capital of New France at Quebec City on the site of a former Haudenosaunee town. The French colony grew slowly. After fifty years, the city of Quebec totaled a mere five hundred residents, many of whom were Jesuits, while neighboring Native towns featured double or even triple the number of inhabitants.[28]

Around the same time, early Dutch colonists began traveling northward into Iroquoia along the Hudson River. In 1614, the Dutch Republic issued a patent for the colonization of New Netherlands to the Dutch West India Company, which established a trading post near present-day Albany, New York, by 1617. The English advanced westward into Iroquoia somewhat later, but eventually took over all of the Dutch positions there following the British conquest of New Netherlands during the Anglo-Dutch War in 1664. Nevertheless, the presence of Europeans in Iroquoia and Wendake remained sparse for another century. The land remained firmly under Native control, mostly thanks to generations of adroit diplomatic maneuvering on the part of Haudenosaunee and Wendat communities.

However, the infectious diseases of the Old World, particularly smallpox, penetrated Iroquoia and Wendake early in the seventeenth century and far in advance of the physical settlement of European colonists. Whereas in the previous centuries most Haudenosaunee died from acute illnesses, accidents, wounds from battle, and occasional sicknesses related to malnutrition, by the 1620s epidemic diseases emerged as the primary cause of death. Historians have estimated that these diseases cut the populations of Iroquoia and Wendake in half within the next several decades. Certainly, from the mid-seventeenth century onward, the colonial-era population of Iroquoia never exceeded more than approximately ten thousand.[29] The dramatic destruction of so many Native lives was often narrated by colonists as a tale of inevitable disappearance, but in spite of the tragedy Haudenosaunee lives and livelihoods continued, and Haudenosaunee social, cultural, and political structures adapted to find new paths for survival.

One of the ways the Haudenosaunee responded to this crisis of death and depopulation was by redoubling their intracommunity alliances and commitments. The feasts and other food rituals that had originally accompanied the mourning wars were soon adapted to the treaty-making processes that the Haudenosaunee embarked upon with European colonists. In order to ensure prosperity, both the Haudenosaunee and Wendat had managed to quell intracommunity violence through the formation of a ceremonial institutions by at least the early seventeenth century. In the case of the Haudenosaunee, the Five Nations established the Great League of Peace, a ceremonial organization dedicated to providing an annual venue for the resolution of blood feuds in a nonviolent manner. According to one Haudenosaunee story, the Deganawidah epic, a man named Hiawatha found it impossible to mourn the wartime deaths of all of his daughters using the standard tools of kidnapping, torture, and death. After wandering in the forest for some time with unrequited grief, Hiawatha met Deganawidah, a supernatural being who taught him new rituals for relieving his sorrow.[30] The practice of these rituals became the basis for the origin of the oldest and longest-standing Haudenosaunee political institution—the Great League of Peace, which had developed by the end of the sixteenth century as an annual conference of approximately fifty ceremonial headmen from the clans of the Five Nations. These rituals were conducted during feasts and were premised around the preservation of good feelings between clans. In short, words of condolences, ceremonial gifts, and requickening rituals performed in a formal, annual setting replaced the mourning wars that terrorized life in Iroquoia in preceding centuries. However, it would not be long until the various pressures of colonialism brought a return of the mourning wars in the seventeenth century—though this time not directed at other Haudenosaunee, but toward their Native neighbors.[31]

With their numbers decreased, but their sense of community and kinship strengthened through the ceremonial structures of the Great League of Peace, the five nations of the Haudenosaunee began to coordinate raids in all directions, transforming the mourning wars that had previously wracked Haudenosaunee society into an institution directed outward as a means of replacing members of clans and families lost from disease and, increasingly, from war. These raids were also intended as a means of plundering neighboring Native communities who, due to geographic proximity, had established a more robust trade with the French, Dutch, and British. From 1624 to 1628, for instance, the Mohawks, easternmost of the Five Nations, waged war against the Mahicans and their Algonquin allies in New England, who had taken up as the original trading partners of the Dutch at Fort Orange (present-day Albany, New York). Although originally outgunned by the Mahicans, who had enjoyed longer trade access to firearms than the Haudenosaunee, the Mohawks quickly overwhelmed the Mahicans, who fled the Hudson Valley and relocated eastward across what are now the Berkshire Mountains. In their place, the Mohawks, along with a substantial number of Mahican captives who were ritually adopted as Haudenosaunees, became the Dutch's new trading partners. Each of the Five Nations participated in similar, independent raids along the St. Lawrence River, attacking Algonquian parties for furs as well as for captives. The Five Nations even plundered the Wendats, their erstwhile cousins, while they traveled up and down the river corridor to trade with the French. The enormous numbers of captives taken by the Haudenosaunee during these so-called Beaver Wars, which lasted for much of the seventeenth century, helped solve the population crisis caused by the introduction of epidemic diseases. However, living in a constant state of war also created significant new struggles for the Haudenosaunee. The Great League of Peace had become, in the words of one historian, a "Great League for War."[32] The Five Nations would have to develop new political and ceremonial structures to contend with the strained relationships that these wars generated with their Native and colonial neighbors.

The peace process was neither simple nor straightforward, however, as the same Haudenosaunee feasts, ceremonies, and rituals that shaped the mourning wars also resided at the core of their treaty-making process and intensified the political significance of food in these diplomatic procedures. Just as the Great League of Peace convened annually to ensure "good feelings" among the diverse peoples of the Five Nations, any kind of peace offered by the Haudenosaunee necessarily required the invocation of familial relationships that tied all parties together through obligations of friendship that surpassed any temporary motives. In other words, the negotiation of any specific details—boundaries on a map, the numbers of soldiers committed to a particular campaign, the transfer of money or other gifts—was an impossibility without first "linking arms," as one Haudenosaunee orator described it, and consecrating a reciprocal brotherhood.[33]

One of the reasons for this complexity was the fact that the Five Nations had no singular leadership easily identifiable to outsiders. From the analytical perspective of the modern political nation-state, for instance, the Haudenosaunee Great League of Peace existed merely as a ceremonial entity. Its fifty sachems met at least once a year, but despite their authority as respected ceremonial leaders, their tasks were limited to issuing ritual condolences and working to adjudicate and end any intratribal enmities. Although most of its members served in diplomatic roles outside of the league, the league itself was never tasked with participating in so low of a mission as politics. The diplomatic and political leadership of the Five Nations emerged far more informally and organically. Beginning at the level of the extended family, a spokesperson for each would represent their family at informal clan meetings. Each clan would also have at least one spokesperson at informal town council meetings. Spokespeople for each of the several dozen Haudenosaunee towns would then be called, on occasion, to make longer trips to major councils, called Grand Councils, where specific issues would be deliberated until all parties reached a consensus. These Grand Councils could take place anywhere that individuals were called to attend, but in the seventeenth and eighteenth centuries most of them took place at one of several major locations in Iroquoia. Perhaps the most prominent of these was Onondaga, a town at the approximate geographical center of the Five Nations (near modern-day Syracuse, New York) that had emerged as the unofficial capital of Iroquoia following the occurrence of many Great League of Peace meetings there.

Grand Council meetings could be sometimes highly regulated by customs and ceremonies aimed at maintaining and expanding the goodwill and friendship between all attendees, and food played a prominent role in structuring the rituals. As travelers arrived in the town where the council was to be held, they were met in a clearing outside and formally welcomed with a ceremonial exchange of gifts. Afterwards, all council members were invited to a feast and then given two days to rest and recover from their journey before other proceedings began. In addition to easing the weary travelers' hunger and thirst, many of these initial rituals, oriented around the mouth and the face, served as a way of facilitating the sensory experiences of conversation. As the historian Mary A. Druke has observed, Haudenosaunee rituals that wiped tears from the eyes, "unplugged the ears," and cleared the throats of the traveling delegates served to open channels of communication and ensure all voices would be expressed and heard.[34]

Special foods were also sometimes prepared for these feasts, including a type of hulled corn that Haudenosaunee cooks prepared by washing off the skins from slightly overripe corn kernels. The process of hulling corn is reliant on the use of an alkaline ingredient like lye, such as in the production of hominy. However, Haudenosaunee cooks instead utilized woven hulling baskets, shaped into sieves, that allowed the skins of kernels to pass through during repeated washings.[35] These hulled kernels were mixed with fat and fruit and boiled into a confection called *onno'kwa*, and then served—as Parker put it—"at [Haudenosaunee] social gatherings as white people use ice cream."[36]

As the meetings of the council progressed over a period of days and even weeks, the rituals continued. For instance, specific rules of oratory protocol required that speakers involved in finding consensus on a divisive issue provided each other with gifts before addressing one another. Customarily, the receiving side of this exchange would listen carefully and then take a day and a night to consider the gift-givers' concerns before providing a response, along with another gift, to the ones who initiated the dialog. Such rules sought to ensure that Haudenosaunee deliberations during council sessions remained respectful and aware of differing points of view. They also ensured that the meetings could drag on for months or longer as all parties sought to familiarize themselves with one another's concerns and to hash out a mutually agreed upon course of action. Ultimately, many meetings ended without such a jointly approved plan but simply with a decision to agree to disagree that nevertheless reestablished the goodwill and friendship between all parties involved. Toward that end, the council meetings and their associated rituals were designed more to maintain Haudenosaunee alliances and internal friendships, no matter the issues at stake, than they were to decide upon and promulgate enforceable decrees. It was a radically democratic form of noncoercive government that reflected the central importance of kinship and family as practiced relationships in Haudenosaunee life.

This familial, noncoercive concept of government particularly frustrated European representatives tasked with securing more modest and venal diplomatic arrangements with Haudenosaunee representatives. When individual Haudenosaunee delegates met European diplomats on colonial turf—Albany, Quebec City, or elsewhere—they unanimously refused to enter into agreements and often even refused to answer direct questions regarding matters of diplomatic policy. They did so not out of obstinacy, as early European (and later American) diplomats inexperienced in Native political negotiation alleged, but due simply to the fact that they did not hold authority to speak on behalf of their kin outside of the highly structured setting of the council meeting. So decisions on diplomatic issues would necessarily be postponed until European representatives either invited an entire Haudenosaunee council (and its associated entourage) or else—as was more frequent—traveled themselves to Iroquoia for a council meeting and participated in its rich array of ceremonies and other events.

When it came to dealing with colonial governments, the heterogeneous social and political formations of the Haudenosaunee meant that the British, French, and Dutch were not able to approach treaty-making as singular moments that defined transfers of land, money, or authority. Instead, treaty-making had to be approached as ongoing alliances—or even a relation of kinship—that required constant care to maintain. Doing so required that Europeans make certain sacrifices to their businesslike sensibilities. In order to earn the trust of Haudenosaunee and Wendats in the seventeenth century, for instance, French Jesuits acceded to reburying the bones of dead missionaries in Native burial pits.[37] This was not a decision taken lightly, but one in which the clergy were forced to engage Native confidence by fulfilling their expectations of what constituted diplomacy. Mixing the sacred bones of the dead offered a powerful way for two peoples to establish a nonhereditary kinship relation—a custom that was necessary for the development of a lasting friendship according to Native practices.

The Haudenosaunee shared their understanding of the essential roots of politics in the establishment of kinship relations not only with the Wendats but also to a large extent with their other Indigenous neighbors to the west, the Ojibwe and the Cree, whose own political structures the historian Michael Witgen has studied in brilliant detail. The political geography of this Native Great Lakes region, what Witgen has described as constituting a "Native New World" in the centuries after colonial contact, was differentiated not by lines on a map designating the abstract possession of land but by kinship obligations that were established either through intermarriage or through reburying the bones of the dead.[38] As late as 1667, the fur trader Pierre Radisson reported a Feast of the Dead consecrating a peace agreement between Ojibwe and Dakota bands, many of whose deceased friends and family members had been slain in battles and raids fought over the preceding years. These fluid diplomatic relationships, and especially the ways that they were embodied and consummated in Native ceremonies, bewildered the European political order. One British official complained that the Haudenosaunee, for instance, were "a rapacious people, composed of many nations, receiving all sorts of outlying Indians, and therefore an ungoverned people, with whom no treaty can be depended upon."[39] Likewise, French diplomats struggled throughout the colonial era to make sense of imbricated and uneven political geographies of the Native New World. This seeming "infinity of undiscovered nations," as the treasurer of New France put it, meant that colonial diplomacy would be impossible to enact from maps in the chart rooms of Versailles. Colonial representatives would need to do it on the ground in ceremonial activities in which travel, food, and drink played major roles.[40]

Neighboring Native communities generally engaged in the Haudenosaunee council process as more sympathetic and active participants than Europeans did. Although the particular protocols of the councils were adapted primarily from the specific, unique rituals of the Haudenosaunee Great League of Peace, many of the Haudenosaunee's friends and enemies with different ceremonial lexicons nevertheless shared a general sensibility toward diplomatic councils as part of a set of ongoing ceremonial practices rather than as a one-time, instrumental task of statesmanship. In fact, it appears that over the seventeenth and eighteenth centuries the Haudenosaunee custom of holding large, face-to-face councils over a period of days or weeks had spread across much of the Native heartland east of the Mississippi River. For example, Wendat and

Algonquian allies of the French to the west invited the Haudenosaunee to a council near Trois Rivierés in 1645 to discuss a peace proposal and followed it up with subsequent council meetings as far west as Detroit. By the American Revolution, Haudenosaunee councilors were traveling as far south as present-day Tennessee, where a Pan-Indian council was held at the Cherokee village of Chota in 1776.[41] The great distances and travel times involved with these council meetings indicated the high value that the Haudenosaunee placed on the face-to-face, ceremonial process of working out diplomatic arrangements in person. As William Johnson had already discovered, these council sessions required logistical acrobatics that severely tested all participants. The advantage was that all parties generally left such meetings with a renewed sense of affection for one another that was built on a set of shared experiences. Regardless of whether all parties left in agreement, at least they had "linked arms" and reconstituted their relationships, an outcome that was expressed wordlessly through the intimate context of cooking and eating in each other's company over the course of weeks or months.

The Haudenosaunee expected European diplomats to enter these kinship relations as well, a factor of diplomacy for which Europeans were generally ill-equipped as a result of patriarchal notions of gender and the family. For instance, the exact political meaning of certain terms like *father* were often lost in translation with European diplomats, whose patriarchal societies harbored a very different set of expectations regarding gender and authority than Native people did. The primary role of the father in Haudenosaunee society was not one of exercising patriarchal power over children and other so-called dependents. Instead, fatherhood represented a series of obligations to serve the needs of their family members. The role of fathers was not to discipline and punish, but to provide and protect. As a metaphor for political relations, then, the father was not a figure expected to use their strength to subordinate their children, but to wield their power on the behalf of their children. Thus, when the Haudenosaunee and other Native peoples addressed one another as "father" in diplomatic councils, the intent, as Witgen has put it, was "to compel those with more power to meet their needs."[42] Perhaps the most effective means of performing the role of a father in Haudenosaunee diplomacy was through generous gift-giving and hosting elaborate feasts. For the most part, it appears that this intention was mostly lost on both European and, later, American representatives, who often relished Indians calling them "father" as a seemingly patriarchal honorific without understanding the phrase's complexity as a sophisticated mode of negotiation. Over time, more capable colonial agents such as William Johnson grew to understand the significance of the Haudenosaunee's kinship diplomacy and developed their own effective responses to facilitate the flow of political negotiations.

The Haudenosaunee viewed the diffusive nature of their political organization as a strength, rather than a weakness. Their resistance to the colonial goal of restricting political sovereignty to a singular mouthpiece ensured that the French, Dutch, and British would need to continuing negotiating with the Haudenosaunee on largely Native terms. This happened in several ways. First of all, colonial representatives would need to meet the Haudenosaunee on Native ground, for agreements could only be made with the consensus of Native participants over days-long deliberation at a council fire. Second, colonial representatives would need to establish some kind of a familiar relationship with the Haudenosaunee before achieving their goal of signing a lasting agreement. Whether for peace or for war, for trade or for land, agreements were not one-time affairs but commitments that would require the performance of ongoing treaty relationship through ritual meetings and the earnest cultivation of the good feelings of friendship. Third, the decentralized authority of Haudenosaunee council meetings ensured that their hosts would need to supply a substantial amount of food. Each official invitee commonly brought an entourage of family and friends who would need to be fed for the duration of the deliberations and these additional persons were vital stakeholders in the diplomatic process. For, after all, their Haudenosaunee spokespersons, whether called *father* or not, entered council discussions on their behalf and would need to consult them. In these ways, the "ungovernable" Haudenosaunee managed to use the ritual feasts of the council to retain control over diplomatic proceedings.

As the seventeenth century progressed, the English responded to the bewildering fluidities of Haudenosaunee leadership by seeking the establishment of the Iroquois Confederacy that existed as a singular political entity. For their part, the Haudenosaunee were willing to play along, provided that the colonial myth of the unification of Iroquoia helped maintain their political preeminence over their Native neighbors, particularly their rivals in New England and New France. The result was the establishment of the Covenant Chain, a series of English-Iroquois alliances from the end of the seventeenth century through the American Revolution. More of a rhetorical device that syncretized Haudenosaunee and English expectations of one another as peacekeepers than a set of hard-and-fast laws denoting boundaries or military obligations, the Chain both was both a reflection of the Haudenosaunee's tradition of bestowing alliances as a fluid kinship relation and a concession to the British demand for diplomatic consistency. Under these circumstances, the significance of feasting as an essential part of the council process grew. As they sought to blend their diplomatic rituals, Indians and colonists found that they shared common ground in food. Although never enough, on their own, to close the wider cultural gulfs separating Haudenosaunee and British expectations of taste and propriety, the feasts of the treaty councils emerged as a major stage for the expression of political power during the eighteenth century because of how the meals fostered senses of kinship, belonging, and reciprocity.

Haudenosaunee and British mediators created a new set of treaty-making traditions that blended the expectations of both cultures without entirely surmounting the differences that distinguished their separate pasts. A cycle of wars in the colonial northeast kept these negotiators on the move throughout Iroquoia. Colonial officials such as William Johnson and Native spokespersons such as Seneca George attended council sessions in all seasons of the year to determine the necessary details of military expeditions and accomplish the ongoing task of maintaining goodwill. Fall was their preferred season for making these trips as it was the mostly likely time of year to find food on the road. With fields full of ripe corn, beans, and squash, these travelers took advantage of a shared custom of generosity toward travelers that had originated in the Native northeast and been adopted by backcountry colonists in New York and Pennsylvania. Peaceful visitors on the trail were welcomed to people's homes and treated not only to a meal but also a customary "double portion."[43] And once hungry travelers made it to their destinations, these woods' edge rituals ensured that they would be liberally fed again and provided sufficient time to rest before conducting serious business.

In some ways, the shared sufferings and stressors of life on the eighteenth-century road helped draw colonists and Indians closer. Mediators often traveled together, and their experiences in one another's cultural environments were often life changing. The close relationship between the Haudenosaunee and the British in particular was the result of a culturally tolerant ambassadorial class that handled the day-to-day diplomatic labor of the eighteenth-century colonial apparatus. Indian or colonist, these representatives all believed fairly earnestly in the necessity of kinship as the pretext for alliance. Some colonial diplomats were even officially adopted members of Haudenosaunee clans. Conrad Weiser, for instance, one of the major representatives of the Pennsylvania colony's Indian affairs efforts from the 1730s through the end of the French and Indian War, had lived with the Haudenosaunee as a child. His family had immigrated to the Schoharie Valley in the 1710s, and his father sent him to live and work for a year in a nearby Mohawk town as a show of goodwill. Weiser remained close to the Mohawk for the rest of his life, and this relationship proved instrumental for the expansion of the Covenant Chain from an agreement centered on New York to one that encompassed Pennsylvania as well.[44] Likewise, William Johnson had originally arrived in Mohawk country from Ireland as a young man. He married Molly Brant, a Mohawk woman, with whom he raised eight children and who worked to maintain British-Haudenosaunee relationships following Johnson's death in 1774.[45]

In spite of the wide cultural tolerance that members of this ambassadorial class had developed over the course of their work, differences in taste sometimes remained a source of discomfort at mealtime. As historian James H. Merrell has put it in his careful study of these eighteenth-century negotiators, the "great obstacles in the way of intercultural understanding were not swollen streams, steep hills, or rotten weather, but deeply rooted perceptions that passage through the woods exposed rather than effaced."[46] For instance, although Native and colonial travelers often shared meals and ate food out of a common pot, their opinions of one another's foods were often shaped by expectations of tastes that revealed their underlying views of cleanliness and sanitation—reflections of more deeply engrained perspectives on the motions of everyday life. Haudenosaunee travelers to English hearths, for instance, were disgusted to find the colonists baking bread and roasting meat with what they saw as dirty ashes, a cooking technique all but ubiquitous in the smoke-filled European homes of the northeastern backcountry. They also objected to eating salted meat, preferring their own custom of preserving meat through drying or smoking. The British complained about "unclean" Native dishes that were "licked by dogs in lieu of washing," and "watched wide-eyed," as Merrell has put it, "as Iroquois cooks dumped lice or entrails into soup." Reflecting on these British glances at Haudenosaunee foodways, it is hard to imagine that they describe anything more clearly than British discomfort. One colonist who accompanied Conrad Weiser into Iroquoia remarked that such a meal of entrails was "no Hardship for Weiser who experienced the like before, [but] was a great one to [those] who never saw Such eatables made Use of before by Mankind, and [were] pretty well pinched with Hunger before he could persuade himself to taste them."[47] Despite what other colonists found to be his impressive ability to stomach Native foods, Weiser's preference for European tastes was evident in his packing lists. When possible, Weiser brought the standard English traveling fare, such as salted meats, bacon, and rice, as well as "Chocolate and Tea and Sugar &c."[48] Exposure certainly helped raise one's tolerance for the tastes of foreign cuisine, but distinct culinary preferences continued to distinguish the palates of Haudenosaunee and British travelers, demonstrating the substantial degree to which the tongue and the stomach helped determine one's sense of political identity.

Nevertheless, this diplomatic world created by Haudenosaunee and British participants was markedly more fluid than the one that replaced it following the Revolutionary War and the formation of the United States. Just ten years after the conclusion of William Johnson's Fort Stanwix Treaty, an army of Americans led by a New Englander named John Sullivan launched a massive invasion of Iroquoia intended to shatter these staunch, longtime allies of the British. The goal of the invasion—or Sullivan's Expedition, as it has come to be remembered—was not just to cripple the Haudenosaunee military, which was led by Johnson's nephew Joseph Brant, but also to destroy the Haudenosaunee and their settlements in western New York so that American colonists could take up their lands. The commander-in-chief of the Continental army, General George Washington, stated in his orders to Sullivan that "the immediate objectives are the total destruction and devastation of their settlements." Furthermore, in a line that could have been written during King Philip's War one hundred years earlier, Washington observed that it would "be essential to ruin their crops in the ground and prevent their planting more."[49] To seal the deal on this command for total war, Sullivan's troops were paid with a land scrip entitling them to Haudenosaunee land in western New York after the war.[50]

Sullivan's vicious invasion in 1779 led to the destruction at least forty Haudenosaunee villages and thousands of acres of corn, beans, squash, and other vegetables, as well as other foods in storage. In total, historians estimate that Sullivan's troops destroyed more than a million bushels of corn, enough to feed one hundred thousand people for a year. Wreaking this almost incomprehensible ruin required immense labor, and entire companies of Sullivan's soldiers spent days burning fields, orchards, and homes across Iroquoia. Sullivan's officers recorded this manic devastation in journals that today reside in the archives at Harvard University and offer a glimpse of Haudenosaunee agricultural achievements. Lieutenant Obadiah Gore, for instance, recorded his men destroying "some hundred acres of extraordinary good corn, beans, pumpkins, squashes, turnips, and potatoes."[51] His colleague Lieutenant Erkuries Beatty remarked on the Haudenosaunee's beautiful homes that were burned: "log homes with stone chimneys and glass windows."[52] Mary Jemison, a colonist who had been adopted by the Seneca Nation as a child after losing her family to the Shawnee during the French and Indian War, recounted Sullivan's invasion years later with sorrow. "A part of the corn they burnt and threw the remains into the river. They burnt our houses, killed what few cattle and horses they could find, destroyed our fruit trees, and left nothing but the bare soil and timber."[53] Unable to defeat the armies of the United States, the British forces abandoned their Native allies, including the Haudenosaunee, in 1783. That year, the new Peace of Paris treaties granted the Americans all "British possessions" east of the Mississippi River and south of the Great Lakes, effectively turning over Haudenosaunee lands to the Americans that King George did not hold title to. Thousands of Haudenosaunee fled for Canada.

In contrast to the British, the Americans had no interest in maintaining the feasts and elaborate treaty rituals that had come to characterize diplomacy in Iroquoia. Instead, the American settler-colonists of the revolutionary generation were most interested in possessing Haudenosaunee homes and farms. The American invasion of Iroquoia in 1779 represented more than just a military campaign borne out of strategic necessity. It was a war driven by the settler-colonial goals of erasing the Haudenosaunee from western New York and replacing them with American colonists. Before Sullivan's troops and their families could settle Iroquoia, they first needed to *unsettle* it. A key element of the unsettlement process was the destruction of Native agriculture. Only by razing the crops in the fields and breaking homes and fences to remove the signs of Indian agriculture could the progressive narrative of colonial agricultural improvement begin anew. This was a pattern that soon repeated itself all across Indian country during the first generations of the early American republic. From the very beginning, the so-called Indian policy of the United States of America was rooted in the goal of removing Native communities and replacing them with colonial settlers. As

Sullivan's invasion of Iroquoia made clear, destroying Native farms was a necessary first act of removal. The next step, as Washington, Jefferson, and other founders made clear, was the disavowal that Native farms had ever existed. This myth that Native Americans never had agriculture was a founding myth of the United States.

3.

Food and the Cherokee Removal

For more than a millennium, Cherokee people and their ancestors grew corn and other crops in the fertile bottomlands of the creeks and rivers that drained the southern Appalachian Highlands. In the soft loam soils and amidst the hardwood forests of chestnut, hickory, and oak trees, the Cherokees built a robust agricultural society that utilized a variety of imported domestic crops as well as an immense catalog of fruits, nuts, and vegetables native to the southeastern forests and amassed an ethnobotanical pharmacopeia of over eight hundred plants.[1] The land was rich, but not necessarily in ways that European colonists initially appreciated. Unlike the soils of New England and of western New York, which carried fertility in the form of minerals and nutrients deposited in broad bands by the glacial tills of the last Ice Age, the best soils of the Cherokee country were confined primarily to the floodplains of the region's waterways: a labyrinth of alluvial streams merging to form major creeks and rivers. Unlike the piedmonts and coastal plains that housed the first ribbons of colonial-era tobacco farms in places like Virginia and the Carolinas, the high peaks and mountain valleys of Cherokee country were a place of extremes. Annual rainfall varied dramatically from one mountain valley to the next, and the rough topography produced a multitude of microclimates stuffed with a biodiverse density of plant and animal life surpassing that of any neighboring physiographic province for hundreds, if not thousands, of miles. The Cherokees utilized these contrasts to fashion rich and varied food and agricultural traditions.

The history of Cherokee agriculture and cuisine, however, was mostly lost on the American leaders who came to power and charted the nascent

United States' Indian policies following the end of the Revolutionary War. Key to their efforts to dispossess and remove Native communities was their insistence that Indians were hunters, not farmers, and so had no valid claim to the fertile lands that they occupied. Thomas Jefferson, for instance, in his *Notes on the State of Virginia*, insisted that "all the nations of Indians in North America lived in the hunter state and depended for subsistence on hunting, fishing, and the spontaneous fruits of the earth."[2] With equal misapprehension, George Washington counseled his "beloved Cherokees" in 1796 that the beneficent United States of America would instruct them on how to "cultivate the earth, and raise corn . . . instead of remaining in a state of hunters."[3] Like most colonial observations of Native livelihood, even those of the most educated and well-traveled elite revealed less about the realities of Native foodways than they did about the warped prejudices of colonial expectations. Historical justifications for Indian removal relied on colonial narratives that misrepresented Cherokee food and agriculture.

The fiction of Indians such as the Cherokees living "in the hunter state" served as a powerful cultural agent of dispossession, for no matter how rich or complex the achievements of Native agriculture were, it was rendered into a logical impossibility by the nation's founders. The Declaration of Independence, for instance, references Native people only once, where they appear as "merciless Indian savages." George Washington, whose own deep familiarity with the heterogeneity of Native peoples should have precluded him from making such statements, observed that Indians were like wolves, "beasts of prey tho' they differ in shape."[4] These statements about the myth of the Indian hunter coalesced during the early nineteenth century into a justification for Indian removal that has persisted in the politics of US-Indian relations in myriad ways ever since. Not surprisingly, President Andrew Jackson used the same logic to justify the Indian Removal Act to Congress and his supporters. In his second annual message to Congress while serving as president in 1830, Jackson stated plainly that his plans to forcibly remove the Cherokee from their Georgia homelands would "place a dense and civilized population in large tracts of country now occupied by a few savage hunters. . . . What good man," he continued, "would prefer a country covered with forests and ranged by a few thousand savages to our extensive Republic, studded with cities, towns, and prosperous farms embellished with all the improvements which art can devise or industry execute?"[5] The power to dispossess Cherokee families from their homes and farms at gunpoint was ultimately premised on the power to deny the Cherokees' very right to possession by casting them, time and again, as savage hunters.

These political visions of the Cherokees as hunters—not farmers—were key to justifying the white possession of Native land not only on the floor of Congress but also in American literary and popular cultures more broadly, where the circulation of the images and texts about the "Indian hunter" expanded from the early nineteenth century onward. A good example of the growing reach of the Indian hunter narrative can be found in a piece published in 1818, most likely by William Wirt writing as an anonymous "gentleman of Virginia." This essay, titled "Reflections on the Institutions of the Cherokee Indians," recounts the author's visit to the Cherokee lands of northern Georgia in 1817 and was published in the *Analectic Magazine*, a touchstone of American intellectual inquiry during the early Republican era.[6] Edited by Washington Irving, the *Analectic* covered a range of topics for educated audiences with a particular taste for exotic curiosities. As such, "Institutions of the Cherokee Indians" would have interested subscribers with its lively pretense as travelogue and ethnography.

The piece presents a standard portrayal of the generalities of Cherokee political and social organization in the early nineteenth century, describing them in vague but not entirely inaccurate terms. Far more problematic are the essay's descriptions of Cherokee domesticity, which center on various aspects of Cherokee life and livelihood intended to shock readers. One of those topics is the supposed sexual freedom of Cherokee women—the "dusky maids of the Hiwassee"—whose polyamorous relations with "three or four men at the same time" meant that "children can consequently never know their fathers with certainty, nor father their children." This titillating observation reflects Anglo-American denials of Indigenous possession and inheritance in addition to marking as sexually available the bodies of Native women alongside Native land.

Wirt's observations of Cherokee food habits generally, and the production of meat in particular, also entertained settler audiences by portraying the alleged bloodlust and savagery of Cherokee men.[7] "Reflections on the Institutions of the Cherokee Indians" provides a clear example of this in an outlandish tale of one Cherokee host (most likely, in fact, a Creek host named William McIntosh) shooting a cow with a rifle to provide meat for his dinner guests:

He took his rifle as I supposed to shoot some wild game which might be near. But while we were standing in a sort of porch attached to his hut, he discharged it at a cow which was eating grass immediately before our eyes; he only wounded the poor animal, which ran bellowing and frantic about the yard. In this situation, two or three half naked negroes, who stood at the corner of the house to enjoy the bloody spectacle, fell upon the cow with axes; cleaved it to the ground; butchered it immediately, and, in two hours after our arrival, part of the very cow which we had found browsing happily on the grass, was stewed for our supper. I need not assure you how utterly unable we were to eat a morsel of an animal which we had seen thus barbarously butchered. But what had sickened and disgusted us, sharpened the appetites of the young warriors, who devoured the flesh with a ferocious avidity.[8]

The account of this cow's "barbarous butchery" richly supports settler expectations of the savagery of Native men, and as a historical source, it raises many questions concerning the ways that settler representations of Native foodways helped cast the Cherokee and other Native peoples as living beyond the pale of civilization. The very first sentence expresses the author's disappointment that his Cherokee host will not be hunting a wild animal like a noble savage from a Montesquieuan fantasy. Instead, shooting a domesticated cow represents the corrupting influence of civilization on Native society; even the introduction of tame livestock cannot raise the Indian above his inclination for brutality. Similarly, the "two or three half naked negroes," standing idly to "enjoy the bloody spectacle," indicate the Indian's inability to assert their authority over chattel slaves, who performed the labor of slaughtering and butchering the cow without discipline or direction. The author's disgust with the meat, so "barbarously butchered," contrasted with the "ferocious" appetites of the Indians further drove home the implicit point. Yet, in an era long before the slaughterhouse, when animals in American cities were often slain, bled, and butchered in public view, the anonymous observer's allegations seem to reveal more about his own insecurities than anything about the presupposed barbarity of the Cherokees.

Settler representations of Native food practices served a powerful cultural role in providing a justification for dispossessing Native people of their land. Chief among these justifications was the assertion that

Native men were savage hunters who roamed the forests and fields, killing animals wantonly and wasting the land by refusing to "settle down" and practice "civilized" agriculture. Even when Native men did, in fact, adopt the agricultural practices expected by Anglo-American conceptions of farming—as was the case with many Cherokees, Creeks, and other Native peoples of the southeast in the early nineteenth century—settler storytellers still emphasized the essential barbarity of the Native family at dinnertime.

The connection between settler representations of Cherokee people as barbaric eaters and the justifications for Cherokee dispossession in the early nineteenth century have been under-acknowledged in popular and scholarly literature. Even the brilliant and esteemed Cherokee historian Theda Perdue, when working with the anonymous gentleman of Virginia's reflection on his dinner at William McIntosh's home, missed an opportunity to consider the significance of representing Cherokee food as a barometer of their failed efforts at civilization and assimilation in the US body politic. She concluded from the passage that "clearly, Cherokee culture did not readily equip men to care for livestock."[9] Whether or not Cherokee men were prepared to take care of livestock is irrelevant, of course. Like most settler sources, the anonymous gentleman of Virginia's "Reflections on the Institutions of the Cherokee Indians" indicated more about the character and prejudices of its author than it revealed about the Cherokee Indians it purported to scrutinize.

The basic immorality and logical inconsistencies of American politics and political culture during the Removal Era meant that proponents of Removal policies had to develop elaborate and tortured rationales for their agenda to appear just. Depicting Indians as hunters provided one instrument for accomplishing this. Representing Cherokee food as uncivilized also provided a key framework for undermining Cherokee claims to having "attained" civilization and being worthy of landownership. Ultimately, settler colonialism in the Removal Era relied on misrepresentations of Native food and agriculture that denied not only the Cherokee's long and dynamic investments in agriculture and agroforestry but also the complex tastes and unique techniques of Cherokee cuisine.

As it had in other Native cultures of the southeast, corn had remained the staple of the Cherokee diet for centuries. Ancient Cherokee agricultural practices were oriented around large, communally planted fields in which the three-sisters combination of corn, beans, and squash were grown. Women planted corn in hills approximately one yard apart, with squash, gourds, and other low-vining crops planted at the base of the hills to provide a natural mulch. In the late spring they planted pole beans at the base of the newly emerged corn stalks so that the beans could use the stalks as a natural trellis. In return, the beans fixed nitrogen back into the soil through their roots. One early nineteenth-century observer estimated that a typical Cherokee bottomland field planted using the three-sisters method could be sustained for about thirty years of successive plantings before requiring a period of fallowing.[10] Cherokee women began substituting watermelon and sweet potatoes for the squash and gourds following African and European contact, adding more diversity to these interplanted, communal fields.[11] Corn, however, remained the single most important Cherokee crop and the focus of most agricultural attention.

Cherokee agricultural work was gendered in ways that emphasized the role of women as farmers and that conferred political authority on them as a result. The corn field remained a place solely for women throughout the growing season. The Cherokee concept of the "bloodiness of men" meant that their presence could harm plants, and so men avoided the fields during the growing season.[12] In order to prevent animals such as crows, deer, and raccoons from eating the corn, women would sit in scaffolds and scare them off. "Usually this [was] the duty of old women," recorded the ethnographer James Adair, "who fret at the very shadow of a crow, when he chances to pass his wide survey of the fields; but if pinching hunger should excite him to descend, they soon frighten him away with their screeches."[13] Perdue has noted that scaring off animals from the field scaffolds was a more dangerous job than it might at first seem, since these women could also serve the purpose of providing an early warning of hostile parties of humans during the summer raiding season. After the introduction of firearms and domesticated livestock like cows, horses, and hogs, Cherokee women armed themselves and used their guns to scare or kill animals that trespassed into the corn fields.

Cherokee women were also responsible for growing a variety of other vegetables, including a special type of sweet corn that ripened in two months and other varieties of beans and peas, in family kitchen gardens that were planted separately from the communal fields. Moreover, in every season Cherokee women were responsible for gathering the fruits, leaves, seeds, and saps of various wild trees and plants. The contributions of these small gardening, foraging, and other food production activities toward the development of a diverse Cherokee cuisine was substantial. Cherokees enjoyed a variety of dishes in every season: salads, soups, heavier nut and bean breads, even fried meats and cakes. By the late eighteenth century at least, Cherokee women had also mastered sugar production from maple sap, using wooden troughs to catch sap from spiked trees and then boiling the sap into sugar.[14]

Precolonial Cherokee cooking focused on the preparation of one daily meal that would be prepared in the morning and then eaten at various times in the day, whenever someone was hungry. Common dishes included soups made with corn, hickory nuts, or beans as well as bread made from corn, nuts, beans, or squash. One missionary described eating a "cold soup of honey locust pods" and a "bread made of corn and beans . . . [consisting] by more than half of black beans," a meal that had a "sweet, but wild, taste."[15] When Cherokee cooks prepared meat, they often did so by roasting it over an open fire rather than by boiling it. According to Perdue, venison was commonly dry smoked over the embers of a fire and then eaten by dipping it into an oil accompaniment. In sum, the dishes were planned to enable Cherokee women to cook once in the morning so that the food would still taste good throughout the entire day. Cooking this one daily meal made a great deal of sense as a way of saving time.

Women's labors in the field, forest, garden, and kitchen provided a source power for Cherokee women in the precolonial era. As Perdue has put it, "Perhaps women willingly performed most of the work in Cherokee society because they also controlled the fruits of their labor, the crops; the means of production, the land; and ultimately, the result of production, the children."[16] The matriarchal society of the Cherokees was underscored by their reliance on plant foods, which were almost solely the product of women's labor. In fact, until the rise of the deerskin trade in the early eighteenth century, the role of hunting in Cherokee society was narrow and assigned significance only for a few ritual occasions. Although Cherokee men were expected to hunt as part of these rituals, eating meat was thought to cause physical debilitation, so it was only eaten infrequently. For instance, while traveling on a raid, Cherokee warriors customarily carried only parched corn, and when playing stickball games, Cherokee men would refrain from participating if they had recently eaten meat because it prevented them from "[enduring] hardships and [bearing up] under fatigue."[17] Likewise, for women experiencing the ordeal of childbirth or even just the routine discomforts of menstruation, meat and its weakening effects were to be avoided. Plant foods were key in the Cherokee diet, and their importance also heralded the significance of women's power in Cherokee society.

As Cherokees began encountering Anglo-American settlers in the early eighteenth century, they also began to incorporate newly introduced plants and domesticated livestock into their agricultural regimens, although the latter grew in significance more slowly. Cherokee women were relatively quick to take advantage of the various seeds brought to their homelands from Africa, Europe, South America, and other corners of the globalizing world. Although many of these vining crops were interplanted as part of the three sisters in the communal fields, they were also grown in the kitchen gardens of individual families. Two introductions that were widely adopted by Cherokee women farmers were watermelons and peaches. By the end of the eighteenth century, peach orchards planted by Cherokees and other Indigenous peoples dotted the Native southeast all the way from the Appalachian Mountains to the west of the Mississippi River. Hogs also made their way into the kitchen garden. As research conducted by the historian Thomas Hatley has demonstrated, Cherokee women were raising hogs by the middle of the eighteenth century.[18] Taking advantage of these new crops and livestock, the Cherokees diversified and expanded their horticultural practices as well as their cuisine during the first half of the eighteenth century, and for the most part women maintained control over these new agricultural pursuits.

At the same time, the rise of a new colonial market for deer skins began to dramatically transform the Cherokee economy. In preceding centuries, hunting in Cherokee society was primarily a ritual activity, rather than a subsistence activity. However, colonial demand for deer skins, as well as other furs and pelts, increasingly brought Cherokee men and others throughout the Native southeast into competition for game animals. The furs of these animals could be traded for Anglo-American goods such as firearms that were initially difficult to acquire within the Cherokee's own internal economy. Additionally, the deerskin trade created a new economic space that existed largely outside of the sphere of women's agricultural labors and through which Cherokee men could support their families. Entire Cherokee families began leaving the communal fields to live independently on a combination of hunting, trapping, foraging, and small-scale farming. Other families stayed and found ways to use new colonial marketplaces for Native goods beyond furs. According to Perdue, Cherokee women, for instance, had begun selling corn to Anglo-American settlers at least as early as the construction of Fort Loudoun in 1756.[19] Colonial armies in the Native southeast relied on this trade with Cherokee women to feed themselves throughout the conflicts of the pre-Revolutionary Era. Alongside a series of catastrophic wars that occurred from the 1750s onward, the prerogatives of commercial hunting and farming had refashioned Cherokee households and social relationships by end of the eighteenth century.

Beginning with an Anglo-Cherokee wars that broke out in 1757 and lasted beyond the American Revolution, Cherokees suffered from continual bloodshed and violence during the second half of the eighteenth century; an experience that necessarily transformed their cuisine by forcing Cherokees to adopt new subsistence strategies in response to wartime destruction. One of the most significant Anglo-American tactics in fighting Native communities in this era remained the destruction of Native agricultural systems of mixed fields, orchards, and livestock that the Cherokees and other Native peoples had assiduously built over several generations of culinary and agricultural hybridization of Native and colonial foods. This "warfare against vegetables," as historian Barbara Graymont has put it, perhaps reached its severest pitch in Cherokee country during the years of the Revolutionary War, when American militiamen destroyed tens of thousands of bushels of Cherokee corn in order to starve Cherokee communities into submission.[20] As was the case in Iroquoia with the Sullivan Expedition, the Americans' assault on Cherokee food and livelihood during the Revolutionary War was devastating. It was also a tactic that had played out time and time again in Cherokee country since the first brutal invasion by British troops in during the Seven Year's War, when General James Grant declared that "destroying a [Cherokee] town may be credible, but 'tis in fact a matter of no great consequence, where the savages have time to carry off their effects."[21] Much more than the independence provided by the deerskin trade, the toll taken by war on the communal corn fields of the Cherokee accomplished their eventual abandonment by end of the eighteenth century, when US Indian Agent Benjamin Hawkins noted that they were fallow and "covered with wild onions."[22] Moreover, as Cherokee towns became the routine targets of British and American armies, many Cherokee refugees chose to stop rebuilding and to live individually on decentralized farms that resembling the pattern of European settlement across most of the colonial southeast, "[separating] and [seating] themselves on plantations suiting their fancies or conveniences."[23] As with the Haudenosaunee in western New York, the American invasions of the Cherokee homeland during the Revolutionary War were temporarily devastating for Cherokee agriculture.

This violent disruption of Cherokee life and livelihood had other consequences as well, including the slow formation of a unified sense of Cherokee ethnic and national identity, as historians such as William McLoughlin, Tom Hatley, and, most recently, Tyler Boulware have demonstrated.[24] In the precolonial era, Cherokee affiliations were often premised on membership within individual towns, each located within one of several distinct regions—Lower, Middle, Valley, Out, and Overhill. Despite speaking a common language and sharing a number of agricultural, legal, and religious practices that bound the various Cherokee towns together in an informal manner, Cherokees were more likely to refer to themselves as members of their local group than as "Cherokees" generically. British and American soldiers refused to make such fine distinctions when hostilities erupted, however, and even erstwhile Cherokee allies of colonial forces found themselves under assault as the blunt and aggressive expansion of the colonists progressed. For instance, a group of Overhill warriors who had initially fought alongside Virginia militiamen against the French and their Native allies in the battles of 1757 were shortly thereafter arrested by Virginian authorities and confined for ten days until they were identified as friendly Cherokees. Even worse, in 1758, backcountry Virginians attacked a party of Lower town Cherokees who fought alongside the British. By the end of the year, Cherokees realized the thanklessness of supporting an ally whose unsophisticated grasp of Native heterogeneity cast all Indians as mortal enemies. They responded to these atrocities by going to war with the British, forging a new sense of unified Cherokee identity in the process. As Boulware has argued, "though town and region remained important markers of collective identity, a broader ethnic and national awareness crystallized in the response to this new age of warfare against the British and their American colonists."[25] To a significant extent, the wars of the eighteenth century not only transformed Cherokee society but also gave rise to the very idea of a singular Cherokee society that spanned the regional divisions that structured Cherokee identities in the precolonial era.

The dynamic creation of a more unified Cherokee identity was also rooted in the persistence of cultural markers associated with food. As a temporary peace returned to Cherokee homelands in the long aftermath of the American Revolution, as some surviving Cherokee people embarked upon their new lives as cotton planters and slave owners while others converted to Christianity, created a syllabary for the Cherokee language, or migrated westward in advance of the forced removal to come in the 1830s, the persistence of certain specificities from precolonial Cherokee dishes was remarkable.

Although Cherokee corn cultivation practices underwent major transformations from the colonial period onward, certain uses of corn as an ingredient in Cherokee cuisine remained relatively continuous. Even into the middle of the twentieth century, for instance, many Cherokee cooks still regularly produced, from scratch, a type of wet, nixtamalized cornmeal similar to Mesoamerican masa that had represented a cornerstone of Cherokee cookery since the precolonial era. In order to make this wet cornmeal, Cherokee cooks used a lye made from the ashes of hardwood trees—hickories and oaks in particular. Cherokee cooks first sifted these ashes into hot water, then soaked corn kernels in this water until their hulls easily separated from the rest of the kernel when the mixture was sieved out. This process combined aesthetic and nutritional enrichment along with culinary expediency into a single step. The wood-ash lye solution strengthened the flavor of the corn, deepened its yellow color, and—as biochemists later determined during the early twentieth century—unbound niacin, or vitamin B3, from corn in a form that made it available for greater absorption into human bodies. As a vital human nutrient that helps prevent inflammation in the skin, the gastrointestinal tract, and the brain, this additional niacin enabled Cherokee people to formulate their diets heavily around corn without suffering symptoms of pellagra and other nutritional diseases common to many other communities that adopted corn as their dietary staple without also adopting their own nixtamalization process. Furthermore, the wood-ash solution also enriched the corn's nutritional characteristics with additional calcium, copper, iron, and zinc. And, of course, using the lye solution to hull the fibrous corn shells from their kernels substantially reduced time spent at the corn grinder.[26]

The cornmeal created from this process provided the base ingredient for a multitude of Cherokee dishes, including various types of steamed, boiled, or roasted "breads" that resembled Mesoamerican tamales but which retained their own particular Cherokee flavor. The most common of these breads consisted of a mixture of cornmeal and either beans, pumpkins, or sweet potatoes. Together with the nixtamalized corn, these ingredients, after being prepared or cooked separately, would be combined in the corn grinder and mashed into a dough. Cherokee cooks then wrapped the dough in individual containers—sometimes the single blades of corn husks, as was customary in many tamal traditions, but perhaps more often in the leaves of oak or other large-leaved hardwood trees common to the forests of the southern Appalachian Mountains. In addition to this variety of tamal skins, Cherokee cooks also took advantage of corn husks in varying physical states. The blades of green husks would be used fresh in the summer and fall when the corn was in season, while unused blades would be hung and dried for later use during the winter. These dried blades would be dipped in hot water during the winter to limber them up before folding in the dough, not unlike working with a modern *hoja de tamal* purchased from a grocery store.[27]

Bean bread, or *tsu-ya-ga*, represents perhaps one the most iconic Cherokee dishes carried from the precolonial era through to our own time. Despite its appellation, the main ingredient of bean bread remains nixtamalized corn; beans were the supplemental ingredient. In fact, it seems possible that the bread was often produced as a means of making dried beans varieties that were better eaten fresh, either as snaps or pods, more palatable. Although their significant space requirements make beans a challenging crop for most backyard gardeners in the urban, suburban, and community garden spaces of the present day, their ability to thrive in a variety of soil types as well as their ability to vine vertically, and prolifically, up and over other plants and obstructions, including corn stalks and miscellaneous brush, made them a ubiquitous feature of not only Cherokee horticulture but also Native agricultural practices across nearly all of North America. Some of the varieties of beans that Cherokees planted not only lasted for years when harvested dry on the vine and shelled from their hulls but also tasted flavorfully sweet when soaked and stewed. Other varieties, however, were best harvested fresh from the vine and eaten boiled, steamed, or roasted. Due to the substantial tasks of other agricultural labors that confronted Cherokee women during the late spring and early summer, when bean pods were ripe for picking fresh, many pods were left unpicked on the vine through the summer and into the fall. When the leaves of the vines withered and died, the hardened pods revealed themselves as a bonus harvest—one that was probably somewhat sour and bitter. The myriad details and diverse characteristics these Cherokee beans reveal the enormous significance of taste in different Cherokee dishes. Different Cherokee beans had very distinct culinary uses, yet historians and other scholars customarily write about beans and other crops in categorical ways that fail to account for this diversity, preventing more sophisticated considerations of Native taste.

Over centuries of seed selection, generations of Cherokee communities had likely acquired and developed dozens, if not hundreds, of bean plant varieties. Several of these beans are widely available in the twenty-first century. The well-known Cherokee Trail of Tears pole bean, for instance, was introduced to the commercial heirloom seed market by a Cherokee gardener named John Wyche in the 1980s. Wyche was a retired dentist in Hugo, Oklahoma, who helped found the organization Seed Savers Exchange.[28] He focused his own gardening efforts on growing and saving the seeds of plants that his Cherokee family members had raised since the nineteenth century. According to oral tradition, the Cherokee Trail of Tears bean was carried by Cherokee people during their forced removal from northern Georgia to Oklahoma in 1838 and 1839. It was a bean adapted through years of selection to grow well in three-sisters cornfields.[29] Not all beans are capable of thriving in three-sisters conditions; the plants need to be adapted to partial shade, and they also need to have a relatively light vining habit so that they do not drag down corn stalks. While the Cherokee Trail of Tears bean does well when interplanted with corn, other bean varieties would have been planted in other conditions. Bush beans, for instance, would have been planted at the edge of a corn field in order to take advantage of the full-sun conditions to set an earlier spring crop.

Both within and beyond the agricultural triad of corns, beans, and squash, plants served significant functions in Cherokee cuisine, not just as ingredients but also as vital instruments of cookery. The fact that corn husks or oak leaves commonly served as vessels for the steaming or roasting of masa was indicative of a culinary practice built around the use of plant fibers in food preparation. Bowls and dippers were fashioned out of gourds that were allowed to ripen and dry on the vine (young, tender gourds were sometimes cooked and eaten fresh). Larger baskets were woven from river cane that grew sometimes to thirty feet in height and was harvested from stands in the bottomlands of southeastern creeks. Before being woven, the cane stems could be stained using pigments and dyes from a variety of nuts and roots, enabling the creation of baskets with colored patterns of yellow, green, orange, brown, and black. Cherokees also produced even stronger, watertight baskets using white oak ribbons that had been laboriously split from young trees to a thickness of less than one millimeter. Durable while still remaining lightweight, baskets such as these played critical roles in Cherokee cooking.[30]

Using a variety of methods, Cherokee cooks developed a rich cuisine with a variety of tastes and flavors. However, given the pervasive colonial myth that Indians did not have a refined sense of taste or cuisine, it can sometimes be difficult for diners in the present to fully imagine and comprehend the meaning of particular flavors in Native cuisines. Take, for instance, the historic Cherokee dish yellowjacket soup, which the celebrity chef Sean Brock recently tweeted that he was "dying to try," generating some interest in the soup's revival.[31] In the spring of 2019, Clark Barlowe, a chef in Charlotte, North Carolina, dug up a nest of ground-dwelling yellow jackets across the street from his restaurant, cooked them according to the recipe in Mary Chiltoskey's *Cherokee Cooklore*, and served them to guests at a fundraiser for the Carolina Farm Trust. The guests reported that the soup had a very unique flavor, like an earthy version of a shellfish broth. But Barlowe's own report was that it tasted "like a yellowjacket—a flavor unto itself." The difficulty of safely harvesting a yellowjacket ground nest was immense, even using twenty-first-century techniques. Barlow and his team used liquid nitrogen to help remove a nest the size of a basketball. "It looked a scene from *Lord of the Rings* or something because the whole ground was smoking," Barlowe recalled.[32] Working with such a unique and difficult-to-procure ingredient indicates the dish's significance as a taste sought out by Cherokee eaters.

In short, by the time the United States of America had been established, Cherokee agricultural and culinary traditions had deep ties to the forests and fields of the southern Appalachian Mountains that had survived more than two centuries of colonial upheaval. The state of Georgia, however, proved a more intractable foe. In the late eighteenth century, the state of Georgia basically existed as an institutional organ for upholding the enslavement of African Americans and for promoting the avaricious demands of American plantation owners hungry for Native land. The original colony of Georgia had been explicitly established for this very purpose in 1732, when King George II agreed to the creation of the new colony tasked with resettling the "worthy poor" of Britain who, according to the colony's royal charter, "would be glad to settle in any of our provinces in America where by cultivating the lands, at present waste and desolate, they might not only gain a comfortable subsistence for themselves and families, but also strengthen our colonies."[33] Structured from the very beginning as a settler colony premised on Anglo-American property ownership, the government of colonial Georgia left very little room for Cherokee political negotiation.

The original boundaries of Georgia that were established by its colonial charter were set to extend inland from the Atlantic Ocean along a broad strip of land between the Savannah and Altamaha Rivers all the way to their respective headwaters, where the boundary lines would then continue westward all the way to the Pacific Ocean. Following the 1763 Treaty of Paris's division of Spanish Louisiana from British North America, Georgia's western boundary terminated at the Mississippi River. Twenty years later, in 1783, following the American Revolution, Georgia's boundaries changed again. While its western boundary stayed intact, its southern boundary was extended to Spanish Florida, at which point the new state of Georgia came to occupy not only its modern territory but also that of Alabama and Mississippi, making it approximately the same size as present-day California.

In the years that followed the American Revolution, which had left states indebted and their citizens' cash greatly depleted, land became the primary reservoir of capital. The state of Georgia wasted no time trying to raise funds by selling the western lands it had been granted in the peace with Britain. Georgia's federal congressional delegation, its governors, and the members of its general assembly unilaterally asserted that they had inherited from Britain the right to own and "dispose of," or sell, this vast amount of land. But since the British had never actually owned this land—it had been owned by Cherokees and other Native communities to the west—Georgia's title to Indian lands remained largely fictious. Nevertheless, this title was vital to Georgia's early history because it represented a veritable cash cow for the state government and the individuals who staffed it.

Beginning immediately after the war, the state of Georgia's political elite set to work devising a variety of plans for conveying Indian land into private ownership with no regard for the fact that it was already occupied by Native peoples. One of these plans for land disposal went awry in 1795 and resulted in a public scandal. Dozens of state officials and members of the general assembly used their powers to quietly sell themselves millions of acres of land in Georgia's far western corner, along the Yazoo River in present-day Mississippi, for a mere fraction of its value—literally for pennies. Then they resold the land at full market value to less prominent individuals in private transactions that netted enormous profits. News of this graft of public resources resulted in a swift condemnation and the passage of a law that overturned the Yazoo land sales. However, individuals who had gotten caught up in the fraudulent scheme were not able to get their money back. The state government, unable to pay, in turn pressed on the federal government to settle these claims, a process that eventually ignited a public furor over Cherokee title to lands claimed by Georgia.[34]

In 1802, a fresh round of negotiations with the US federal government resulted in the Compact of 1802, a new agreement in which the state of Georgia would cede its vast western lands—the future states of Mississippi and Alabama—to the federal government in return for the federal government paying to settle the claims of the victims of the Yazoo land fraud. The terms of this agreement included a cash payment of $1.25 million from the federal government to the Georgia state treasury. The federal government also promised to work to extinguish Indian title to all Cherokee and Creek lands within the new borders of the state of Georgia, a task that they would accomplish "as soon as the same can be peaceably obtained on reasonable terms."[35] Although other states also settled with the federal government in similar compacts regarding the cession of lands conveyed by eighteenth-century colonial charters, Georgia's was the only such agreement that also included a promise to extinguish Indian land title. At first this federal promise meant little in the way of concrete action, but the state of Georgia began pressing for more by the end of the 1810s as its political elite again tried to mastermind new schemes to privatize their state lands. The fact that the Cherokees owned millions of acres of Georgia lands obstructed the general assembly's schemes and aggravated Georgia officials so much that they made Indian removal one of their top political priorities by the end of that decade.

In 1803, one year after the compact between the state of Georgia and the federal government, the Georgia General Assembly created a land lottery—the only one of its kind in the United States—to dispose of the lands ceded to the state by Native people as the federal government extinguished their title. Such a lottery system encouraged public goodwill and trust in the state government after the scandal of the previous decade. It also produced a popular fervor for the removal of Indians from the state of Georgia. Interested citizens of the state of Georgia could subscribe to the lottery by purchasing a ticket for as little as ninety cents, or roughly the same price as a pound of coffee. These tickets were kept in a barrel until drawing day, when particular lots of land ranging from two hundred to five hundred acres would be assigned owners among those whose names were drawn out of the barrel. Tens of thousands of these "fortunate drawers," as they came to be euphemized, eventually occupied 23,992,058 acres of Indian lands within the state of Georgia. Lotteries in 1805, 1807,

1820, and 1827 concerned lands recently ceded by treaties with the Creeks, but the infamous Cherokee lotteries of 1832 and 1833 disposed of the lands contested with the Cherokee Nation.

Just as the land scrip awarded to Sullivan's soldiers motivated the destruction of Haudenosaunee agriculture during the Revolutionary War, these land lotteries helped to make Indian dispossession the single most sought-after goal of the state of Georgia in the years following the War of 1812. From the conclusion of the war until the middle of the 1820s, Andrew Jackson and other federal officials assisted in the effort to "extinguish" Indian title and mostly achieved this goal in the Creek lands of the southwestern and central portions of the state. By 1826, the Cherokee Nation's five million acres in the northernmost reaches of the state were all that remained of Native holdings in Georgia.

The refusal of the Cherokees, under the leadership of principal chief John Ross, to sell this land outraged Georgia officials, who in turn directed their fury toward the federal government and its failure to carry out the removal provision of the Compact of 1802. The federal response was unwavering, however, and stuck to President James Monroe's interpretation of the compact: in short, that the federal government was under no obligation to forcefully remove the Cherokee. The fact that the Cherokee steadfastly refused to cede their lands and leave their homeland was proof enough that the state of Georgia would need to wait for a "peaceable outcome," as the initial agreement stated.

The political saga of Cherokee Removal has been retold often, no doubt because its legal absurdities remain difficult to comprehend no matter how many times they are repeated. In short, the election of Andrew Jackson to the presidency in 1828 brought a sympathetic ear toward the state of Georgia. Jackson himself had expressed impatience with the treaty-making process of the previous decade, even arguing with President Monroe while serving as his Indian agent that Congress should simply pass laws to take Indian land. "Circumstances have changed," Jackson wrote. For the president and his supporters, treaty-making with Indian polities was an antiquated diplomatic approach used by Britain and other European powers to govern from afar. The United States, however, was poised for a different role. Its "arm of government was sufficiently strong to carry [a new policy] into execution."[36] Once in the presidency, Jackson set to work implementing his new model of Indian dispossession through legislative action. In the summer of 1830, he signed into law the Indian Removal Act, which had passed in the Senate with a vote of 28–19 and narrowly passed in the House of Representatives with a vote of 102–97.[37]

John Ross and other Cherokee officials were present in Washington, DC, to summon opposition to the Indian Removal Act. Their very presence, however, infuriated the Georgia delegation and its allies. Adamant that the state of Georgia was the rightful owner of all Cherokee lands, the former governor of Georgia John Forsyth famously blustered that "the lands in question belong to Georgia. She *must* and she *will* have them." His testimony in Congress referred to the Cherokees as a "useless and burdensome people" whose constitution and presumptions of nationhood amounted to an "intrusive sovereignty of a petty tribe of Indians."[38] The fiction that the uplands of northern Georgia were an uninhabited, uncultivated, and unpeopled "waste" was impossible to maintain when so many white Georgians greedily eyed their chance to win Cherokee homes through the land lottery. These expectations were even articulated in a popular rhyme: "All I ask in this creation / Is a pretty little wife and a big plantation / Way up yonder in the Cherokee Nation."[39] The Georgians had demanded the lands of the Cherokee Nation and it was clear they would persist in stealing it using any available means.

In the years after the 1830 passage of the Indian Removal Act, federal negotiators worked with delegations of Cherokees to try to reach an agreement about Cherokee removal to the Indian Territory. Meanwhile, armed bands of white Georgians attacked, arrested, murdered, and terrorized Cherokees in their own homes and farms, prompting approximately three thousand Cherokees to flee Georgia for the Indian Territory. However, the majority of Cherokees—nearly twenty thousand—stayed and resisted the incursions of white Georgians while battling the Indian Removal Act in the courts on the basis of the Cherokee Nation's status as a sovereign nation through treaties signed with the United States. In 1832, the US Supreme Court case *Worcester v. Georgia* ruled that the Cherokee Nation was a sovereign polity and that the laws of the state of Georgia had no jurisdiction on Cherokee Nation lands or citizens. Federal troops arrived in Georgia to enforce the ruling, but their presence was ineffective, and the continuing violence put pressure on the Cherokee Nation to negotiate a treaty.

By the winter of 1835, the worsening situation drove a minority faction of Cherokees, called the Treaty Party, to sign a removal treaty of their own making with the United States at the Cherokee capital of New Echota. The Treaty Party was not authorized by the Cherokee Nation, and thousands of Cherokees signed a petition demanding that the removal treaty they signed be rejected. Ross as well as the members of the Cherokee National Council wrote to members of Congress informing them that the treaty was unauthorized and should not be ratified. Nevertheless, the Senate ratified the Treaty of New Echota by a margin of one vote in March of 1836, and President Jackson signed it into law. Legislators in Congress as well as President Jackson and the members of his administration were aware that the Treaty of New Echota was unauthorized and that more than 80 percent of Cherokee citizens had signed a petition rejecting it. But those in Washington, DC, carried through with its ratification nonetheless because the treaty provided a pretext for the forcible removal of the Cherokee Nation from northern Georgia.

The Treaty of New Echota imposed a deadline requiring that all Cherokees leave their homes in Georgia and relocate to the Indian Territory by May 31, 1838. Most Cherokees had no intention of leaving Georgia, believing that the treaty was unauthorized by the Cherokee Nation and that their government's challenge to the treaty's ratification would be upheld in court. However, in May of 1838, Jackson's successor, President Martin van Buren, ordered seven thousand troops, including militia from the state of Georgia, to prepare for an invasion of northern Georgia in order arrest and expel the sixteen thousand Cherokees who remained in the homes. The US Army also supervised the work of building internment camps for the Cherokees in southern Tennessee, where they planned to gather them before the forced march to Oklahoma.

These state and federal soldiers entered the Cherokee Nation on May 23, 1838, and began making arrests. They forced entire families from their homes at gunpoint. One woman remembered that the soldiers entered her home and "drove us out of doors and did not permit us to take anything with us not even a second change of clothes, only the clothes we had on."[40] Rebecca Neugin, who was small child during the invasion, recalled a similar experience. Her family had planned to fight removal, but when faced with soldiers they surrendered, knowing that the soldiers would kill them if they resisted. Her mother was able to grab some bedding and "a few cooking utensils she could carry," but forced to "leave behind all of our other household possessions."[41] The sudden appearance of troops demanding that families vacate their homes immediately meant that more than just household possessions were left behind; some families lost children or other family members. When soldiers approached one home, for instance, two small children ran into the woods out of fear, and the soldiers denied their mother's pleas to go find them. They arrested her and forced her into the internment camp without her children.[42] These horrors continued until early June. The soldiers arrested around fifteen thousand Cherokees and confined them in the thirty-one stockades that they had built in Tennessee.

While thousands of Cherokees spent the summer of 1838 imprisoned in these concentration camps, the "fortunate drawers" of Georgia opened the front doors of these Cherokees' homes and took ownership of them. Cherokee possessions were plundered and stolen. White Georgians took over the Cherokee families' cultivated fields and other agricultural improvements. This repeated the pattern of the Pilgrims occupying Patuxet in the 1620s and Sullivan's troops staking claim to Haudenosaunee fields in the 1780s. While Patuxet had been temporarily abandoned by Wampanoags due to disease and Iroquoia had been disrupted by the ravages of the American Revolution, the dispossession of Cherokee homes was the primary goal of the invasion of the Cherokee Nation. In many respects, the Cherokee Removal illustrates most vividly the scholar Patrick Wolfe's contention that central goal of settler colonialism is to "erase and replace" Native people, for the "fortunate drawers" of Georgia, supported by the military power of both the United States and the state of Georgia, intended to replace Cherokee people literally in their own homes during the summer of 1838.

The "fortunate drawers" also took Cherokee stores of corn and other grains. Perhaps as much as 250,000 bushels of corn were stolen from the Cherokees in the spring of 1838. In the meantime, the Cherokee were suffering immensely from food shortages in the army stockades. Nearly two thousand Cherokees perished during this internment, dying of malnutrition and its multitude of related diseases. Finally, in the fall of 1838, the survivors embarked on a circuitous, 2,200-mile forced march from southeastern Tennessee to northeastern Oklahoma during the six coldest months of the year. Those who survived this treacherous journey arrived in Oklahoma in more than a dozen different groups during the spring and summer of 1839.[43]

After months of incarceration and forced march, Cherokees who survived the Trail of Tears had to rebuild their society literally from the ground up. Several major physiographical differences distinguished the new Cherokee reservation in Indian Territory from their ancestral homelands. First, the Cherokee lands in Indian Territory existed on the western edge of the Ozark Plateau, where the peaks and ridges of the Ozark Mountains flattened out onto the Great Plains, a dry grassland radically different from the forests and meadows of the southern Appalachian Highlands. On average, the new territory of the Cherokee received one-third less rainfall than did their homelands back east, a difference that represented a significant obstacle to the successful re-creation of Cherokee agriculture without major interventions in irrigation or crop substitution. An even more noticeable climatological difference, however, was the fact that the new lands were substantially hotter. During the summer especially, daily high and low temperatures were warmer by an average of about ten degrees Fahrenheit without a substantial difference in relative humidity. This heat provided its own limits to the re-creation of Cherokee agriculture. Heirloom crops that had thrived in the wetter and cooler eastern homelands withered and died in the hot summer sun. Planting dates and methods needed adjustment so that spring crops could survive the summer drought and heat, and the plants themselves needed adjustment as well—a process that would take years of seed selection and saving. Moreover, the hard, clay soils of the Indian Territory differed even more markedly from the sandy loams of the southern Appalachian valleys. The clay soil was difficult to plant, warmed more slowly in the spring, and was relatively poorer in nutrients and minerals. Cherokees struggled to adapt their corn, beans, squash, and other crops to this new agricultural landscape and developed a new, deeper plowing technique that broke the clay soils and allowed the root systems of plants to reach deeper into earth, where they would be better able to reach moisture during the dry summer.[44] Within a generation, the Cherokee succeeded in re-creating their basic agricultural triad in Oklahoma.

Less easy to re-create were the foraging activities that had brought diverse plant ingredients into the Cherokee diet for centuries. For instance, the hardwood forests of the eastern Cherokee homeland, dominated by large chestnuts, hickories, white oaks, and a variety of other nut-bearing trees, were replaced by shorter stands of post oaks and blackjack oaks, which together comprised about 70 percent of the forest cover of an ecological zone of eastern Oklahoma known today as the Cross Timbers.[45] Frustrated nineteenth-century travelers referred to this thick band of stout post oaks with its dense and scrubby understory of blackjacks as the Cast Iron Forest.[46] The acorns produced by these western oaks were fewer and of an inferior quality compared to the white oaks of the eastern forests. The absence of chestnuts and other eastern nut trees, however, was partially recompensed by the presence of several nut-bearing western hardwoods, especially black walnut trees in the hills of the Ozarks and pecan trees along the creeks and river bottoms.

Ironically, in the celebratory idioms of American settler colonialism, these Cherokee refugees might have been dubbed "pioneers." Although their eventual successes in adapting their old customs and developing new ones suited to this unfamiliar land would rarely be acknowledged by their settler-colonial neighbors as a triumph, the Cherokee certainly proved their adaptability in creating a new world for themselves despite the violence and trauma their communities had suffered.

The nineteenth-century white prejudice against the Cherokee as inherently "uncivilized" was an "amorphous disability," as Theda Perdue has aptly described it; an epithet whose power rested in its vagueness.[47] It also relied on a mythology of the Cherokee as hunters, not farmers, and as a culture without taste and therefor worthy of hunger. No matter how the Cherokee demonstrated their ownership of their homelands—either through their agricultural improvement of its forests and fields or through the creation of a political system of elected representatives—the narrative of the nomadic Indian hunter, a symbol of savagery rooted in expectations of food and agriculture that permeated American culture, was used to justify their dispossession. "It is a mistake to imagine a nation civilized because it has black cattle, or plants a few potatoes in the weeds, or spins a gross of broaches of very indifferent cotton," wrote the anonymous gentleman of Virginia.[48] The dispossession of Native property required a willful denial of Native agricultural and culinary labor.

The American Revolution is traditionally considered to have been a historic victory for democracy and decolonization. After all, the American colonists overthrew the colonial authority of King George III and Great Britain, creating their own independent nation based on the rule of the people. But as the histories of both the Cherokee and Haudenosaunee indicate, the creation of the United States established a nation that was committed to settler colonialism and that relied on the ongoing dispossession of Native peoples to pay its bills and fuel its growth.

The United States that emerged after the Revolutionary War excluded Native people from the body politic. But the fact that hundreds of thousands of Native people lived within these newly drawn political boundaries—as recorded in the 1783 Peace of Paris signed with Britain—meant that the United States would have to reckon with the sovereign claims of Native people. Throughout the first century of its history, the United States worked to resolve this contradiction by removing Native people from their homes and relocating them outside of state boundaries; a process that occurred throughout the entire continent but perhaps most violently in the Cherokee homelands of southern Appalachia. In 1838, the US Army forced more than sixteen thousand Cherokees from northern Georgia to abandon their homes and relocate to the Indian Territory in modern-day Oklahoma. In the course of making a new home there, they adapted their agricultural practices in ways that blended their traditional foodways with new innovations. A small group of around one thousand Cherokees remained in western North Carolina and maintained a continuous presence in the southeastern mountains that endures to the present day.

The Cherokee's struggle to resist forced removal is, for complicated reasons, simultaneously an often-repeated and underappreciated saga of American Indian history. The historian Andrew Denson has recently argued, for instance, that white southerners in particular have commemorated the Trail of Tears as a tale of Indian disappearance because it undergirds notions of northern Georgia as a white possession.[49] Dour remembrances of the Trail of Tears provide moments to reflect on the historic removal of Indians from the southeast, highlighting Native disappearance rather than the continuation of Native communities. In large part, the historical scholarship on the Cherokee Removal has also followed this path, with dozens of works published on the removal process in Georgia for every volume published on the creation of a new Cherokee homeland in northeastern Oklahoma.

In the generations following removal, Cherokees built new communities and maintained many agricultural and culinary traditions that were adapted as necessary to suit new circumstances. Ironically, the admonition of George Washington and other early American statesmen that the Cherokees should "take up the plow" revealed the limitations of a settler-colonial gaze that failed to see the ongoing presence of Cherokee agriculture despite a century of war and other upheaval. The adaptation of Cherokee foodways from the east to the west was a historic accomplishment that exemplifies the challenges faced by many other Native American communities during the nineteenth century. Although not removed from their homelands in the same manner as the Cherokee, many Native communities in the Great Plains were also forced to confront transformations to food and agriculture that accompanied the expansion of settler-colonialism and capitalism across the North American continent in the nineteenth century.

4.

Food and Adaptation on the Blackfeet Reservation

Throughout the nineteenth century, just as the Cherokee and other communities of the Native southeast adapted their foodways to new homelands in the Indian Territory, the Blackfeet of the northern plains similarly negotiated radical transformations to their foodways as a result of the geographical upheavals accompanying settler colonialism. The Indian Removal Act of 1830 set a pattern for federal Indian policy that repeated for most of the rest of the nineteenth century as the United States pushed its land claims westward. Following the removal of many Native communities from their homelands east of the Mississippi River in the 1830s and 1840s, federal removal efforts shifted westward, first to the Pacific Coast, where a series of wars, treaties, and forced removals accompanied the land rush to the Oregon Territory. Following the end of the war with Mexico in 1848, the California gold rush and the expansion of slavery and statehood to the greater southwest accelerated the process of removal even further. As was the case in Georgia, these federal Indian removal actions often followed the demands of white settlers whose local, state, and territorial governments cohered around aggressive desires to possess Native lands—a political process the historian Gray Whaley has called *folk imperialism*, a term that more accurately represents the colonial spirit of the age than the exhortation of *manifest destiny* first coined by John L. O'Sullivan in 1839 and preserved even today as a common euphemism in many American history courses.[1]

In the two decades following the US Civil War, these removal policies reached another violent climax on the Great Plains when the colonial demands of American settlers came into conflict with the Blackfoot,

Comanche, Sioux, and other powerful Native polities. Rather than "fading away" according to the expectations of American colonizers, these Native empires had been expanding their influence and authority across the vast, grassy interior of North America ever since acquiring guns and horses in the previous centuries.[2] US military forces, often joined by irregular settler militias, launched a series of chaotic and horrific wars in the last decades of the nineteenth century intended to forcibly remove Native communities from their Great Plains homelands and confine them to Indian reservations created through federal treaties that rarely, if ever, represented genuine Native assent. Thousands of deaths accumulated from these battles, massacres, and raids.[3] Moreover, US forces under the command of George Custer, Philip Sheridan, William Tecumseh Sherman, and other Union veterans and associates of President Ulysses S. Grant eagerly laid waste to Native homes, farms, and resources, applying the same scorched-earth tactics that marked the final years of the Civil War.[4]

Accompanying this death and destruction were larger transformations in the global agricultural economy that relied on the subordination of Native land and labor on the Great Plains to suit new geographical regimes of food production. The industrialization of wheat, corn, and other grains proceeded only through the enclosure and conversion of hundreds of thousands of acres of North American grasslands into privately owned farms, a process subsidized by federal legislation such as the Homestead Act and the Pacific Railway Act, which were both passed by Congress in 1862. The industrialization of meat also relied on reconfiguring the political economy and ecology of the Great Plains. The arrival of railroads connecting the Great Plains to massive new animal processing factories in Chicago, Fort Worth, and other cities had largely ordered the grasslands into a capitalized garden of meat by the end of the nineteenth century. Within the span of no more than thirty years, this transformation, occurring from north of the Saskatchewan River to south of the Rio Grande, was most evident in the wholesale replacement of wild bison with domesticated beef cattle that could be more easily owned and controlled as private property and whose flesh and entrails were better suited to the industrial machinery that processed their bodies for export to a growing global marketplace.[5]

On the far northwestern plains, the Blackfeet, or Amskapi Pikuni, navigated these disruptions of war, settler colonialism, and industrial agriculture through some of the most rapid and profound sets of foodways adaptations in modern history. From their forced confinement on the Blackfeet Reservation in the 1880s to the federal recognition of the Blackfeet Nation in the 1930s, in a single generation the Blackfeet shifted from a centuries-old subsistence food economy based on an extensive seasonal round that included bison hunting, to a market-centered, mixed agricultural economy defined by private property that included cattle ranching and wheat farming. To a certain extent, these adaptations mirrored the common experiences of millions in America and elsewhere who negotiated the dramatic changes to global food systems that occurred as the nineteenth century transitioned into the twentieth. But the pressure of these transformations on Blackfeet food, life, and livelihood demanded innovations that blended specific, often traditional, Blackfeet sensibilities toward food and community with the opportunities and possibilities offered by consumer capitalism and industrial agriculture. Although colonial observers, and the many historians who later took their words at face value, emphasized the intransigence, recalcitrance, and dismay of Blackfeet people struggling to subsist in a world of modern foodways, in reality, Blackfeet producers rapidly and effectively created a new agricultural world on the Blackfeet Reservation that utilized the prerogatives of colonial agricultural capitalism—such as the forced privatization of landownership—to serve Blackfeet needs and desires. In many cases, these adaptations drew from longstanding Blackfeet experiences with herding animals and growing crops—elements of Blackfeet foodways that were commonly ignored or willfully forgotten by colonial administrators, ethnographers, and artists. George Catlin's famous paintings of Blackfeet bison hunting from the 1830s and 1840s, for instance, helped cement a public imagination of the Blackfeet as a quintessential wild people living in a "hunter state." These misinterpretations of the history and culture of Blackfeet foodways have held sway even in our own century.

Chief among the colonial misconceptions that undergirded American ignorance of Blackfeet foodways was the popular characterization of the Blackfeet as a nomadic people who followed bison, living solely "by the chase." In the years that followed the Civil War, American colonists and settlers who entered the Blackfoot homeland derided them in much the same way as previous generations of colonists had derided the Cherokees and Haudenosaunee in the years that followed the wars of the late eighteenth century. One federal official visiting the Blackfeet Reservation in 1885 claimed the Blackfeet were "nearer to barbarians than anything I have ever seen."[6] The colonial narrative that casts Indians as nomadic hunters has always served the dual colonial purposes of justifying the dispossession of Native lands and elevating Euro-American agricultural practices as the only legitimate form of labor in nature. Moreover, the mischaracterization of the Blackfeet as nomads obscures the realities of their environmental relationships and other horticultural practices.

Rather than following the bison, the Blackfoot had, over centuries, developed methods of making bison come to them. Evidence for these methods can be found in the archaeological record, in ethnographic studies, and, of course, in Blackfoot oral traditions and cultural practices. This ability to make animals "come dancing," as the anthropologist Howard Herrod has described it, was, to a certain extent, an aptitude shared with other Native communities on the Great Plains.[7] However, the Blackfoot may have developed their traditions of calling bison earlier than their neighbors and in ways that made hunting so central to their ritual discourses that it distinguished their culture from those around them. As such, the violent, colonial project of transforming the Plains Indians from hunters to herders during the late nineteenth and early twentieth centuries struck the Blackfeet particularly hard as in their case this also entailed significant cultural and phenomenological changes.

Unlike most other iconic "buffalo peoples" of the Great Plains—who had either lived historically along fertile floodplains of the Great Plains rivers or else migrated to the plains from the Great Basin or the Mississippian woodlands following the widespread reintroduction of horses—the Blackfoot people had been living on the northern Great Plains and hunting bison there for thousands of years. In the rolling foothills of the northern Rocky Mountains frontcountry, ancient Blackfoot communities located steep escarpments, called *pisskans*, where hunting parties could cooperatively drive entire herds of bison to their deaths over the cliff edges. It was possible to kill hundreds of bison at once using this tactic, and archaeological "bone banks" scattered at the bottom of the numerous steep ridges and cliffs of Blackfoot country bear testimony to the method's effectiveness. In the 1950s, for instance, the archeologist Tom Kehoe found fifty-four such bison kill sites while conducting a survey of the southern half of the Blackfeet Reservation, a mere fraction of the total pisskan range that extends roughly from Yellowstone National Park in the south to Edmonton in the north.[8] The consensus among anthropologists today is that the ancient success of bison hunting in this manner contributed to the development of a sophisticated and stratified Blackfoot culture based on a unique understanding of shared kinship with bison and other animals. And because this form of hunting bison was organized around fixed geological features, Blackfoot understandings of food, place, culture, and history all emerged as mutual constituents of a complicated social relationship with landforms that were both naturally and culturally determined.

Driving entire herds of bison off of cliffs by running after them was a difficult and dangerous task that required a substantial division of labor, a high degree of social commitment, and a constant manipulation of the physical environment. Blackfoot communities selected buffalo runners, men whose task was get the bison herd to charge in the proper direction—toward the cliff. Archaeological evidence suggests that these drives often took place over distances of up to twenty miles.[9] Other men of the hunting party were responsible for the dangerous task of keeping the bison herd moving the right direction over the course of this painstaking and dangerous rush toward the pisskan. Using their own fragile bodies as a sort of human fence, the hunters could not actually stop the bison if they changed course and decided to trample through their cordon, but they could frighten the animals from a distance. Blackfoot women awaited the bison at the bottom of the pisskan where, as their communities' traditional butchers, their work was to carve up the bodies of the felled animals while still another group of men at the bottom of the cliff slaughtered the maimed and mortally wounded.

The gendered division of labor that marked men as hunters and women as butchers is reflected in Blackfoot origin stories. In these stories, immediately after the creation of men and women, members of each gender lived homosocially in separate camps. The men's camp learned to drive bison off pisskans, while the women's camp learned how to butcher the carcasses to make meat and bison robes. Napi, the son of the creator, lived in the men's camp, and after a while convinced the other men that they should live with the women in the women's camp so that men and women could share their complementary skills, as well as cooperate in the reproduction of new generations of Blackfoot people.[10]

Properly listening to animals like bison and wolves was one of the key aspects of Blackfoot hunting practices. This activity extended beyond the auditory function of listening to animal calls and movements; it was a listening that entailed deeper sensory and observational engagements with the nonhuman world during both waking and dreaming life.[11] A basic principle of Blackfoot cosmology is that humans are powerless until they establish "natural alliances" with nonhuman agents.[12] One of the best-established methods of building these alliances is to listen for animal voices in one's dreams. Within the realm of hunting especially, what an individual experienced during their dreams was just as potent and real as a moment from their waking existence. As late as the early twentieth century, dreams still retained their influence over Blackfoot life in ways that colonial anthropologists struggled to comprehend. For example, in a letter to Franz Boas, Clark Wissler (an eminent anthropologist and Boas's successor as curator of the American Museum of Natural History), remarked simply that the Blackfeet were "dream mad."[13] Once these natural alliances had been established through dreaming or waking life, the knowledge and power ("medicine" or *mokaksin*) originally granted from one nonhuman patron to an individual human person could be collected into a bundle of objects and transferred to other members of the community who sought to borrow or purchase it. Beaver bundles were perhaps of the most famous of these Blackfoot medicine bundles. As one of the most powerful members of the nonhuman world, beavers were believed to exert control over bison. If properly utilized in association with the correct ritual practices, a beaver bundle would enable its bearer to summon the beaver's help in controlling where bison would move and how they would behave when hunters sought to drive them. In short, the Blackfoot did not hunt by wandering around the plains in vain, nor did they live, as Blackfeet scholar Rosalyn LaPier writes, " 'in harmony and balance with nature' the way we portray them today." They listened to animals with the intention of finding ways to "change and control" them.[14]

According to oral traditions, Blackfoot communities learned to drive bison by watching wolves stampede bison herds, and the practices developed by Blackfoot hunters recapitulated this wolfish performance. Bison are armed with keen senses of hearing and smell but handicapped by dull vision. When Blackfoot hunters disguised themselves in wolf skins, bison could not easily tell the difference from a distance. Catlin's paintings depict Blackfoot buffalo runners on foot and wearing wolf skins in such a manner. This mimetic performance during the hunt encouraged a special relationship with wolves among ancient Blackfoot, who left meat for wolves to scavenge at their kill sites.[15]

As Blackfoot communities refined their methods for driving bison, they embarked on elaborate stone construction projects to reinforce their human fences. Although it was impossible to commit the labor necessary for building impenetrable stone walls along the entirety of a twenty-mile drive lane, the Blackfoot managed to build large stone cairns that were spaced at distances that made it difficult for charging bison to exit the drive lane. The cairns also provided escape routes for buffalo runners, who could climb on top of them in the event of a disaster, as well as waiting stations where members of the hunting party could have a commanding view of the plains as they awaited the herd. And when the bison herd did come charging along, hunters standing atop the cairns could more easily signal the animals' imminent arrival to those stationed farther down the drive lane.

Constructing the stoneworks along these drive lanes took generations and required a significant social investment of labor. Recent archaeological research has demonstrated that ancient Blackfoot drive lanes were far more extensive than scholars had formerly realized. For example, a study published in 2014 documenting stoneworks in the Two Medicine River valley, located on the southern half of the Blackfeet Reservation, found more than fourteen thousand cairns and rock rings, all marking many of the drive lanes established by Tom Kehoe's studies during the 1950s.[16] Many of these rock features appear invisible to the untrained eye, both because of centuries of weathering and because they appear to be continuous with much of the upland landscape of the northern Rocky Mountain frontcountry. The anthropologist Jonathan Driver has suggested that this complementarity of Blackfoot stoneworks with surrounding landforms may have provided Blackfoot communities with an additional aesthetic impetus for legitimating their claims for holding power over the natural world by hiding their landscape engineering in plain sight.[17] Whether or not this was the case is impossible, of course, to determine using archaeological evidence alone. In any event, however, it is clear that the Blackfoot extensively modified thousands of square miles of drive lanes with stoneworks in order to facilitate their method of hunting bison by driving them off cliffs. It is also clear that this Blackfoot landscape engineering occurred on a scale that was comparable to, albeit less visible than, the mounds, pueblos, and fields associated with the Native agricultural communities of other North American regions, features that Western and colonial scholars have been trained more easily to see.

Over time, Blackfoot people came to define their communities by which pisskans they used to hunt bison and produce meat. By the historic period, the Blackfoot people comprised four main tribal groups, each consisting of fifteen to twenty-five smaller bands of around two hundred people.[18] Although they all maintained seasonal rounds that saw them traveling hundreds of miles every summer, each of these bands also occupied regular winter camps in close proximity to a set of pisskans that helped determine their geographical identity. For instance, members of the Lone Eaters band would return each year to a campsite near specific pisskans on the Marias River, while neighboring bands returned to their own pisskans near surrounding creeks and rivers.

In the Blackfoot language, the word for bison is *inii*, which can be translated idiomatically into English as "the real food." The staple foods produced from the bodies of bison dominated the ancient Blackfeet diet. One of the most important Blackfeet dishes was pemmican, a dried mixture of flesh, fat, and flavoring ingredients that had variations among nearly all Native communities of the North American subarctic interior. The word *pemmican* first emerged as a French derivation of the Cree word *pemigan*, and both its taste and its portability earned it an important place in the diets of those in the intercultural fur trade, from the Great Lakes to the Pacific Coast. One agent of the US Office of Indian Affairs (OIA), for instance, described it as "the national dish, so to speak, of a population composed of many nationalities; and like everything else in this peculiar country, it is a wonderful mixture."[19]

The Blackfoot and other Native people on the northern plains had been making pemmican for more than five thousand years by the time the French first encountered it during the seventeenth century. It was one of the ultimate travel foods, packing more than three thousand calories per pound and providing quick nourishment without cooking while resisting spoilage for years. The British and French encounters with this hardy road food revolutionized the fur trade during the early nineteenth century in ways that scholars are only beginning to unravel. Historian George Colpitts, for instance, has demonstrated that pemmican fueled the expansion of the Hudson's Bay Company (HBC) north through the Canadian Shield by providing calories for the company's canoemen. Whereas French voyageurs on the Great Lakes in the preceding centuries subsisted primarily on the rich flora and fauna of the woodlands through which they traveled and—when desperate—ate parched, pounded corn foods like the Wampanoag *nocake* that they could bring with them, the low biotic carrying capacity of the subarctic meant that hungry laborers needed to carry the vast majority of their food with them. By Colpitt's estimates, the average HBC canoeman in Rupert's Land consumed between four and seven thousand calories per day, a staggering amount of food that the HBC struggled to provide.[20] At first, the firm outfitted its employees with eight-gallon barrels of salt beef, but procuring a steady supply of these rations from London proved impossible. When the salt beef plan failed, they imported "digesters"—portable pressure cookers designed for the poor houses of England—to their supply depots, but the production of rations in this manner also proved uneconomical. Finally, the HBC decided to trade with Native people not only for furs but also for pemmican—the preeminent food of the northern plains and the Canadian Shield. Beginning in 1821, the HBC even began manufacturing and selling their own pemmican.

In a way, pemmican comprised the process of reducing of an entire animal: disassembling it, melting it, pounding it, and pouring it into a container—sometimes a bag made from a stomach, but more often a bag made from skin. Like other pemmicans, the Blackfoot version consisted primarily of bison flesh and hard tallow to which other ingredients were added. Blackfoot cooks pounded the dried flesh into a powder and then filled it into a rawhide bag called a parfleche by French-speaking fur trappers. Next, Blackfoot cooks added chokecherries and serviceberries for flavoring, as well as peppermint leaves to act as an additional preservative. The hard tallow, however, accomplished the bulk of the preserving duties. After melting the fat over a fire, Blackfoot cooks poured the molten tallow into the filled parfleche bags. When it cooled, the bags contained pemmican—a solid, nutritious, and easily portable food that had a distinct Blackfoot flavor.[21]

In addition to pemmican, the Blackfoot cooked a number of other bison-based foods that included dried jerkies, a smoked back fat called *dupuyer*, blood sausages, and any other number of dishes that astonished and sometimes horrified colonial observers who, by the late eighteenth century and certainly by the nineteenth century, had grown increasingly accustomed to industrial efforts to "vegetalize" meat, as the anthropologist Noelie Vialles has put it—to separate "the animal" from the edible.[22] One such horrific dish, for instance, was a fetal calf roasted whole in a bath of hot ashes. Indeed, when the OIA built slaughterhouses on the Blackfeet Reservation in the late nineteenth century, they justified the expense partly on the grounds that the centralization of slaughter and butchery would force the Blackfeet to use only desirable parts of flesh and fat and eschew the "animal refuse," as agency administrators put it.[23]

Colonizing the Blackfeet meant not only confining them to the reservation and subordinating their land and their labor, but also assimilating their sensibilities to Anglo-American standards of taste.

Bison played a prominent role in providing not only food but also cookware and other necessary household items. One OIA agent, Henry Rice, observed with humor that it was sometimes difficult "to tell where the buffalo terminates and the pemmican begins."[24] In addition to serving as the vessel for pemmican and other foods in the form of parfleche bags, the body parts of bison were used by the Blackfoot to craft other utensils and paraphernalia, from their homes to their stirrups (one Blackfeet man, according LaPier, informed Clark Wissler's assistant in the early twentieth century that in the old days they used the scrotums of bison bulls to cover their stirrups).[25] In order to re-cover their tipi each year, one family would need between twelve and fourteen whole bison skins, which meant, in turn that the entire band of extended family would need to hunt a substantial number of bison each summer just to procure these skins. LaPier has estimated this number to be somewhere between 280 and 420.[26]

The Blackfoot seasonal round was dominated by bison hunting, but in order to succeed in the hunt, members of Blackfoot communities had to coordinate a series of related ritual and subsistence tasks. Foremost among these tasks was the annual planting of tobacco, which occupied a vital and central role in hunting preparation. In order for the owners of beaver bundles to activate the mokaksin necessary for a successful hunt, they would need to smoke tobacco from their bundle and replenish their bundle with tobacco leaves and tobacco seeds from the coming year's crop. Thus, the Blackfoot annual seasonal round began with the opening of the beaver bundles in late winter and the sowing of tobacco seeds.

Although the Blackfoot did not practice formal gardening or farming of grain or vegetable crops until the introduction of European agricultural practices during the reservation era, Blackfoot people had practiced the annual horticulture of tobacco for centuries. Before the arrival of commercial tobacco in the early nineteenth century, the type of tobacco planted by the Blackfoot was *Nicotiana quadrivalvis*, known more widely as Indian tobacco on the West Coast, and probably originally introduced to the Blackfoot from Native communities along the Columbia River. *Nicotiana quadrivalvis* is lower in nicotine than the *tabacum* tobaccos cultivated on the Atlantic coast. After acquainting himself with *quadrivalvis* tobacco grown by Arikara farmers along the Missouri River in 1804, for instance, Meriwether Lewis reported that the effect was "very plesent, [although] it does not affect the nerves in the same manner that the tobacco cultivated in the U'S. dose."[27] The historian Joseph Winter estimates that the nicotine content of *quadrivalvis* rested at about 0.16 percent of the total weight of dried leaves, versus the whopping 8 percent that became the common figure for commercial *tabacum* tobacco in the twentieth century.[28]

At first glance, it seems surprising that the Blackfoot cultivated tobacco—a finicky crop with a reputation for fragility—when they eschewed the cultivation of corn, beans, squash, and other comparatively low-maintenance crops that had been raised for centuries by their Great Plains neighbors to the southeast, such as the Arikaras, Hidatsas, Mandans, and Pawnees. The Blackfoot's reluctance to farm these staple crops did not reflect a lack of social development, as colonial administrators alleged, but instead reflected the Blackfoot's sophisticated understanding of their comparative advantage as purveyors of bison products within the greater food economy of the northern plains. The "horticultural tribes" to the southeast, as historian Elizabeth Fenn has described them, found themselves at the center of this burgeoning trade in foodstuffs by the seventeenth century, when Siouxan people and other communities from the eastern woodlands arrived to hunt bison on the plains after being displaced from their homelands by colonial war with the Iroquoian and Algonquin peoples of the Great Lakes region. This new trade in corn and other foodstuffs spurred an intensification of Native agriculture along the floodplains and bottomlands of the Great Plains rivers. Like a reprise of the transformations that had occurred in Native New England a generation earlier, the newcomers were farmers turned hunters, and the old-timers who occupied the prime agricultural lands largely gave up hunting and became full-time farmers. By the end of the eighteenth century, for instance, the British fur trader David Thompson reported that the Mandan "killed very few Bisons and lived as much on Corn as on Meat," trading their grain for meat produced by neighboring communities of hunters. Before leaving their village, Thompson purchased three hundred pounds of corn himself.[29] And when a group of Sioux confronted the Lewis and Clark Expedition on their path along the Missouri River, the Corps of Discovery used corn to purchase their safe passage. Corn was an especially desirable trade good on the plains, and it is likely that Blackfoot travelers to the southeast traded pemmican and other bison-based products for Mandan corn.

Clearly, Blackfoot communities would have been capable of growing their own corn had they wished to do so, as their experiences raising tobacco demonstrated their horticultural skill. As LaPier has noted, the Blackfoot ability to cultivate tobacco in "a dry, arid landscape required intimate knowledge of the environment and the climate."[30] Moreover, Blackfoot communities did not put in the effort to grow tobacco merely for its own sake, but for the purpose of deeper rituals intended to summon mokaksin from their natural alliances with the Beaver people. It was essential that owners of beaver bundles have adequate tobacco to smoke in order for them to control the bison during the summer hunts. So as soon as the last of the spring snowstorms passed, Blackfoot bands pulled tobacco seeds out of their beaver bundles and sowed them into a fertile creek bank. As one Blackfeet informant described to George Bird Grinnell, this was the task of Blackfeet women, who planted the tobacco seeds with a mixture of dung and dried berries to serve as a fertilizer.[31] After planting the tobacco, the entire community would enjoy a ritual feast and then depart on their summer travels to their pisskans and various other seasonal campsites, only returning to the harvest their tobacco in the fall.

The contrasts between Blackfoot tobacco horticulture and the intensive, plantation cultivation of tobacco on the colonial Atlantic seaboard were stark. Not only were the labor inputs of Blackfoot cultivation minimal, but the Blackfoot farmers themselves were not even present with their crops throughout the entire growing season. The tobacco was not fenced or directly monitored. However, as LaPier has noted quite brilliantly, the Blackfoot did not simply "leave it to nature." After planting the tobacco, Blackfoot communities relied upon their ritual connections to the supernatural world to tend to their crops. What this meant, in concrete terms, was that a community of miniature people, or *ni-wax-sax*, each standing about one foot high, protected the tobacco fields in exchange for miniature clothing and food that Blackfeet women left for them in fields following the tobacco planting ceremonies. These supernatural beings were also friends of the beaver and could be relied upon to keep the crop safe.[32]

Over the next six months, as the Blackfoot embarked on their summer travels, families would complete a seasonal round that carried them hundreds of miles and that engaged them in food production pursuits far beyond bison hunting. One of the most important components of the seasonal round was gathering fruit from specific sites of informally cultivated stands of chokecherries, huckleberries, serviceberries, and other plants that were visited annually during the times of the year when the fruits were ripe. These fruits were not only important ingredients in pemmican but also constituted some of the main ingredients of Blackfoot teas and medicines. Serviceberries played a particularly prominent and distinctive role in Blackfoot cuisine. According to the ethnographer Walter McClintock, Blackfoot families would eat the berries raw, as well as boiling them down into a thick stew. Additionally, the Blackfeet would make a tea from serviceberry leaves that they used to treat certain symptoms of diabetes, such as hunger, fatigue, and blurred vision. Fascinated with Blackfeet herbal medicines, McClintock collected a total of sixty-six different plant species utilized by the Blackfeet during his research on the reservation in the 1890s, sending them to the Carnegie Institute for identification and study.[33] Outsider interest in Blackfoot pharmacology has continued to the present day. For instance, medical researchers from the University of Washington recently published a study in the *Journal of Ethnopharmacology* about Blackfeet medicinal plants used to treat symptoms related to Parkinson's disease, and another team of scientists has likewise demonstrated that the efficacy of Blackfeet serviceberry tea in delaying the absorption of carbohydrates into the stomach is similar to that of the trademarked antidiabetic drug Acarbose.[34]

The colonial confinement of the Blackfoot to reservations in both the United States and Canada during the late nineteenth century precipitated dramatic transformations to Blackfoot foodways. Confinement not only circumscribed hunting but also brought an end, essentially, to the seasonal round. In place of these institutions, federal agents intended that Blackfoot communities assimilate to Anglo-American standards of agricultural land tenure. At first, this meant transforming the Blackfoot from bison hunters to cattle herders, a reform in keeping with the broader ecological revolution sweeping the northern plains from the 1860s onward as Anglo-American stock raisers began introducing cattle by the hundreds of thousands. South of the US-Canada border, OIA agents envisioned the Blackfeet Reservation as a grand cattle ranch where Blackfeet men would labor as the keepers of a tribal herd, managed by agency personnel, that would pay for the reservation's administration with proceeds from the sale of beeves to eastern markets in Chicago and beyond. The next phase of the OIA's plan to colonize the Blackfeet through their stomachs hinged on efforts to assimilate Blackfeet families as farmers. To this effect, the agency hired farmers to operate demonstration fields and to model state-of-the-art horticultural practices. Compared to most of the other heavy-handed colonial efforts to rapidly remake Blackfeet culture on the reservation, the agency's farming initiatives were generally well received by many Blackfeet people. This changed, however, with the final major stage of agency politics during the assimilation era: the execution of the allotment act and the push to privatize Blackfeet tribal landownership, a drama that played out from 1908 until 1919. In the end, the Blackfeet charted their own path forward, managing to forge a new, mixed agricultural economy founded on a combination of the subsistence production of vegetables, the commercial production of cash crops, and, for some, the management of cattle herds. Although the long-term adverse effects of the reservation's allotment have persisted and even worsened up to the present day, the Blackfeet were also able to make the forced privatization of landownership work toward their own ends to a surprising extent.

The colonial groundwork for confining the Blackfeet to a reservation began in 1851 with the congressional ratification of a treaty in which no Blackfeet were themselves represented. The Treaty of Fort Laramie, signed on the Platte River nearly eight hundred miles south of the core Blackfoot homeland, established the first formal colonial boundaries of Blackfeet country but included no Blackfoot signatories. Alexander Culbertson, an American fur trader based at Fort Union on the far eastern end of Blackfoot country—at the junction of the Yellowstone and Missouri Rivers—and married to a Blackfoot woman named Medicine Snake, had been tasked with gathering Blackfoot delegates but was, for unknown reasons, unable to travel west to collect Blackfoot representatives for the journey south to attend the treaty proceedings. Culbertson himself agreed to be the Blackfoot's representative, and along with representatives of the Arikara, Assiniboine, Hidatsa, and Mandan peoples proceeded to carve out the Blackfoot's portion of the northern plains. The treaty proceedings had been tasked with defining Native claims to that portion of the Great Plains south and east of the Missouri River, a region that the Blackfeet had contested with these other tribes over the previous generations. The ultimate outcome was to define the southeastern portion of Blackfoot country to a relatively insignificant region of land between the Yellowstone and Musselshell Rivers.[35]

Four years later in 1855, the new commissioner of Indian Affairs, George Manypenny, proposed that the agency use a new round of treaty-making to assimilate the Blackfeet and other Native peoples of the northwest by "reclaim[ing] the Indians from a nomadic life," and "encourag[ing] them to settle in permanent homes and obtain their sustenance by agriculture and other pursuits of civilized life."[36] Isaac Stevens, governor of the Washington Territory (which encompassed most of present-day Montana at the time) appointed none other than Alexander Culbertson to facilitate the new treaty-making process with the Blackfeet. Culbertson hesitated in his endorsement of Stevens and Manypenny's plan to assimilate the Blackfeet to American standards of agriculture, mainly out of a pragmatic observation that the Blackfeet had already been capable of farming but chose not to. "The day is far off," he announced to Stevens, "when the Blackfeet will turn the Sword into the Ploughshare and make the wilderness bud and blossom like the Rose."[37] Nevertheless, Stevens pushed his assimilationist plans, laying bare what would become, over the following decades, the blueprint for federal assimilation efforts on the reservation. "We want to establish you in your country on farms," Stevens said in addressing the Blackfeet. "We want you to have cattle and raise crops. We want your children to be taught, and we want you to send word to your Great Father, through us where you want your farms to be. . . . Bye and bye," he concluded, "the Blackfeet would not be obliged to live on poor Buffalo Meat but would have domestic Cattle for food."[38] The Blackfeet took Stevens up on his offer, but they drove a hard bargain, establishing a reservation larger than the state of Pennsylvania and negotiating a decade's worth of annuities payments and other concessions that totaled $35,000 per year.

Unfortunately for the Blackfeet, the terms established in the 1855 treaty came under assault almost immediately after its ratification. In short, the annuities payments were a boon for white merchants, both those located in Fort Benton on the upper Missouri River as well as their suppliers thousands of miles downriver in St. Louis. The Blackfeet's annuities were paid in the form of trade goods, which federal contractors purchased from private sellers. The scale of graft and the corruption of this annuities trade extended all along the Missouri River watershed. Along with Fort Benton, the city of Bozeman, Montana, located in the fertile river valleys of one of the Yellowstone's upper tributaries, was also a center for this trade. Originally established as a terminus for gold miners and cattle drivers arriving to Montana from Texas, Bozeman also became the home of Nelson Story, the real-life inspiration for the protagonist of Larry McMurtry's novel *Lonesome Dove*. Story made his first fortune on the daring cattle drive, but he made his second fortune from his work as a banker and a merchant with a penchant for buying Indian annuities goods cheap and selling them profitably to the Indian agency.[39] Throughout the 1850s and 1860s, the annuities funds of the Blackfeet, Crow, and other parties to the Fort Laramie treaty and its subsequent amendments were frittered away in a manner that enriched white middlemen in the growing mining and cattle towns of present-day Montana and Wyoming.

The annuities goods themselves were often rejected by the Blackfeet. Annual distribution of fishhooks, for instance, provided no practical benefit to a community who, in the nineteenth century, categorically resisted eating fish despite the efforts of colonial administrators to try to encourage Blackfeet eaters to acquire the taste. Likewise, early annuities payments in the form of hardtack, purchased in St. Louis, spoiled by the time they reached the agency's initial storage depot in Fort Benton. Letters written to the commissioner of Indian Affairs suggested that the hardtack be replaced by distributions of wheat flour, and the agency obliged by purchasing ten thousand pounds of it annually, much of which, in later years, came from Story's own mill. Although it probably beat rotten hardtack, the flour also proved to be of limited usefulness. Without ovens or yeasts, the Blackfeet could not bake bread, nor did they seem all that interested in frying the flour or eating it, mixed with water, as a porridge. Instead, the majority of annuities goods wound up being traded right back to white merchants in Fort Benton in order to obtain more useful products, such as ammunition for bison hunting.[40]

The character of bison hunting itself began to change during these years as well. The arrival of American fur traders seeking bison robes to the upper Missouri River during the 1850s finally brought the Blackfeet into the fur trade. Just as they had eschewed fishing due to the sanctity of the denizens of the Water World, so too had the Blackfeet refused to participate in the beaver pelt trade, keeping them out of the orbit of the Hudson's Bay Company and other enterprises in the first half of the nineteenth century. Merchants of the American Fur Company in St. Louis, however, developed a profitable European market for bison robes as well as a steady source of willing suppliers among the Blackfeet and other Native communities of the upper–Missouri River watershed. During the winter, at least, hunting was no longer premised primarily around subsistence but increasingly around the fulfillment of American demand for bison robes, for only during the late winter months did bison fur on the far northern plains reach the unique thickness desirable for the robes, which were worn as clothing or else used to upholster furniture and carriage seats.

Unlike the ancient days, when Blackfoot communities drove bison to pisskans as a community endeavor, the introduction first of horses and then of firearms enabled individual Blackfoot families to hunt bison for robes. While men did the hunting on horseback armed with rifles, women continued to perform their traditional art of butchering the animals and transforming their bodies into meat, robes, and other goods. The anthropologist David Nugent has argued that this transformation in Blackfoot hunting practices accompanied a new set of practices governing the community management of horses as private property. The relative scarcity of horses in Blackfoot communities compared to plains peoples farther south (such as the Comanche, who were closer to the animal's original source of diffusion in northern New Spain), meant that horses required comparatively more effort and expense for Blackfoot families to acquire. By the late eighteenth century, this dynamic had led to the emergence of a type of "horse-banking" whereby Blackfoot men who owned large numbers of horses (typically more than ten) would loan horses for a period of a year to poorer men in their band, who would be responsible for returning the horses along with additional horses as a kind of interest. This custom of horse-based debt drove the Blackfoot demand for horses even higher, and Blackfoot men began embarking on seasonal raids of neighboring peoples, both near and far, with the intent of stealing horses. This led to a series of wars from the late eighteenth century through the early nineteenth century that threw the ratio of men to women among the Blackfoot remarkably off balance, so much so that Blackfoot households transformed over the course of several generations from monogynous and matrilineal to polygynous and patrilineal. As surviving men married additional wives, these women set to work turning the household into an ever-more elaborate facility for the production of bison robes, the wealth from which in turn fueled additional wealth in horses. Thus, the colonial cycles of robe hunting and horse raiding became central components of Blackfoot society during the middle of the nineteenth century, radically altering previous hunting and food production practices.[41]

While in later years the contracting boundaries of the Blackfeet Reservation would greatly circumscribe the Blackfeet's ability to hunt successfully, the relatively large size of the reservation that was established in 1855 provided ample room for Blackfeet families to manufacture bison robes. The Blackfoot homeland was essentially an ocean of grass that extended from the Yellowstone River in the south to the upper tributaries of the Saskatchewan River in the north. The international boundary on the forty-ninth parallel separating the United States from Canada existed as a mere fiction, a line on the maps adorning colonial offices. The reservation boundaries were perhaps more meaningful, for day-to-day matters at least, as they adjudicated the legal jurisdictions policed by US marshals and Indian agency personnel. But the Blackfeet crossed all these boundary lines largely at will, leaving the reservation to visit friends and family members, to trade in cities such as Fort Benton, to hunt, and to raid for horses.

By the 1870s, enforcing the reservation boundary as a hard line became a priority of the Office of Indian Affairs. Confining the Blackfeet to the reservation served colonial interests by subordinating Blackfeet land and labor, and federal officials grew ever-more impatient to assimilate Blackfeet people as colonial subjects. By breaking the Blackfeet of their habits as bison hunters and transforming them into proto-Anglo yeomen farmers and ranchers, not only could federal officials claim the successful completion of the longstanding Jeffersonian impulse for cultural assimilation but they could also "free up" Blackfoot lands for white settlement. The ultimate goal of the colonial plan to turn the Blackfeet into farmers was to open the possibility of dispossessing them of their customary hunting territory. Federal agents attempted this first by establishing a tribal cattle herd. After these efforts failed, they embarked on the allotment process—the forced privatization of tribal landownership. Both federal initiatives served to colonize the Blackfeet by radically altering the means by which they produced and consumed food.

The OIA began issuing cattle to the Blackfeet during the 1870s and continued the process for the next two decades. The plan to transform the Blackfeet Reservation into a grand cattle ranch was implemented initially by John Young, who was placed in charge of the OIA's Blackfeet agency operations in 1871. Young held a low estimation of the agricultural capabilities of the Blackfeet Reservation's land. Located on the high, windswept backbone of North America, literally on a triple divide that separates rivers draining to the Pacific, Atlantic, and the Arctic, Young assumed that the reservation's horticultural potential was slim; an estimation that proved incorrect over the following decades as Blackfeet farmers mastered the art of growing a wide variety of both cash crops and garden-variety vegetables.[42] Like the demonstration fields that had been established on the floodplain of the Sun River in the late 1850s, Young's cattle served, initially, as a type of experimental herd for demonstrating the capacity of the reservation as grazing space for domesticated beef cattle. However, as populations of bison on the northern plains began to diminish dramatically during the late 1870s, the reservation cattle herd took on a new, unintended role as a surrogate bison herd for the Blackfeet to hunt. But the construction of an agency slaughterhouse in 1884, and a second slaughterhouse in 1895, centralized the production of meat and provided federal personnel with an instrument to enforce circumscriptions against hunting.

At the same time the OIA confined and centralized the production of beef inside the agency slaughterhouse, a new cadre of Indian office personnel decided to lease the Blackfeet Reservation's grazing lands to neighboring white ranchers. The outbreak of the Civil War had brought a further influx of settlers, mainly draft dodgers from the Missouri River border states and some Union Army deserters—what Stanley Davidson and Dale Tash termed Montana's "confederate backwash."[43] These men settled primarily in the gold-mining towns surrounding Virginia City and Helena. Within a few years the white population of north-central Montana had trebled, and by the 1870s a new influx of stock-growers trailing cattle northward from Texas and the southern plains had made the grasslands of Blackfoot country suddenly desirable.

By the early twentieth century, leasing Blackfeet Reservation grazing lands to neighboring ranchers proved a more profitable way to raise revenue for the Indian office administration than the Blackfeet agency herd, and the federal officials charged with managing the Blackfeet's tribal lands more eagerly conducted business with the non-Native farmers and ranchers whose lands abutted the reservation. In 1909, Clarence Churchill, one of the many federal agents who presided over the Blackfeet Reservation during this era, explained to his supervisor, the commissioner of Indian Affairs in Washington, DC, that there was "no better grazing in any part of Montana than the Blackfeet Reservation."[44] Within three years, more than twenty thousand head of cattle had been stocked on the reservation's grasslands, and the Office of Indian Affair's livestock supervisor, Oscar Lipps, suggested it could handle an additional eighty thousand. In making this recommendation, Lipps also endorsed a plan conceived by Churchill's successor, Arthur McFatridge, to sell the reservation's unallotted lands to non-Native stock raisers and to use the funds from the land sales to purchase more cattle for the tribal herd.[45] This plan was never executed, however. In 1914, McFatridge stole $1,200 of tribal funds and fled to Canada after finding out that he had been fired for, among other violations, using Blackfeet money to buy himself a Buick.[46]

The politics of beef on the Blackfeet Reservation were tied to larger conversations about private property, individual responsibility, and landownership that were animating controversies over land allotment on reservations across the American West. Authorized by Congress with the Dawes Act of 1887, allotment was intended to forcibly privatize Native landownership on Indian reservations, aiding in the colonizing mission of assimilationists like the bill's author, Henry Dawes, who wished to dissolve the communal cultures of Native peoples and replace it with an ethos of personal responsibility and individual economic agency. Allotment also served the interests of non-Native farmers and ranchers who eyed the vast expanses of tribal lands as one of the last vestiges of "public land" that could be disposed into private ownership. After carving communally owned reservations into privately owned parcels—or allotments—which would be granted under a trust arrangement to each enrolled tribal member, the allotment act provided for all "surplus" unallotted land to be retitled by the state and sold to non-Native buyers. Although the exact outcome of each allotment agreement varied from one reservation to the next, by the time the OIA ended the allotment process in 1934, more than ninety million acres of reservation land had passed into non-Native ownership, representing roughly two-thirds of the aggregate acreage that tribes had owned communally in 1887.[47]

On the Blackfeet Reservation, the battle over allotment raged for more than a decade. Most tribal members supported the privatization of reservation landownership, and they looked forward to owning their own allotments where they could build their homes, farms, and ranches. The surplus unallotted land sales, however, pitted many of the Blackfeet against the OIA and its allotment plan. Robert J. Hamilton, a Blackfeet graduate of the Carlisle Indian School, spent much of his adult life (from about 1898 until 1932) fighting the Indian office on the Blackfeet Reservation and working with legislative allies in Washington, DC, in order to achieve Blackfeet self-governance. Born sometime during the 1870s, Hamilton's origins remain somewhat mysterious. At various points in his life he claimed to have been orphaned in infancy by the death of his Blackfeet father and mother, while at other moments he claimed that this biological father was a white man and that his Blackfeet mother had died in childbirth. In any case, Robert Hamilton and his brother Joseph were raised by A. B. Hamilton, a white man who was married to a

Blackfeet woman and owned a successful mercantile store in Browning, the reservation's largest town. In about 1890, Robert and Joseph traveled to Pennsylvania and entered Carlisle Indian School along with two other young Blackfeet men from middle-class families on the reservation—Charles Buck and Malcolm Clark.[48] Joseph died at Carlisle in 1894; Robert graduated two years later and returned to Browning.[49]

Once Hamilton returned home with his Carlisle diploma in hand, he was hired to work as an Indian office interpreter and tasked with assisting the reservation agent with translating between the English and Blackfeet languages. Hamilton had a natural talent for verbal expression, excelling as a writer and orator during his school days, and seemed to enjoy his new career as a translator despite the fact that he understood his complicity as an Indian office employee in the agency's militant efforts to suppress the Sun Dance and other important Blackfeet rituals. In 1898, Hamilton received permission from his boss, Agent Thomas Fuller, to regularly host meetings of a Blackfeet literary society in one of the agency buildings, presumably for Indians to practice their English and discuss works of American literature. In reality, however, Hamilton operated the society as a safe space for Blackfeet elders to share their oral traditions with Hamilton and his young friends and to train them in the outlawed Sun Dance rituals. When word got around about this betrayal, a furious Agent Fuller fired Hamilton on the spot from his job as agency interpreter.[50] Hamilton spent the rest of his life on the opposing side of the Indian service working to undermine its powerful grip on reservation politics.

Over the next several years, Hamilton's commitment to preserving Blackfeet cultural institutions, like the Sun Dance, that were under assault by the assimilative forces of the Indian service helped him establish a political constituency on the reservation. With his own livelihood relatively secure thanks to his family's business and other resources, Hamilton devoted himself to political and social revolution, leading successful strikes on federal construction projects administered by the Indian agent that brought Indian wages to parity with those of white workers and convincing other Blackfeet to condemn the Indian office's policy of allowing white ranchers from off the reservation to graze their cattle on tribal grasslands. In 1905, following the death of his father, Hamilton inherited a modest fortune that included a large herd of horses, a culturally significant form of wealth that signaled the prereservation days of the Blackfeet and placed Hamilton into even higher esteem among opponents of the Indian office. Chafing at the continuing ascendance of this young activist, the reservation agent James Monteath had several of his non-Indian, off-reservation friends allege that A. B. Hamilton's horses had really belonged to them, and that Hamilton had acquired them unlawfully. Monteath used these allegations as his pretext to arrest Hamilton and charge him with horse stealing, an incident that, ironically, only served to enhance Hamilton's rising reputation on the reservation as a powerful horse thief in the mold of an old warrior.[51] Monteath dropped the charges.

The next reservation agent failed even more in his efforts to constrain Hamilton's activism. Like Monteath, the new agent, Clarence Churchill, was committed to running the Blackfeet Reservation as a reservoir of public grazing land for neighboring white ranchers. In order to ensure the legality of such grazing leases, Hamilton convinced Churchill to organize a small voting committee of elected Blackfeet representatives, called the Blackfeet Tribal Business Council (BTBC), that would serve to provide the Indian office with the tribe's official permission for such decisions. Councils like this had been set up widely on other reservations to help side-step issues of the Indian office's legal authority over tribally owned lands. Although they were intended to be puppets for the exercise of the agent's colonial power, Hamilton had other ideas for the BTBC and used the council as an instrument to voice the grassroots desires of Blackfeet people for agricultural reforms on the reservation.[52]

By 1908 the single most important issue on the reservation was its pending allotment. While Hamilton and his supporters did not oppose allotment per se, and all eagerly selected their own allotments, they objected to the provisions for the sale of surplus unallotted land that would have opened up more than half of the reservation's remaining acreage to non-Native buyers. The extent of this surplus unallotted land, amounting to an area larger than the state of Rhode Island, marked the allotment proceedings as an aggressive land grab by non-Native stock-growers and wheat farmers in northern Montana, who were represented in Washington, DC, by Montana senator Thomas J. Walsh, one of the Blackfeet allotment act's leading supporters and sponsors. Over the following years, Hamilton used the BTBC as a vehicle for organizing reservation opposition to the surplus unallotted land provisions.[53] During this time, as the historian Thomas Wessel claims, Hamilton "used the committee as a forum to turn the Blackfeet from a fragmented tribe, frequently at war with itself, to an issue-oriented, politically-minded community."[54] The Carlisle graduate used his boarding school connections to communicate with Indian and non-Indian allies alike across the country, explaining the Blackfeet's political struggles and emphasizing his desires to use federal law to carve out a just space for Native self-determination on reservation politics. For instance, in response to an alumni survey sent by the new superintendent of the Carlisle school, Hamilton described not only his frustrations with the Indian service back home but also his optimism that other organs of federal power could operate fairly. "If a return student happens to criticize a rascal Indian agent," he quipped, "he is at once stamped as a horse and cattle thief. . . . When such a student attacks any government employee, he sees something which may be detrimental to both the Indians and the Government, but not because he is against this great and good government."[55] Instilled with a love and respect for American democratic principles, but still not an American citizen under federal law, Hamilton proposed to the new superintendent of Carlisle that all boarding school diplomas should come with citizenship.

Churchill and his successor, Arthur McFatridge, fought back against Hamilton and the BTBC by using the old agency weapon of withholding rations from their supporters. They also charged Hamilton with allegations of financial fraud and had him arrested. In 1910 Hamilton spent much of the year in the agency jail awaiting a federal court to overturn Churchill's absurd charges. During this time, Hamilton plotted his next move. Upon his release, he began writing directly to legislators in Washington, DC, including Harry Lane, the former mayor of Portland, Oregon, and Oregon's recently elected senator, detailing the various abuses of Indian people that Churchill, McFatridge, and their administration had overseen on the Blackfeet Reservation. Lane served on the Senate committee that oversaw the activities of the OIA and befriended Hamilton, inviting him to visit Washington, DC. Hamilton took advantage of this relationship, visiting Lane in DC for the first time in 1912 and returning on eight other occasions before the end of the decade.[56]

During one of these visits in 1914, Hamilton presented Senator Lane's committee with blunt testimony about the Indian office's custom of withholding treaty rations from certain Indians in order to starve out political opposition. Hamilton's allegations that McFatridge had starved 149 Blackfeet to death during the previous winter's battles over the surplus unallotted lands provisions raised a public uproar. Although subsequent investigations failed to officially document all of these deaths, a survey of the reservation revealed widespread starvation and malnutrition. Senator Lane himself visited the reservation during one of these inspections, taking private tours with Hamilton and meeting Hamilton's supporters, and this trip burnished Hamilton's reputation as the Blackfeet's de facto grassroots leader. Lane's committee had McFatridge fired. Their investigations also turned the tide against Senator Walsh's allotment bill. Within the next few years, Hamilton and Lane managed to get another bill passed that finally awarded the Blackfeet their allotments while also allowing the Blackfeet to retain tribal ownership of their surplus unallotted lands. For Hamilton and his supporters, their twenty-year fight against the abuses of the Indian office had yielded a major victory.

In the aftermath of allotment, Blackfeet farmers took their individual allotments and reworked them not only to serve Congress's ostensible goals of assimilation into private property ownership but also to serve more traditional tribal ends and meet cooperative needs. Families and friends selected adjacent allotments in an effort not to exclude others from their property but to aggregate their allotments into larger parcels that could be more practically utilized to grow food and livestock at a multifamily scale. In 1921, the creation of the Piegan Farming and Livestock Association, or PFLA, established twenty-nine chapters across the Blackfeet Reservation that formalized these cooperative agricultural units into an official organization recognized by the Office of Indian Affairs. PFLA members jointly owned a central flour mill as well as two threshers that traveled to the each of the twenty-nine member cooperatives during the wheat-harvest season. Individual chapters purchased their own shared hay rakes, binders, and other machines.

A review of the PFLA program after the first year impressed federal agents, including Oscar Lipps, the former Indian Affairs livestock supervisor. In the fall of 1921, he reported that one of his Blackfeet acquaintances, now an old man, had raised "40 bushels of wheat, 30 bushels of oats, 50 sacks of potatoes, some rutabagas, beets, carrots, peas, corn, etc. They put up hay, sold 20 tons and have one stack left," producing enough food for his family to eat as well as garnering a cash income of more than $200. "Thus stands the record of the efforts of these old buffalo-eaters and hunter-sportsmen in their first attempt at subsistence farming," he concluded. In total, PFLA members harvested 1,100 bushels of wheat and oats in 1921; they harvested more than 15,000 bushels the following year.[57]

As the concept of mutual aid societies swept rural communities across the United States during the farm crisis years of the 1920s, the Blackfeet's agricultural adaptations marked the PFLA as one of the darling programs touted across the nation by the Office of Indian Affairs. Not only did the program seemingly reflect the success of the OIA's long-term efforts to transform the Blackfeet into farmers, but, from the Blackfeet perspective, the PFLA represented a Native reorganization of food and agriculture on the reservation that continued the communal food traditions that had marked Blackfeet society since the days of the pisskans. Hamilton's allies in Congress increased their resistance to the surplus unallotted land sales, leading eventually to the end of allotment in 1928. The Indian Reorganization Act, or the "Indian New Deal," passed in 1934, ending allotment and promoting Native self-governance, and the newly organized Blackfeet Nation was the first Native group to pass a tribal constitution under this law. Meanwhile, a new generation of American Indian activists from across tribal boundaries worked together to set a new agenda for Native food sovereignty that would play out across the rest of the twentieth century.

5.

Food and Activism in the Twentieth Century

When he was five-years old, Naawakamig, an Anishinaabe boy from the Leech Lake Reservation, saw a man from the United States Office of Indian Affairs (OIA) arrive in a yellow school bus. Pounding on the door, the man entered Naawakamig's home and confronted the boy's mother, grandmother, and grandfather. He demanded that Naawakamig, along with his older brother and sister, leave with him on the school bus immediately. Within a few minutes, amidst a flood of tears and screams, the man had forced the children from their mother's arms and locked them on the school bus. After driving for many hours, they arrived at their destination: the Pipestone Indian School, three hundred miles away from Naawakamig's home on Drumbeater Lake. The year was 1942, the same year that the United States began, in earnest, to reverse the global tide of fascism during the Second World, halting the Japanese drive across the Pacific at Midway and Guadalcanal and defeating Germany in North Africa. The same year as well that the War Relocation Authority incarcerated eighty thousand American citizens of Japanese descent into ten internment camps across the American West. Imprisoned himself in an Indian boarding school that he would later describe as a "concentration camp," Naawakamig would not see his mother again for eleven years; a reunion he achieved only after a frenzied escape from Pipestone.[1]

In 1962, Naawakamig, now known by his English name, Dennis Banks, helped found the American Indian Movement, or AIM, in an American Indian neighborhood of south Minneapolis. Banks was just one of thousands of Native activists of his generation whose defiance of American colonialism and assertions of American Indian nationalism were irrevocably shaped by their experiences in the federal boarding school system, including those of food and both literal and metaphorical hunger.

Although the stories of Banks and the fellow militants in AIM are perhaps some the most familiar accounts of twentieth-century American Indian activism, many other Native activists engaged state authorities and public opinions throughout this same period. Boarding school students used their compulsory educations for anti-colonial ends. When they returned home to their reservations after their long, forced removals, they squared off against corrupt reservation agents who unlawfully withheld federal food rations and other treaty resources from Indian people. Like Robert Hamilton, who traveled to Washington, DC, to lobby against the allotment act's provisions for the sale of surplus unallotted land that threatened to further reduce Native landownership and erode Blackfeet food sovereignty, other students also returned home to their communities as the century progressed to press Indigenous calls for social equality and political sovereignty. They formed new professional associations and organizations devoted to pursuing the legal claims of Native communities for past and present violations of federal treaties that had crippled American Indian food sovereignty by cutting off access to customary hunting, fishing, foraging, and farming grounds. In the case of AIM, this twentieth-century diaspora of hungry former boarding school students also occupied dozens of federal and state facilities during the early 1970s—including, most famously, the site of the Wounded Knee Massacre and the Bureau of Indian Affairs headquarters in Washington, DC—hoping to turn the tide of public opinion against a colonial American government that continued to subjugate Native people in the midst of increasing Cold War–era commitments to freedom and civil rights.

Food and hunger played central roles in all of these activist endeavors. The political radicalization of boarding school students occurred, in part, not only because many students had been taken from their families against their will but also because this trauma was commonly justified by the presumptions of federal personnel that Indian parents were unable to feed their children. The widespread poverty and hunger on American Indian reservations from the late nineteenth century onward was often manufactured by federal personnel in order to subordinate tribal leadership.[2] Dependence on the reservation agent for food supplies was a crucial weapon in the Indian service's colonial quiver, an instrument that had been wielded on the Blackfeet Reservation during Hamilton's era, for instance, as a cudgel for silencing tribal critics of the agency's sale of surplus unallotted land. Although food rations were guaranteed by the very treaties that had confined Native communities to reservations in the first place, the agents tasked with administering food rations and other entitlements routinely withheld them from so-called "problem" Indians who advocated for tribal sovereignty or who flouted the Indian service's various efforts towards cultural assimilation. Likewise, when boarding schools needed to fill their rooms with children to justify their funding, reservation agents could reduce tribal rations as if turning off a faucet and collect hungry students from desperate mothers and fathers deemed incompetent by social workers; a scenario that played out periodically across the entirety of Native America during the eighty years of federal boarding school operations.

Withholding food as an administrative weapon continued at the boarding school. Once enrolled, students were not often adequately fed unless they learned to negotiate institutional systems that were at once chaotic, stressful, and authoritarian. Food at boarding schools was meager, and students suffered from numerous nutritional deprivations. Students were responsible for the almost all of the labor of meal preparation, as well as the growing, harvesting, milking, killing, and butchering all raw ingredients that did not arrive in the schools' infrequent, palletized deliveries. Mealtime itself could be an unruly nightmare. After reciting their enforced blessings, hungry students jostled with one another to eat as much as possible before their teachers rang the bell and marched them back to class. As on the reservation, the authorities at the boarding school used food and hunger strategically as instruments of subordination.

Native students who managed to survive the boarding school life (and there were thousands who did not) emerged from their experiences with a new understanding of the significance of food sovereignty to the freedom struggles of Native communities. At the heart of much of twentieth-century Native activism was a political commitment to restore Native self-determination and political authority, objectives that could be achieved only if Native people could take back control of their bare subsistence from the federal government. Activists sought to accomplish this through a variety of approaches. For instance, in the early twentieth century Robert Hamilton, himself a Blackfeet graduate of the Carlisle Indian Industrial School, embarked upon a successful twenty-year activist career to prevent the sale of so-called surplus unallotted lands on the Blackfeet Reservation, a sale that would have devastated the Blackfeet's agricultural base. After serving three years in the Minnesota penal system for stealing groceries to feed his hungry family, Dennis Banks committed himself to the anti-colonial agenda of AIM, publicizing the struggle of Native peoples to eat in an unequal society committed to their impoverishment and subjugation. Other activists, such as Lorelei DeCora Means, directly contested the United States' colonial food regimes in Congressional hearings over welfare and food stamp reform. By the 1980s, all of these struggles had culminated in a broad measure of success for Native activists in their effort to achieve Indian self-determination through food sovereignty. By framing access to food not only as a human right but also as a treaty right, Indian activists over the twentieth century reshaped political conversations over the significance of food in the processes of settler colonialism.

For more than fifty years, the federal government had mandated that Native children's attendance in federal boarding schools was compulsory as a part of their sweeping efforts to assimilate Native people into the American body politic. This colonial assimilation, however, was never premised around the full incorporation of American Indians as American citizens—as fully free and fully functional legal and economic agents of American society. It was assimilation through subjugation; assimilation as a means of perfecting American Indians as colonial subjects within the unequal spaces of American society. As the historian Philip Deloria has noted, "Americans meant to bring Indian people within social and cultural boundaries only to the extent that they could be shaped using the same institutions and ideologies that made white citizens into subjects —schools, churches, wage labor, and literacy, among others."[3] In this sense, the boarding school was an essential instrument of the assimilation process as it undertook an educational project that sought to void Native children of their tribal identities and to acculturate them instead with the expectations and tastes of middle-class white society. Proponents of this boarding school project, such as Richard Henry Pratt, the superintendent of the Carlisle Indian Industrial School in Pennsylvania, evoked the violent process through which this transformation was supposed to occur. As Pratt infamously remarked, boarding schools worked to "kill the Indian in order to save the man."[4] Tearing Native children from the arms of their mothers, fathers, and other loved ones was an integral step in this cruel process of cultural conversion.

Although Congress passed the compulsory Indian education law in 1891, boarding schools had been a vital component of federal Indian policy since the years immediately following the Civil War. Pratt himself had played a pivotal role in the creation and evolution of the schools in the late nineteenth century. Inspired by the Reconstruction-era freedmen's schools for African American students and emboldened by his experiences as a white second lieutenant in a "buffalo soldier" cavalry regiment of enlisted African American troops serving under George Armstrong Custer out of Fort Sill in the Indian Territory, Pratt's philosophy of education emphasized the remaking of supposedly racially inferior men through military drill and the enforced acquisition of white, middle-class cultural values. After the end of the Red River War, his final active-service military campaign, in 1875, Pratt relocated hundreds of captured Arapaho, Comanche, and Kiowa men from the Indian Territory to St. Augustine, Florida, where they were imprisoned at Fort Marion, a coastal fortress built of stone by the Spanish in 1672 that had been periodically used through the nineteenth century to incarcerate Native American prisoners. Pratt experimented on these imprisoned men with his educational methods for several years, achieving enough progress on English language and "craftwork" skills that he later sent seventeen of them to the Hampton Institute in Virginia where they studied under Booker T. Washington alongside African American students. In 1879, the opening of the OIA's Carlisle Indian Industrial School provided Pratt with a permanent home for his program of Indian reeducation. He served as Carlisle's superintendent for the next twenty-five years.[5]

In the meantime, the boarding school model of Indian education rapidly grew into one of the foundational programs of federal assimilation efforts. By the end of the nineteenth century, tens of thousands of Native children were enrolled in one of twenty-four off-reservation boarding schools, and the institutions' prevalence persisted well into the twentieth century. In 1931, six years before Dennis Banks's birth, enrollment in Indian boarding schools peaked with more than 29 percent of Indian children living in a boarding school.[6]

In retrospect, it is remarkable that Indian families managed to prevent their children from being wrenched away from their homes by federal agents and other members of the Indian service. Indian children over several generations were instructed by their parents and families to hide from these authorities, which constituted a federal crime according to the compulsory Indian education act. One example from northern Arizona illuminates the aggressive cruelty with which government personnel, tasked with stocking the new schools with Native children, carried out their mission. In 1890, a troop of US cavalry raided the Hopi community of Oraibi, kidnapping 104 children to intern at the new boarding school in Keams Canyon. Four years later, the cavalry returned to kidnap more Indian children, but they were met with an empty village, abandoned by families who had left their homes and fled with their children to hiding places in the mountains and canyons. Rather than leave empty-handed, the soldiers arrested nineteen Hopi men who they charged with violating the compulsory education law. These men were then transported eight hundred miles away to California, where they were held in the federal penitentiary on Alcatraz Island.[7] In short, for more than half a century, federal laws accorded Native parents no guardianship over their children. In both childhood and adulthood, Indian people were wards of the state, their lives subjected to any whim or exercise of federal power.

By forcibly taking children from their homes, the Indian service undermined the concept of *home* for Indian families. In the wake of the intergenerational trauma of forced removal from their ancestral homelands, just as new reservation communities had adapted to produce new forms of agricultural independence and open up new possibilities for the intergenerational transfer of wealth, the federal boarding schools came along to steal Indian children with the fundamental goal of severing Native peoples' ties to their tribal lands and reservation communities. Alongside the practical outcome of federal allotment policy—the massive transfer of Indian land into the non-Native ownership—the federal boarding school served as a tool for breaking up the possibility of permanent Indian land tenure by assaulting social and cultural cycles of family reproduction. From the perspectives of food, agricultural, and settler colonialism, the removal of children from Native communities into boarding schools served much the same devastating function as the removal of entire Native communities had earlier in the nineteenth century.

In addition to military force and the threat of arrest, federal agents also coerced Indian families to give up their children through systematic campaigns of hunger. By withholding the delivery of treaty rations on remote reservations during the winter, for instance, superintendents forced Native parents to give up their starving children in the hope that they would at least be able to eat at the boarding school. Such was the case on the Hopi Reservation, where federal agents essentially laid siege until village families returned to deliver their children, as well as on the Ojibwe reservations of northern Minnesota, where Banks and many other children were taken.[8] Depending on the sagacity of the Indian service agent, children could also be compelled from their parents' loving hands when families arrived, reluctantly, at OIA agencies in order to ask for rations, annuities, and other resources that were legally entitled to them according to federal treaties but that were often only issued at the command of reservation superintendents. At one of these meetings in the late 1930s, for instance, the young Dennis Banks recalled how his mother pleaded with a social worker to issue her family some commodity foods as well as enough fabric to clothe her three children with one outfit each. The social worker responded with a script of questions designed, essentially, to ascertain whether she was fit to remain as the custodian of her children. Banks's mother, he remembered, abruptly responded by saying: "I don't have to answer any of those questions. I came here for help. But if you're not going to help me, we will leave." The family had walked into town from their home thirteen miles away and had nowhere to stay, so they slept on the street before returning, empty-handed, the following morning.[9]

A variety of other domestic situations were also leveraged to force the separation of parents from their children, including divorce. For instance, D'Arcy McNickle, the celebrated author of *The Surrounded* and other works of Native fiction and non-fiction, was born on the Flathead Reservation in northern Montana to a white father and a Cree mother. In 1913, after his parents divorced, McNickle found himself, at the age nine, shipped off to the Chemawa Indian School in Salem, Oregon. Despite his mother's ongoing legal battle to maintain custody of her son, she could not prevent the Flathead Reservation agent from ordering McNickle off to Chemawa. When McNickle escaped from the reservation's train platform on the day of his departure and returned home to his mother, the reservation agent had her arrested for kidnapping, and McNickle was forced to board the next train to Oregon.[10]

Once at the boarding school, children like McNickle discussed one another's forced relocations and began to realize commonalities to their experiences as colonial subjects that transcended their tribal differences. Experiences at the boarding school further recapitulated broader stories of resilience and refashioning that marked the historical evolution of Native communities in the wake of the Removal Era. In short, the boarding school experience did not "kill the Indian" as administrators like Pratt had intended, but instead served as an incubator for new forms of pan-Indian culture and identity adopted by children of many tribes whose only assured common characteristic was their compulsory removal from their homes and families. As the historian Brenda Child has observed, "Children did indeed enter 'the unfamiliar world of the white man's school,' but the power of home was so intense and comforting that few students left that world behind."[11] And in remembering home together, these children introduced the ways and memories of their cultures to each other, learning each other's languages and ceremonies and inventing their own.

One of the most important areas in which Indian students both practiced their Native identities and developed new ones was in the domain of food. Feeding students at the boarding school was a time-consuming and complicated task that required immense amounts of child labor from start to finish. Female students were primarily responsible for all aspects of kitchen preparation, from provisioning ingredients to cooking and cleaning, and male students were required to participate in all aspects of the "agricultural industry" that not only put food on the schools' tables, but also put money back into their underfunded account books. In short, life at the boarding schools reflected the same colonial mentalities that had shaped the reservation agents' admonitions that Indians must "work or starve." Just as the many agents on the Blackfeet Reservation had tried to manipulate tribally owned lands for the commercial production of export beef cattle—in part to help pay for the costly administration of the OIA's colonial surveillance and oversight of the Blackfeet community—the superintendents of Indian boarding schools around the country resolved to bridge their own budgetary shortfalls by selling off agricultural goods produced by their students. At the Chilocco boarding school in northern Oklahoma, for instance, farm products raised by students accounted, on average, for around $35,000 of school income per year—an amount equal to roughly 10 to 15 percent of the school's annual appropriation from the federal government.[12] In 1925 at the Haskell boarding school in northern Kansas, where many male students were commonly "put out"—that is, consigned to serve as farmworkers for white communities as far as away as Colorado during seasonal shortages in agricultural labor—students still managed to generate $14,000 of supplemental income for the school's coffers. "This school," observed its superintendent, "could not long continue without the great amount of free labor contributed by the pupils."[13] Indeed, without the free agricultural labor of tens of thousands of Native children, the federal government's underfunded experiments in Indian education would have gone bankrupt within just a few budget cycles.

Thus, in order to eat at school, Native students had to do all the work of feeding themselves (and others), illuminating their plight, of course, as captive forced laborers, but also at times revealing new strategic places from which they could challenge and circumvent institutional authority. In all matters food related, students effectively transformed their schools into Native institutions. Demonstrating remarkable resourcefulness, students supplemented their boarding school diets with the meat of wild game that they had hunted in secret and with vegetables, milk, eggs, and other products of their labor that they reappropriated from the school farm before it could be taken to the institutional kitchen or sold to outside communities. They found ways to rehearse certain food rituals from home, recreating their Native traditions within the walls of a place designed to shear them of their Native identities. Ponca girls at Chilocco, for instance, consumed peyote in their dormitory rooms, both introducing the unique ceremonies to students from other regions of Native America and providing a means of covert resistance to the boarding school's suppression of their Native identities.[14] As the historian Tsianina Lomawaima has put it, "Indian people at boarding schools were not passive consumers of an ideology or lifestyle imparted from above by federal administrators. . . . An institution founded and controlled by the federal government was inhabited and possessed by those whose identities the institution was committed to erase."[15] By performing the labor required to feed the schools, Native students also gained familiarity with the institutions' most intimate spaces, finding opportunities to plant the seeds of their culinary projects in ways that emboldened resistance to colonial authority and nurtured new expressions of American Indian identity.

One of the most popular of these clandestine culinary pursuits was the production of alcohol. In the early twentieth century, an era of widespread state and federal prohibitions on alcohol production, do-it-yourself methods of making beer, cider, and liquor were generally widely known . Especially in Indian country, where alcohol had been widely consumed despite its illegality for many decades, the craft of making alcohol at home had helped supply meet demand. In boarding schools, Indian children used drunkenness as a means of resistance and rebellion both by breaking the law and by incorporating the production and consumption of alcoholic drinks into social rituals. In getting drunk, the children mocked the puritanical authority of their reform-minded teachers and principals. For many, the actual beverage they were drinking often mattered less than the effects of the drink itself. One student at Chilocco, under the pseudonym Edgar, remembered the first time he got drunk, at the age of eleven, drinking a cocktail mixed with vanilla and lemon extract, which his friends procured several cases of by breaking into the school bakery. In order to reach their desired state of drunkenness, they had to drink an enormous amount of extract. "There's no need telling you," he remarked, "how long it took to get rid of the smell." After experimenting with various other flavoring extracts, Edgar and his friends decided to brew their own beer with stolen sugar, yeast, and barley malt. They mixed these ingredients with water in a lidless wooden keg that had been used to store nails in the dairy barn, then wrapped the top of the keg tightly with sacks and buried it "four or five inches" below the ground. The mixture bubbled away for several weeks, fermenting and stinking, but its strategic burial near the dairy barn hid its olfactory tells. Had the school's dairy instructor not accidently stepped on the cache and broken through, landing with one leg in the soil-fermented keg of beer, Edgar and his friends would have had their first batch of homebrew.[16]

Female students, unlike their male peers, spent much of their days laboring in the boarding schools' institutional kitchens. As part of their required domestic science training, the task of cooking for thousands of people each day kept these students extremely busy. At Chilocco, for instance, a typical breakfast required cooking seventy-five pounds of dried oatmeal in ninety-gallon kettles over a four-by-nine-foot gas burner. In 1932, a feature article on these Chilocco student cooks in *Oklahoma Indian School Magazine* described a rare occasion when all the students were served eggs; the girls cracked and cooked 1,020 of them.[17]

This heavy kitchen labor, masqueraded as domestic training, was also racialized and gendered in ways that corresponded to longstanding colonial expectations of Native women as drudges. For instance, in a recapitulation of seventeenth-century English rhetoric describing Wampanoag women, at the National Congress of Mothers in 1898, Sylvanus Stall, the noted antimasturbation sexual hygienist, declared the suitability of Native girls as domestic servants given their ability to "endure effort, exposure and hardship which would kill the white woman."[18] This public image of Native women as servants also circulated and expanded throughout the United States during the height of the boarding school era, spread by popular Hollywood movies, such as Cecil B. DeMille's *The Squaw Man* (1914)—a film in which a Native woman named Nat-u-rich saves the life of an English immigrant to Wyoming, marries him, then bears him a son and serves as his ranch wife until his long-lost love from England, Diana, arrives on the scene, at which point Nat-u-rich takes her own life. This film exemplifies a pattern of binary expectations for Native women in the twentieth century as either "dominated drudges" or "feisty natural princess," as Philip J. Deloria as observed.[19]

The link between domestic training and household servitude was formalized in boarding schools with "working out" programs. In these programs, students temporarily left their everyday routines either to work off-campus as domestic servants for local white families, as at the Carlisle school, or, as was the case at Chilocco, to take turns living together in cottages and role-playing the daily domestic life of an idealized white, middle-class family. This system had its roots in the educational programming of the Hampton Institute and other post–Civil War freedmen's schools. Students at Booker T. Washington's Tuskegee Institute in Alabama, for instance, also participated in cottage projects as part of their domestic science training. At Chilocco, Indian girls spent six weeks each year in such cottages, tasked with managing a household of four family members on $4.50 per week. The students took turns playing the roles of father, mother, son, and daughter, an educational activity intended both to help transfer the culinary skills acquired in the institutional kitchen to a single-family, residential setting, and to provide tacit cultural training in the heteronormative, nuclear family relationships to which middle-class white reformers at the turn-of-the twentieth century aspired.[20]For Native students, life in the cottages provided another space for the reassertion of their tribal identities. It opened an opportunity for them to recall the comforts of their own homes as well as an opportunity to mock, by "play-acting," the expectations of white people. Rather than achieving the elimination of Native identity, this cottage exercise, along with so many other activities of the boarding school, instead provided Native girls with a sense of cultural mastery and cultural mastery that would serve them well in their future careers as reformers and activists.

Despite both formal and anecdotal testimony from Native students on the substandard diets at the boarding schools, official inspections and accounts of tours given by Indian service personnel often waxed poetic about the high quality of food served at the boarding schools. These reports corresponded more with Indian office desires for administrative streamlining than with the reality of mealtimes at the schools. At one school in Montana, for instance, an inspector wrote to the commissioner of Indian Affairs that "hot cocoa [was served] at 10:30 every forenoon," followed by a lunch featuring "macaroni and tomatoes, mashed potatoes, beef extract with gravy, butter, hot baking powder biscuits and syrup." The following day the same inspector reported that the menu featured "escalloped potatoes, creamed peas, stewed peaches, whole wheat bread, butter and syrup. . . .The students," he continued, "told us that they were amply supplied with food. We found no complaint on this whatever."[21]

Such stories from inspectors masked the serious problems with boarding school meals, however, and student accounts differed substantially from the official reports. One student remembered that "we'd have stew, once in a while, I suppose cooked with vegetables, potatoes and carrots, onions . . . but never a fresh vegetable, never a fresh fruit . . . every Sunday you'd have what they called cake which was really just bread." Other students discussed the difficulty of getting anything to eat at all during meals that were served "family" style. Even when a varied menu was present, it was often difficult to get enough to eat. For instance, one Creek student recently arrived at Chilocco was introduced to the customary system of "trading out," where individual students would immediately take an entire serving bowl into possession once mealtime started, refusing to share any of the food in the dish unless someone else with a different dish offered to trade them a bite. If a student found themselves "shut out," without a dish to trade, then they would likely go hungry during that meal. As a young, small boy, the only way that this student eventually managed to eat during mealtime was by volunteering to be a waiter—one of the students who brought the dishes into the dining room from the kitchen. For all these reasons and countless others, mealtime was "a story unto itself," as Lomawaima has put it.[22]

By the end of the 1920s, the federal government's forced privatization of tribal landownership on Indian reservations under allotment policies had exposed a widespread crisis in the governance of reservations placed under the sole authority of agents of the OIA. In response to many longtime concerns about the corruption and incompetence of Indian agents on western reservations during the allotment process, in 1926 the US Secretary of Interior, Hubert Work, commissioned a federal statistician, Lewis Meriam, to gather data and other insights into Native life and livelihood across Indian country. Meriam's efforts led to a wide-ranging, eight-hundred-page account that was published in 1928 titled *The Problem of Indian Administration* and that laid blame for Native poverty squarely at the foot of the Indian agency system.[23] The effects of Meriam's report reverberated throughout the twentieth century as federal administrators and Indian activists sought to address the many problems, both visible and invisible, in Indian country.

At the same time, the diaspora of boarding school graduates had begun returning to their homes on reservations, where they confronted Indian office personnel who had systematically starved their families, facilitated the sale of tribal lands into non-Indian ownership, and sent them off to the boarding schools years earlier as young children. During the end of the allotment era in the 1910s and 1920s, controversies over the sale of surplus unallotted lands dominated reservation politics all across Indian country, and members of this new generation of boarding school–educated Indian activists, such as Robert Hamilton, took center stage in these confrontations. Not only did they emerge as the youthful leaders of their reservation communities but they also traveled to Washington, DC—and, in fact, across the entire globe—in their efforts to raise public awareness of the mistreatment of Native American communities as well as to work, specifically, within the legislative structures of the federal government to address issues related to Native hunger, poverty, and landownership. By the 1920s, these efforts had developed into a series of compromises between the federal government and Indian communities that set the stage for ongoing contestations over the meaning and practice of Indian sovereignty and self-determination throughout much of the rest of the century. Food played a vital role in these political confrontations. By publicizing the issue of Native hunger, activists convincingly demonstrated the basis for Indian poverty not in the distant colonial past but in America's recent dispossessions of Indian landownership.

In response to these problems, federal legislators and American Indian activists devised a new system of representational government on Indian reservations by laying out a process for the creation of tribal constitutions, a major transformation in the history of federal Indian policy that was enacted into law under the Indian Reorganization Act of 1934. Widely heralded as the "Indian New Deal," the Indian Reorganization Act (IRA) officially ended the allotment process. It also led to the establishment of many of the tribal councils and other Native governing bodies that have represented federally recognized tribes up to the present day. On the one hand, the IRA offered the possibility of a radical return to Native sovereignty by replacing the colonial authority of an OIA agent with an administration of democratically elected members of the tribe.

On the other hand, the fact that the OIA held the authority to accept or reject tribal constitutions meant that the radical possibilities of Native sovereignty were contained by OIA approval. Over the next several decades, Indian activists increasingly worked both within and beyond the mainstream political systems set up by the IRA to advance a broad policy agenda of maintaining the federal recognition of Indian treaty rights. Given its foundational importance to welfare-state visions of economic and social development, food played a central role in the politics of Native sovereignty from the era of the IRA onward.

The IRA promised much, but for many Native communities it failed to deliver. As a result, Indian activists formed the National Congress of American Indians (NCAI) in 1944. While the scope of the NCAI's policy interests was wide, their overall goals were straightforward, emphasizing the defense of tribal rights, as defined by protecting the federal recognition of existing tribes, and the defense of the civil rights of individual Indians. In the context of the New Deal and the emerging national politics of social welfare, the NCAI also took pains to dispel the notion that Native communities were recipients of welfare aid, instead contextualizing federal "aid" to tribes as a matter of upholding specific treaty relationships dating back to the nineteenth century.

Nevertheless, the late 1940s and 1950s were marked by a concerted federal effort to cancel these treaty obligations through a process called termination. Officials in the Eisenhower administration sought to work out arrangements with the tribal nations organized under the IRA that would terminate their treaty relationship with the United States and their status as sovereign governments in return for cash payments that would be distributed per capita to enrolled tribal members. The terms of proposed terminations were largely determined by regional political and economic forces. In the case of the Klamath termination, for instance, a major paper manufacturer—the Crown-Zellerbach company of San Francisco—acquired 90,000 acres of timber lands previously owned under tribal trust while another 525,000 acres were transferred to the US Forest Service and became the Fremont-Winema National Forest in 1961. The Klamath regained federal recognition status in 1986, but their reservation lands, which contained some of the most productive pine forests on the west coast, were not returned. In the intervening twenty-five years, private corporations contracting with the Forest Service cut a total timber harvest valued at more than $500 million. In contrast, the one-time monetary payments sent to roughly two thousand individual members of the Klamath under the termination agreement amounted to about $44,000 each.[24]

For Native activists concerned with self-determination and food sovereignty, the threat of termination for further dispossessing and alienating Native communities from their agricultural homelands was substantial. The NCAI and other organizations lobbied throughout the 1950s and 1960s to oppose the policy, as well as to seek the re-recognition of tribes that had been terminated. For these Native activists, the recognition of federal treaty rights was essential for the protection of Native food sovereignty. Treaty rights, for instance, adjudicated hunting and fishing access on public lands, exempting certain tribal members from state and local laws.[25] Likewise, for many Native communities, treaty status also provided for the continued tribal management of reservation lands and agricultural resources.

These debates over treaty status and food sovereignty reached a climax in the 1970s and 1980s as Native activists navigated the efforts of federal officials jockeying for food stamp reform as part of a broader effort to erode the political economy of the midcentury American welfare state. On a July afternoon during the United States' bicentennial summer of 1976, President Gerald Ford invited a delegation of American Indian activists and community leaders into the White House dining room for refreshments. Ford addressed his audience with a few generic stanzas on the historical role of Native foodways in American culture, a contribution that was, as he put it, "both material and spiritual. . . . Your ancestors," continued Ford, "introduced settlers not only to new foods and plants, but to Indian ways of life and Indian values, which they absorbed."[26]

For the Native men and women gathered at the White House that day, concerned with recent changes to federal food stamp and commodity distribution programs on Indian reservations, Ford's claim that Indian ways of life were "absorbed" into the political economies and ecologies of America's food systems must have seemed absurd. To them, Ford's bicentennial celebration might as well have marked two centuries of colonial policies premised around ongoing efforts to dispossess and subordinate Native land and labor for the benefit of non-Native agricultural production. And a recent decision by the US Department of Agriculture to replace commodity food distribution on Indian reservations with food stamp programs administered by state governments added a deeper insult to this historical injury, as the decision reflected the Ford administration's misunderstanding of food distribution in Indian country as a welfare project rather than a matter of treaty obligation.

Indian activists had a strong case for interpreting federal food provisioning as a treaty obligation rather than an act of charitable welfare. The confinement of Native people on western reservations during the nineteenth century had opened up enormous tracts of prime agricultural soil for non-Native farmers and ranchers. This massive dispossession—of literally hundreds of millions of acres—was rendered legal according to federal law by a series of over six hundred treaties signed among hundreds of Native communities. In these treaties, the federal government pledged to provide public services—usually including food distribution—on Indian reservations, and this was particularly important on the relatively barren reservations of the high plains, where bison and other traditional sources of subsistence had been hunted to near extinction by the end of the 1870s. Balking at the expense of actually delivering on these treaty obligations, however, federal officials soon neglected to do so. By the 1950s and 1960s, Congress clamored to establish a new policy of termination through which remaining Indian land titles and treaty relationships might be liquidated through lump-sum payments. It was in this context that a new coalition of American Indian activists who opposed termination came of age. By the summer of 1970, this activist movement had achieved its goal of reversing termination policy, ushering in a new era, which the Indian Bureau and President Richard Nixon famously called the era of "Indian self-determination," focused on a return to treaty rights and a recognition of the special relationship between Native communities and the federal government.

Nevertheless, when it came to food, by the early 1970s both the American public and most federal officials associated food distribution not with treaty obligations but with the federal social welfare institutions developed during the New Deal. In fact, in the 1970s, the USDA's commodity food distribution system that was administered by the Bureau of Indian Affairs on Indian reservations had its roots in the Commodity Credit Corporation Act of 1933, which authorized the USDA to purchase surplus commodities from farmers in order to shore up agricultural prices from overproduced crops. During the New Deal and the Second World War, these crops were distributed as commodity foods to schools, needy families, and charitable institutions. Beginning in 1949, the Bureau of Indian Affairs also distributed these commodity foods on reservations. But despite the source of these commodity foods being the same agricultural surplus that fed non-Native recipients on USDA distribution lists, the Indian food distribution program was not part of the welfare state; it was part of a much older federal treaty obligation to provide public services on Indian reservations. Or as one Lakota activist put it, citing the 1868 Treaty of Fort Laramie, the commodity foods distributed to Lakota communities were not "free," and were certainly not handouts from the federal government, but instead represented a portion of the annuities that the United States committed to pay in return for the ceded lands of the Cheyenne River, Standing Rock, Rosebud, and Pine Ridge Reservations.[27]

With the passage of the federal Food Stamp Act in 1965, policymakers had sought to replace commodity food distribution with a new model of social welfare food provisioning better suited to an American postwar landscape of shopping malls and supermarkets. In 1973, the USDA tried to replace commodity distribution with food stamps on Indian reservations as well, a move that was delayed through a series of injunctions over the next four years and eventually halted by a legislative decision in 1977 that preserved the food distribution program on reservations, alongside the implementation of a new food stamp program, and put both programs under tribal administration.

The implementation of the food stamp program on reservations suffered from a number of substantial the challenges, however. Perhaps most obviously, a near-total lack of retail grocery stores on rural Indian reservations in the early 1970s, along with reservation unemployment rates surpassing 40 percent, hampered the reform efforts envisioned by food stamp supporters. Moreover, the historical legacies of the roles that food played in delegating power between Native and non-Native people on Indian reservations across rural America presented a wide field of unseen obstacles for USDA administrators to negotiate.

Perhaps the most obvious problem with the USDA's plan to replace commodity food distribution with food stamps was the fact that there were very few existing locations on reservation lands where food stamps might be accepted. For instance, a 1973 survey of the Cheyenne River Reservation in South Dakota—a reservation roughly the same size as the state of Connecticut—revealed only six small grocery stores, mostly scattered along the reservation's boundaries. By comparison, the same survey found sixteen commodity distribution points, evenly situated across the reservation, that each served approximately

2,500 eligible participants.[28] The plan to replace commodity distribution with food stamps would have forced the majority of these participants to drive thousands of additional miles per year to purchase food with their stamp benefits. This situation was not unique to South Dakota. On the Blackfeet Reservation of north-central Montana, one single grocery store in Browning would have been responsible for serving twelve thousand eligible food stamp participants.[29]

Although these reservations were fairly typical in terms of size and population density—and in these characteristics alone did not appreciably differ from neighboring non-Native rural communities—several other reservations presented geographic obstacles to implementing an effective food stamp program that were more shockingly obvious, and yet these obstacles did not immediately dissuade the USDA.[30] The Havasupai Reservation, for instance, located at the bottom of the Grand Canyon, presented its own unique challenge to using food stamps. Reaching the community required a six-hour hike down canyon walls from a trailhead located sixty miles down a dirt road. The nearest grocery store lay many miles further down the highway, and the nearest food stamp issuing office was located an additional hundred miles away in Flagstaff, Arizona. For decades, the Bureau of Indian Affairs had supplied commodity foods to reservation residents using mule pack trains, and, more recently, occasional helicopter deliveries. Nevertheless, in 1972 a well-meaning food stamps program coordinator traveled to the reservation and came down the canyon on horseback. "The people were so hostile that they wouldn't even come to meetings where food stamps were explained," she reported with exasperation.[31]

The application and interview process for gaining admission to the food stamp program posed a slew of both cultural and administrative challenges for eligible Indian applicants. For starters, the administration of the food stamp program by state agencies, rather than federal agencies such as the USDA or the Bureau of Indian Affairs, fostered much confusion, especially on reservations that straddled state boundaries. Just north of the Cheyenne River Reservation, for instance, Native people on the Standing Rock Reservation were forced to reckon with the process of determining whether to apply to issuing offices in North or South Dakota.[32] Living on the largest reservation by both land area and population, eligible Navajo participants had to negotiate with the rules and regulations of three different state governments: Arizona, New Mexico, and Utah. Rather than offering Navajos additional choice or flexibility, the state certification administrations tasked with enrolling Navajo participants in these overlapping jurisdictions instead inspired dread. Many Navajo applicants could not read or write in English, and officials rejected Navajo food stamp applications for any number of technicalities, one of the most common being an inability to document wages from informal work such as hauling wood and water.[33]

Even in situations where Native food stamp enrollment worked as the USDA had intended, participants shared concerns about their forced supplication to state bureaucrats for access to the federal program, a situation described by Charles Trimble, the executive director of the National Congress of the American Indian, as an "on your knees" begging.[34] The federal treaty right of food distribution had been diminished into an arbitrary offering of state-level social welfare. In response, Native activists pressed for federal legislation to remove the administration of the Indian food stamp program from state agencies and to place it, preferably, within the jurisdiction of tribal councils.

But the campaign to pursue tribal administration of food stamps did not enjoy clear-cut Native support. Other activists pointed to their own distrust of corrupt tribal councils—what they considered to be puppet regimes of the Bureau of Indian Affairs—for administrating a Native food stamps program. Lorelei DeCora Means, for instance, expressed her opposition to tribal management to the Senate Select Committee on Nutrition, chaired by George McGovern, in 1974. A veteran of the American Indian Movement's armed occupation of Wounded Knee the previous spring, Means delivered her testimony while seven months pregnant. She expressed her concern that Richard Wilson, the tribal chairman of the Oglala Lakota Sioux of the Pine Ridge Reservation who was widely regarded as a puppet for the Bureau of Indian Affairs and the FBI's counter-insurgency actions against Red Power activists, would simply deny the claims of his political opponents. Couching Native food sovereignty in the context of tribal council management of food stamps was simply not enough, and Means boldly proclaimed to the Senate committee that if both federal officials and the Wilson administration were going to starve her and her allies through the denial of food aid, especially one couched in the liberalized rhetoric of freedom and the marketplace, then "you might as well just shoot me in the back."[35]

The diverse positions of Native food activists also encompassed those who recognized significant problems with the commodity food distribution system, particularly in regard to its deficient nutritional composition. The USDA only grudgingly maintained the Indian commodity food distribution program after its decision to switch entirely to food stamps had been blocked, and their deliveries grew increasingly monotonous after 1973. Observers on the Pine Ridge Reservation remarked that the main deliveries each month consisted of flour, rice, and macaroni. Little or no meat or other sources of protein had been delivered aside from dry beans and split peas, and canned fruits and vegetables—let alone fresh ones—were even less frequently delivered.[36]

In the meantime, Native activists enlisted public allies to campaign on behalf of adding nutrition to reservation diets—a human rights mission that might resonate more with the hearts of the American public than the legal issues of treaty rights. For instance, Jean Mayer, professor of nutrition at the Harvard School of Public Health, visited the Navajo Nation and several other southwestern reservations, producing a series of editorial essays that were published in the *Washington Post* and other prominent forums and that featured scathing indictments of the commodity program's nutritional failures. Improving the Native "state of health," wrote Mayer, "would cost a mere pittance," and yet it was an effort "that we as a society seem unwilling to make."[37]

From the perspective of the USDA, commodity foods were never intended to provide a complete diet, but rather to provide supplemental calories. In fact, the monthly commodity food distribution was determined far more by which specific agriculture markets were oversupplied than by the dietary needs of those who received them. In the wake of the Food Stamp Act, the USDA planned to use the commodity program even more aggressively as a means to subsidize agricultural surpluses in corn and other cash crops to the near exclusion of fruits and vegetables. This was another reason, according to federal officials, for Indians to transition to food stamp program, which, in theory at least, provided access to better and more complete nutrition.

In practice, many Indians did not rely on commodity foods for their nutritional requirements, nor did they even necessarily eat their commodity foods. Instead, they disposed of the often monotonous rations by trading them with various businesses, individuals, and institutions both on and off their reservations for fresh foods. For instance, in a series of cartoons titled *Being Indian Is . . .* drawn by the noted Reuben Snake, one cartoon represents a Native man wrapped in a blanket with lugging a crate labelled "USDA commodities surplus—since WW2" towards a non-Native farmer with flies buzzing around his unshaven face. Although the thought bubble hovering above the Indian's head makes it clear he really wants a jug of wine, the caption reads: "Being Indian is . . . Trading your surplus commodities to a local farmer (who uses them for hog feed) in exchange for fresh eggs, butter, milk, etc."[38]

In modern American Indian history, the tumultuous 1970s are perhaps best known for the armed confrontations between Red Power activists and federal troops that punctuated the ongoing colonial relationship between Native Americans and the United States. The occupations of Alcatraz Island, the Bureau of Indian Affairs headquarters in Washington, DC, and the Wounded Knee compound all demonstrated the tenacity of the new generation of Indian activists who envisioned themselves not only through pan-tribal identities but also as members of a global community of colonized indigenous peoples. By the middle of the 1970s, many of these activists also focused their efforts on improving reservation food security, an effort that inevitably led to deeper questions about food and Native sovereignty.

Resisting the USDA's plan to replace commodity distribution on reservations with food stamps was a galvanizing moment for American Indian food activism. The legislative victory in 1977 established tribally run food distribution programs alongside tribally administered food stamp programs. These programs remained imperfect. However, this activist effort was not only a political action to provide for the humanitarian needs of some of the nation's poorest communities through the mechanisms of the welfare state but also part of a broader reassertion of Native treaty rights; an effort to remind President Ford, for instance, of the fact that the nation's legal obligations to Indian communities persisted in spite of his platitudes. Controversies over food stamps and commodity distribution on Indian reservations in the 1970s were emblematic of the fact that Indian activists conceived of food security beyond the idioms of social welfare, framing it instead as an issue of treaty rights and Native sovereignty and laying the foundation for a future of American Indian activism oriented not around food security but around food sovereignty.

That afternoon in the White House state dining room, Ford ended his bicentennial address with what must have been envisioned by his speech writers as a friendly but vacant banality: "1976 is a year for all of us to realize what a great debt we owe to the American Indians."[39] Activists had their own understandings of the specifics of this great debt, however, as well as how it ought to be repaid.

EPILOGUE

Reinvention

In 2000, at the age of sixty-three, Dennis Banks—still field director of the American Indian Movement—came home to his birthplace in Federal Dam on the Leech Lake Reservation. After decades spent in Canada, California, New York, Kentucky, and other places evading federal prosecutors who wanted to put him in prison, Banks returned home not to retire but to expand his political activism into the domain of Native food sovereignty by tapping sugar maples and manufacturing maple syrup. Starting with 1,500 trees near his childhood home on Sugar Point, Banks updated centuries-old Anishinaabe sugaring techniques with twenty-first century equipment, sealing the final, cooked product into decorative glass syrup bottles to be sold to tourists and exported to natural foods markets in the Twin Cities and beyond.

Banks remarked that the syrup practically sold itself: "Joe Blow could probably sell it because people love it . . . because Dennis Banks is selling it, my name adds a little sales value." His friend Horst Rechelbacher, the founder of the Aveda beauty products company, echoed the observation: "[He's] a celebrity, an American hero." Banks also began marketing wild rice grown and harvested on Leech Lake and traveled to Japan to discuss the possibility of distributing his syrup and grains to a chain of eight hundred Japanese grocery stores. Spokespeople for the maple sugar industry predicted that, with a stand of more than thirty thousand prime sugar maples located on Leech Lake tribal lands, Banks's company, the Dennis Banks Wild Rice & Natural Organic Foods Co., would grow into the largest producer of maple syrup in the entire state of Minnesota. Members of the Leech Lake Tribal Council expressed their own hopeful support, praising the company for their efforts "to provide jobs for the young people" and for continuing "the Indian way of wild-rice harvesting and tapping maple trees."[1] Although these lofty predictions that the company would dominate the rice and sugaring industries while serving as a panacea for Leech Lake's struggles with underemployment never came true, Banks nevertheless ran a successful business until his death in 2017, marketing Anishinaabe food products to thousands of people across the world who recognized Banks's maple syrup as a distillation of decolonial activism.

In the absence of any indicating iconography or label copy, however, the Indigenous origins and histories of Native foods such as maple syrup often go unrecognized in their global travels as twenty-first century commodities. More than five hundred years of settler colonialism have worked to establish Native foods as non-Native possessions by conditioning views of the agricultural landscape in ways that foreground the productive capabilities of settler society and minimize the knowledge and expertise of Native peoples as a lost past. This process began almost immediately upon the arrival of English settlers to the Atlantic seaboard in the seventeenth century, as Pilgrims and other colonists occupied and refashioned the Indigenous farms and fields of southern New England. It continued into Iroquoia during and after the last years of the American Revolution, when Sullivan's Expedition waged war against Haudenosaunee agriculture to uproot and dispossess Haudenosaunee communities . Similar processes continued in the Cherokee Removal from northern Georgia in the early nineteenth century and in the debates over allotment and the forced privatization of Native landownership a century later. In all these instances, settler-colonial fictions of Native land tenure as wasteful and unproductive obscured the historical realities of Indigenous agriculture in order to justify dispossessions of Native land and labor.

Likewise, the settler-colonial myth that Native food traditions were dominated by hunting and gathering persists in a capitalist society that frames the outcomes of waged labor and private property as productive, in part, by identifying competing possibilities of work and livelihood as unproductive—as predatory, primitive, or otherwise beyond the pale of legitimate economic concern.[2] Thomas Jefferson's absurd observation, for instance, that all Indians lived "in the hunter state" and relied on the "spontaneous fruits of the earth" for their survival, reveals that by the eighteenth century these misrepresentations of Native food and livelihood already held hegemonic sway in an American political discourse premised on defining production as the sole province of property owners. From the nineteenth into the twentieth century, similar misrepresentations of Native people as wasteful hunters and predators were used by various American partisans of settler colonialism to justify Indian removal, the sales of surplus unallotted lands, and the kidnapping of Native children under mandatory Indian education laws on the premise that Indian ways of life were inefficient and wasteful.

These insinuations of an inherent Native wastefulness in the domains of food and agriculture also framed settler-colonial assumptions that Indians were always hungry and that, therefore, they had no opportunity to cultivate taste. Defining hunger as a timeless property of Native peoples enabled colonial policy makers not only to disavow Native malnutrition and mass starvation as the outcome of their policies but also to use this hunger to justify further colonial intervention. For instance, federal efforts to assimilate the Blackfeet by transforming them first from hunters into herders, and then from herders into farmers, were devised, at least in part, as solutions to address not only the starvation that accompanied forced confinement to the Blackfeet Reservation but also the hunger and disruption caused by off-reservation cattle leases, the consolidation of meat production into the reservation slaughterhouses, and policies such as land allotment that exacerbated the problems they meant to fix. By the middle of the twentieth century, these paradoxes had become embodied in a food security paradigm that assessed Indians as poor, nonproductive beneficiaries of the federal welfare state—a paradigm that early food-sovereignty activists confronted head-on in debates over food stamps and tribal self-determination in the 1970s.

Perhaps above all, the history of Native food and agriculture in America over the last five centuries is most characterized by adaptation and reinvention. Colonial disruptions to Native foodways and culinary practices made provisioning traditional ingredients difficult and sometimes impossible, forcing Native peoples to adapt their agricultural and culinary practices in order to survive. Fry bread, for instance, emerged as a pan-Indian dish across western reservations where commodity flour rations had to somehow be cooked and consumed without easy access to other ingredients. In some respects, what constitutes Native cuisine is no longer best defined by the use of particular ingredients or cooking techniques deemed traditional, or locked in the timeless past. Native cuisine represents a diverse set of sensibilities, tastes, ingredients, and approaches that are defined by survival and innovation.

The work of Native activists and allies over the last century has helped build a foundation for new generations of Indigenous chefs and entrepreneurs who have reinvented Native cuisine, taking tastes and techniques, new and old, to eaters around the United States and the rest of the globe. The noted Oglala Lakota chef Sean Sherman exemplifies many of these transformations. Born on the Pine Ridge Reservation in 1974, one year after the Wounded Knee occupation, Sherman recounts the persistence of traditional Lakota foodways in spite of the widespread poverty that kept his family and most of their neighbors dependent on federal commodity goods while growing up in the 1970s and 1980s. While most of their pantry was "lined with government-issued canned corn, canned carrots, canned peas, canned salmon, chipped beef, saltines, white flour, and bricks of bright orange commodity cheese," Sherman also recalls foraging for vegetables such as the roots of timpsula (*Psoralea esculenta*) with his extended family and preparing traditional Lakota dishes like *wojape*, a tart sauce made from chokecherries.[3] These foundational influences from Pine Ridge are present in Sherman's cuisine.

Rather than seeking to conform to a rigid set of rules and expectations about what counts as Native food, Sherman's dishes reveal Native food as a dynamic, creative, and forward-looking cuisine that is alive and evolving. His menus showcase Native ingredients and techniques whenever possible and incorporate them into items that are recognizable to a broad audience. The rice bowls served from his popular Tatanka Truck, for instance, feature a "Dakota MirePoix" comprised of squash, turnips, and wild onions served over wild rice and seasoned with maple syrup and sunflower oil.[4] His reinvention of the "Indian taco" (the old frybread-based staple) as the "Indigenous taco" substitutes corn cakes for frybread and bison for commodity hamburger; a vegan version offers beans braised with cedar branches and seasoned with ground juniper.[5] The brilliance of Sherman's dishes is not just in these fusions, however, but also in bringing to light what is, for many eaters, the surprising revelation that common American dishes already have Native tastes and techniques hidden in plain sight. Sherman's trick is to accentuate the Native ingredients and techniques already on the plate with others that are less familiar.

The significance of these lesser-known Native foods beyond their immediate communities remained somewhat hidden to Sherman for many years, and the very food knowledges that he learned from his parents and grandparents had been themselves transformed over a massive period of reconfigurations in Oglala Lakota life and livelihood. Raised by a veteran of the Battle of Little Bighorn, Sherman's great-grandfather had started a cattle ranch in the early twentieth century on Pine Ridge land that was seized by the US Department of War in 1918 to serve as a bombing range for Army Air Corps pilots training at nearby Ellsworth Airfield. Sherman grew up on the ranch where his family was forced to relocate and where his grandfather had grown up. They raised cattle and hunted and foraged to supplement their diet of commodity foods.[6] But even though Sherman and his family practiced many components of Lakota foodways from the previous century, these experiences were mostly routine; their historical lineage was not immediately clear to Sherman.

Likewise, as Sherman embarked on his culinary career, his training emphasized settler cuisines. He learned to cook during summer jobs in restaurant kitchens in the Black Hills and Rapid City after moving off the reservation with his mother while she finished her college degree. In the early 1990s Sherman ended up in Minneapolis and made his home on the southside, a vibrant community that was "crowded and diverse," where he "no longer stood out" for being an Indian. He worked at Broder's Pasta Bar and other celebrated Uptown restaurants, climbing the ranks and earning a position as an executive chef before the age of thirty, becoming a central force in the city's millennial reinvention as young and hip destination for foodies.

After taking a year-long vacation to Mexico, Sherman came home to the United States eager to explore the Native influences of American cuisine. He had been impressed with the restaurants and food culture of Nayarit, where "much of the indigenous foodways remained intact," unlike the United States, where the connection between popular dishes, ingredients, and their Native pasts seemed obscure at best. "I realized," Sherman recollected, "how grossly underrepresented Native American foods are in the United States. Mitsitam Cafe in the National Museum of the American Indian in Washington, DC, was the only Native restaurant I could find."[7] When Sherman returned to Minneapolis, he decided to change things up. He moved to Red Lodge, Montana, an upscale tourist town in the Beartooth Mountains, near Yellowstone National Park, where he worked for a while at a farm-to-table restaurant before returning to Minnesota and opening up his food truck and catering businesses under the name the Sioux Chef.

Native foods are infused with Native histories, of course, but they are also living manifestations of the Native present, and Sherman's style of cooking challenges settler society's implicit notion that Native American foodways disappeared as part of the colonial process. Native foods are not fixed in time or place. Native tastes and Native cuisines are ceaselessly created, recreated, and transformed. On the one hand, many Native American foods are familiar today to eaters around the world. On the other hand, as Sherman and so many other Native people have demonstrated in both the past and present, Native foods are not necessarily ancient, or even old; they can be novel, hip, and desirable for many reasons beyond their supposed function as touchstones of Native culture. Native foods are also widely eaten by people who may not even realize their Native origins, but identifying those origins helps showcase the presence, persistence, and fluidity of Native American communities and cultures in a settler society conditioned to consign Native people to a static past. Native foods offer an intriguing window for curious people to rethink their own relationships to food, culture, and the environment in the present. In fact, this reconsideration may be one of the fundamental missions that Sherman and others suggest with their millennial reinventions of Native cuisine.

As the expansion of colonial capitalism over the last two centuries drives our planet toward environmental exhaustion, all would do well to learn from the history of Native foods—not in order to romanticize a lost past but in order to appreciate the possibility for humanity's successful adaptation to a future marked with inexorable changes in the geographies of our resources, climates, and structures of power. The history of Native foods is full of stories large and small of individuals and their communities finding new ways to cope with radical transformations to their economies, ecologies, and societies.

One of the most significant historical contributions of Native communities to current efforts to grapple with the effect of climate change on global agriculture is the sheer diversity of the food crops Native American farmers have selected, cultivated, and saved for centuries. When it comes to selection and genetic adaptation, there is simply no substitute for time. While the great northern bean emerged as the favored Hidatsa white bean for industrial production when it was acquired by Oscar Wills more than a century ago, Native farmers continued to save seed from other bean plants—black, red, yellow, and, of course, the famous Hidatsa shield bean. The number of Native seeds maintained and preserved is astounding, and many are tough varieties selected and improved by Native farmers over generations to suit specific ecological niches. As climates change and agricultural footprints transform, the biodiverse pantry of Native crops will continue to function as a major storehouse of genetic traits used by agronomists in their efforts to adapt local agricultures to changes in weather and climate.

The violence, hunger, dispossessions, and denials that have accompanied more than five centuries of settler colonialism in America deserve acknowledgement. Yet, the frame for writing Native food history should not just be a chronicle of disaster and decline but also a narrative that identifies and analyzes ongoing struggles to negotiate specific food relationships that have centered Native lives, bodies, places, and identities across this time period. Such a project offers more than just a new set of historiographical quibbles. It promises a scholarly conversation that takes seriously how Native understandings of food, in its multitude of relations, have continually engaged modern transformations in agricultural land and labor, in industrial processing and production, and in distribution, retailing, marketing, cooking, and other realms of continental and global food systems. It also forces food studies scholars to take up the challenge of reconsidering some of the boundaries and interconnections of those very categories. For instance, what exactly counts as agriculture? Turning Indians into farmers was one of the stated goals of nearly two hundred years of federal assimilation policies in the United States. But all throughout the heterogeneous communities of Indian country, Native people responded by reworking their own understandings of agriculture to fit within the new colonial parameters, creating alternatives to the emerging industrial food system that were hidden in plain sight. Even radical colonial programs like allotment and the forced privatization of Native American landownership were reengineered by Native communities to suit their own agricultural needs and desires in ways that far exceeded the expectations of Indian office personnel. It isn't just the wapiti and the wapato eaten by Native people of the past that deserves our attention, but also the food histories of Native people who lived, died, thrived, and struggled along with other American communities in a modern, and not prehistorical, world.

On a recent trip from Texas to Washington, DC, I stayed at a bed and breakfast run by a health food and fitness buff. When he learned that I was a historian who studied food and agricultural history, he asked in me, in all earnestness, if I could give him any tips about secret "Native superfoods" that scholars like me had recovered from the dustbin of history. Not only did his question indicate a misconception of the work I had just tried to explain to him (hey, he asked!), but it also rankled my early morning acerbity. So—I responded, straight-faced, with "pizza," dropping this seeming non sequitur in part because I was curious to witness his reaction and in part because I had wanted to deliver the joke for a long time, having heard it in a very different context from a friend who is a professional bike racer and always provided it as a one-word description of his nutritional regimen when fans asked him about which superfoods they should be eating to get in shape. ("Pizza *is* a super food," he would insist. "It's *super* delicious.") This quip had always appealed to my critical sensibilities as a food studies scholar. Nevertheless, when I saw my host's reaction, I felt guilty about my intrusion into his foodie dreamworld. With the so-called food revolution in full swing, it seems like there will be popular demand for "Native superfoods" for quite some time, along with plenty of products to round out the supply. The task for food historians, however, is to bring Native food histories out of the timeless past, out of the settler-colonial myths, and to give them the critical, historical attention they deserve.

NOTES

Introduction

1. This work was originally published as Gilbert L. Wilson, "Agriculture of the Hidatsa Indians: An Indian Interpretation," in *Studies in the Social Sciences*, no. 9 (Minneapolis: University of Minnesota, 1917). It was a revised version of Wilson's dissertation and was reprinted, seventy years later—with a critical introduction by Jeffrey R. Hanson—as Gilbert L. Wilson, *Buffalo Bird Woman's Garden: The Classic Account of Hidatsa American Indian Gardening Techniques* (St. Paul: Minnesota Historical Society Press, 1987). More recently, the work has also been reprinted as Gilbert L. Wilson and Waheenee, *Native American Gardening: Buffalobird-Woman's Guide to Traditional Methods* (Mineola, NY: Dover Publications, 2005). There are likely other published editions, and digitized versions of the original are widely available online.

   Maxidiwiac (ma-hidi-we-ash) was born with the Hidatsa name Waheenee. She took the name Maxidiwiac—which translates into English as Buffalo Bird Woman—when she was still a girl, sometime after her mother died of smallpox in 1845. See Gilbert L. Wilson, *Waheenee: An Indian Girl's Story* (Lincoln: University of Nebraska Press, 1981).

   Although Wilson has often been attributed as the sole author of these works of Hidatsa ethnography, it is important to note that Maxidiwiac provided the entire narrative that Wilson transcribed, both in *Waheenee* and in *Buffalo Bird Woman*, as well as in many of Wilson's other publications. Edward Goodbird, Maxidiwiac's son, also served as Wilson's interpreter, and provided translations of his mother's descriptions from the Hidatsa language into English. Wilson admitted this indebtedness in his own characterization of his ethnographic methods, explaining that he "sought to preserve all narratives as the informants gave them, merely arranging materials and putting Goodbird's Indian-English into proper idiom. Bits of philosophy, personal and humorous observations are as they fell from the informants' lips. The writer has sincerely endeavored to add nothing of his own." See Wilson, "The Horse and the Dog in Hidatsa Culture," in Anthropological Papers of the American Museum of Natural History, vol. 15, ed. Clark Wissler (New York: American Museum Press, 1924), 125–312, 132.

   In fact, Wilson's emphasis on publishing the verbatim descriptions provided to him by Maxidiwiac (as interpreted by Goodbird) even struck his contemporaries as an odd application of ethnography. Claude Lévi-Strauss, for instance, remarked on the unfiltered nature of Wilson's work as a starting point for thinking through the problematic structures of anthropological observation. After Wilson's death, Robert Lowie—with a hint of condescension—remembered that Wilson was "neither cultivated nor in any sense an intellectual, but he was a superb observer." For a discussion of Lévi-Strauss's remarks, see Carolyn Gilman and Mary Jane Schneider, *The Way to Independence: Memories of a Hidatsa Indian Family, 1840–1920* (St. Paul: Minnesota

Historical Society Press, 1987), 347. For Lowie's description, see Robert H. Lowie, *Robert H. Lowie, Ethnologist: A Personal Record* (Berkeley: University of California Press, 1959), 104.

2. Son of Star providing these beans to Oscar Will is a story that is widely shared in the seed catalogs and other literature of the heirloom vegetable gardening community, which has long revered Will for the colorful catalogs and seed collections that his company maintained during the early twentieth century. The anthropologist Fred Schneider read these seed catalogs alongside Will's unpublished records at the North Dakota Historical Society research center in Bismarck, which seem to confirm the story's accuracy. See Fred Schneider, " 'Corn in the Crib is Like Money in the Bank': George F. Will and the Oscar H. Will and Company, 1917–1955," *North Dakota History* 76, nos. 1–2 (2010): 2–25; and Schneider, "Oscar H. Will: North Dakota's Pioneer Seedman," *North Dakota History* 68, no. 1 (2001): 2–19.
3. For a classic study of the Pick-Sloan saga, see Michael L. Lawson, *Dammed Indians: The Pick-Sloan Plan and the Missouri River Sioux, 1944–1980* (Norman: University of Oklahoma Press, 1982), as well as Lawson, *Dammed Indians Revisited: The Continuing History of the Pick-Sloan Plan and the Missouri River Sioux* (Pierre: South Dakota State Historical Society, 2009). For an institutional history of the Pick-Sloan plan in the context of broader American federal flood control, see Marc Reisner, *Cadillac Desert: The American West and Its Disappearing Water* (New York: Penguin, 1986). Another informative source on the specific economic and environmental outcomes of the Pick-Sloan dams is David C. Campbell, "The Pick-Sloan Program: A Case of Bureaucratic Economic Power," *Journal of Economic Issues* 18, no. 2 (1984): 449–56.
4. See Vine Deloria Jr., "Foreword," in Lawson, *Dammed Indians*, xi–xvii, xiv. Gerald Vizenor once described Lake Sakakawea as a "flood of white men and their pleasure boats." See Gerald Vizenor, "Firewater Labels and Methodologies," *American Indian Quarterly* 7, no. 4 (1983): 25–36, 26. More recently, scholars in Indigenous studies have reconsidered the cultural legacy of the lake in terms of its potential as "culturally viable property." See Wendi Field Murray, María Nieves Zedeño, Kacy L. Hollenback, Calvin Grinnell, and Elgin Crows Breast, "The Remaking of Lake Sakakawea: Locating Cultural Viability in Negative Heritage on the Missouri River," *American Ethnologist* 38, no. 3 (2011): 468–83.
5. Conceptualizing rivers as systems of energy flows has been a prominent approach among environmental historians for the last several decades. One of the classic statements in relation to energy and settler colonialism is Richard White, *The Organic Machine: The Remaking of the Columbia River* (New York: Hill & Wang, 1996).
6. I originally purchased these I'itoi onions from Native Seeds/SEARCH, a non-profit seed conservation organization in Tucson, Arizona, that was founded in 1983 to save and distribute free seeds to Native farmers and communities across the Southwest.
7. David Treuer, *The Heartbeat of Wounded Knee: Native America from 1890 to the Present* (New York: Penguin, 2019), 11.

8. For a provocative discussion of these legal structures and their codification into everyday settler-colonial culture, see Aileen Moreton-Robinson, *The White Possessive: Property, Power, and Indigenous Sovereignty* (Minneapolis: University of Minnesota Press, 2015). For a discussion of how expectations of "able-bodiedness" structure the political economy of colonialism, see Dan Goodley, "Dis/entangling Critical Disability Studies," *Disability & Society* 28, no. 5 (2013): 631–44.
9. Cheryl I. Harris, "Whiteness as Property," *Harvard Law Review* 106, no. 8 (1993): 1707–91, 1721.
10. Williams first coined this phrase in Raymond Williams and Michael Orrom, *Preface to Film* (London: Film Drama Limited, 1954). For an overview of how "structures of feeling" evolved over Williams's career, see John Higgins, *Raymond Williams: Literature, Marxism and Cultural Materialism* (New York: Taylor & Francis, 2013), 37–45.
11. My approach has been influenced by the work of anthropologists who have critiqued scholarly historical narration as a central aspect of colonial projects of representation, in particular, Keith Basso, *Wisdom Sits in Places: Landscape and Language Among the Western Apache* (Albuquerque: University of New Mexico Press, 1996); Dipesh Chakrabarty, *Provincializing Europe: Postcolonial Thought and Historical Difference* (Princeton: Princeton University Press, 2000); Timothy Ingold, *The Perception of the Environment: Essays in Livelihood, Dwelling, and Skill* (New York: Routledge, 2000); and Eric R. Wolf, *Europe and the People Without History* (Berkeley: University of California Press, 1982).
12. Jean M. O'Brien, *Dispossession by Degrees: Indian Land and Identity in Natick, Massachusetts, 1650–1790* (Cambridge: University of Cambridge Press, 1997), 9.
13. For a sophisticated explanation of the differences between food security and food sovereignty, as well as how these approaches to Native foods relate to historic settler-colonial policies, see Devon A. Mihesuah and Elizabeth Hoover, eds., *Indigenous Food Sovereignty in the United States: Restoring Cultural Knowledge, Protecting Environments, and Regaining Health* (Norman: University of Oklahoma Press, 2019), 7–12.
14. See for instance Taiaiake Alfred, "Sovereignty," in *A Companion to American Indian History*, eds. Philip Deloria and Neil Salisbury (Malden, MA: Blackwell, 2002), 460–74; Joanne Barker, ed., *Sovereignty Matters* (Lincoln: University of Nebraska Press, 2005); Kevin Bruyneel, *The Third Space of Sovereignty: The Postcolonial Politics of U.S.-Indigenous Relations* (Minneapolis: University of Minnesota Press, 2007); Jessica Cattelino, "The Double Bind of American Indian Need-Based Sovereignty," *Cultural Anthropology* 25, no. 2 (2010): 235–62; and Heidi Kiiwetinepinesiik Stark, "Nenabhozo's Smart Berries: Rethinking Tribal Sovereignty and Accountability," *Michigan State Law Review* 339 (2013): 339–53.
15. Kyle Powys White, for instance, has argued convincingly that destroying Native capacities for production and then disavowing them has been a core effort of food colonialism. See Kyle Powys White, "Food Sovereignty, Justice, and Indigenous Peoples: An Essay on Settler Colonialism and Collective

Continuance," in Anne Barnhill, Tyler Doggett, and Mark Budolfson, eds., *Oxford Handbook of Food Ethics* (Oxford: Oxford University Press, 2018), 345–66.

16. For a critical study of the Morrill Act and the political economy of agricultural and settler colonialism, see Margaret A. Nash, "Entangled Pasts: Land-Grant Colleges and American Indian Dispossession," *History of Education Quarterly* 59, no. 4 (2019): 437–67. For the text of the Morrill Act, see "Act of July 2, 1862 (Morrill Act), Public Law 37–108, which established land grant colleges," Enrolled Acts and Resolutions of Congress, 1789–1996, Record Group 11, General Records of the United States Government, National Archives.
17. Michel Foucault, *The History of Sexuality, Volume 1: An Introduction*, trans. Robert Hurley (New York: Pantheon Books, 1978), 138.
18. Portions of this research at the Newberry were originally published in Michael D. Wise, "Colonial Beef and the Blackfeet Reservation Slaughterhouse, 1879–1895," *Radical History Review* 110 (2011): 59–82.
19. The work of historians and geographers who have interrogated the farm as a landscape that values labor differently on the basis of race and gender has greatly influenced my approach. See Don Mitchell, *The Lie of the Land: Migrant Workers and the California Landscape* (Minneapolis: University of Minnesota Press, 1996); and Laurel Thatcher Ulrich, *Good Wives: Image and Reality in the Lives of Women in Northern New England, 1650–1750* (New York: Alfred A. Knopf, 1982).
20. See, for instance, the classic discussions of Cherokee women's political roles in relation to their agricultural duties in Theda Perdue, *Cherokee Women: Gender and Culture Change, 1700–1835* (Lincoln: University of Nebraska Press, 1998). For a recent, critical appraisal of the patriarchal expectations that have framed settler-colonial legal agendas, see Sylvia McAdam Saysewahum, *Nationhood Interrupted: Revitalizing nêhiyaw Legal Systems* (Vancouver: University of British Columbia Press, 2015).
21. The historian Coll Thrush, for instance, has used the phrase "unseen gardens" to remark on the Native agricultural sites of Northwest Coast during the period of colonial encounter in the late eighteenth and early nineteenth centuries. See Coll Thrush, "Vancouver the Cannibal: Cuisine, Encounter, and the Dilemma of Difference on the Northwest Coast, 1774–1808," *Ethnohistory* 58, no. 1 (2011): 1–35, 4.
22. For a discussion of this process in the late nineteenth and early twentieth centuries, see Frieda Knoblauch, *The Culture of Wilderness: Agriculture as Colonization in the American West* (Chapel Hill: University of North Carolina Press, 1996).
23. A good introduction to these Native agricultural techniques is Enrique Salmón, *Eating the Landscape: American Indian Stories of Food, Identity, and Resilience* (Tucson: University of Arizona Press, 2012).
24. The "spontaneous fruits" quotation comes from Thomas Jefferson, *Notes on the State of Virginia* (Boston: Lilly and Wait, 1832 [1787]), 214. For a crucial critique of the colonial differentiation between wild and cultivated plants, see M. Kat Anderson, *Tending the Wild: Native American Knowledge and the Management of California's Natural Resources* (Berkeley: University of California Press), 241.

25. Quoted in William Least Heat-Moon and James K. Wallace, eds. and trans., *An Osage Journey to Europe, 1827–1830: Three French Accounts* (Norman: University of Oklahoma Press, 2013), 50.
26. See Philip J. Deloria, *Indians in Unexpected Places* (Lawrence: University Press of Kansas, 2004).
27. See, for instance, Virginia DeJohn Anderson, *Creatures of Empire: How Domestic Animals Transformed Early America* (Oxford: Oxford University Press, 2006); William Cronon, *Changes in the Land: Indians, Colonists, and the Ecology of New England* (New York: Hill & Wang, 1983); and Andrea L. Smalley, *Wild By Nature: North American Animals Confront Colonization* (Baltimore: Johns Hopkins University Press, 2017). Also see Michael D. Wise, "Meat," in *The Routledge History of American Foodways*, eds. Michael D. Wise and Jennifer Jensen Wallach (New York: Routledge, 2016), 97–112.
28. See, for instance, J. F. Organ, V. Geist, et al., "The North American Model of Wildlife Conservation," *Wildlife Society Technical Review 12-04* (Bethesda, MD: Wildlife Society, 2012).
29. This generalization requires more precise distinctions, of course. For Blackfeet examples, see discussions in chapter 4. For a broader discussion of hunting and reciprocity that considers Indigenous approaches to animals in the context of the circumpolar north, see Rane Willerslev, *Soul Hunters: Hunting, Animism, and Personhood Among the Siberian Yukaghirs* (Berkeley: University of California Press, 2007).
30. See, for instance, Erik R. Seeman, *The Huron-Wendat Feast of the Dead: Indian-European Encounters in Early North America* (Baltimore: Johns Hopkins University Press, 2011).
31. See Douglas Hay, "Poaching and the Game Laws on Cannock Chase," in *Albion's Fatal Tree: Crime and Society in Eighteenth-Century England*, ed. Douglas Hay et al. (New York: Pantheon, 1975); and E. P. Thompson, *Whigs and Hunters: The Origin of the Black Act* (New York: Pantheon, 1975).
32. See Karl Jacoby, *Crimes Against Nature: Squatters, Poachers, Thieves, and the Hidden History of American Conservation* (Berkeley: University of California Press, 2001); Mark David Spence, *Dispossessing the Wilderness: Indian Removal and the Making of the National Parks* (Oxford: Oxford University Press, 1999); and Louis Warren, *The Hunter's Game: Poachers and Conservationists in Twentieth-Century America* (New Haven: Yale University Press, 1999).
33. For a recent consideration of the role of gender and leisure in nineteenth-century American hunting, see Karen R. Jones, *Epiphany in the Wilderness: Hunting, Nature, and Performance in the Nineteenth-Century American West* (Boulder: University Press of Colorado, 2016).
34. This quotation is from Barbara Graymont, *The Iroquois in the American Revolution* (Syracuse: Syracuse University Press, 1972), 213. For a more recent scholarly interpretation of hunger and power in era of the American Revolution, see Rachel B. Herrmann, *No Useless Mouth: Waging War and Fighting Hunger in the American Revolution* (Ithaca: Cornell University Press, 2019).
35. See United States, Office of Indian Affairs, *Annual Report of the Commissioner of Indian Affairs, for the year 1891* (Washington, DC: Government Printing Office, 1891), 17.

36. For a discussion of Indian agents see Cathleen D. Cahill, *Federal Fathers and Mothers: A Social History of the United States Indian Service, 1869–1933* (Chapel Hill: University of North Carolina Press, 2011).
37. See, for example, Mike Davis, *Late Victorian Holocausts: El Niño Famines and the Making of the Third World* (London: Verso, 2001); and Paul E. Minnis, *Famine Foods: Plants We Eat to Survive* (Tucson: University of Arizona Press, 2021).
38. Arthur C. Parker, *Iroquois Uses of Maize and Other Food Plants* (Albany: University of the State of New York, 1910), 64.
39. For a scholarly introduction to the literature on twentieth- and early twenty-first-century Native American dietary and nutritional concerns, including popular applications of the "thrifty gene" and western pattern diet hypotheses as explanations for Native malnutrition, see Michael Milburn, "Indigenous Nutrition: Using Traditional Food Knowledge to Solve Contemporary Health Problems," *American Indian Quarterly* 26, nos. 3–4 (2004): 411–34. Also see Devon A. Mihesuah, "Decolonizing our Diets by Recovering our Ancestors' Gardens," *American Indian Quarterly* 27, nos. 3–4 (2003): 807–39; and Mihesuah, *Recovering our Ancestors' Gardens: Indigenous Recipes and Guide to Diet and Fitness*, 2nd ed. (Lincoln: University of Nebraska Press, 2020 [2005]).

    For a sophisticated consideration of these processes at work in colonial New Spain, see Rebecca Earle, *The Body of the Conquistador: Food, Race and the Colonial Experience in Spanish America, 1492–1700* (Cambridge: Cambridge University Press, 2012).
40. John Gerarde, *The Herball or Generall Historie of Plantes* (London: John Norton, 1597), 76–77.
41. See Raymond Darwin Burroughs, *The Natural History of the Lewis and Clark Expedition* (East Lansing: Michigan State University Press, 1995 [1961]), 282–83. For the Lewis quotation, see Meriwether Lewis, April 13, 1806, *The Journals of the Lewis and Clark Expedition*, ed. Gary Moulton, accessed June 29, 2021, https://lewisandclarkjournals.unl.edu//item/lc.jrn.1806-04-13.

Chapter 1

1. See William Bradford, *Of Plimoth Plantation* (Boston: Wright and Potter Printing, 1898), 127; and Edward Winslow and William Bradford, *Mourt's Relation or Journal of the Plantation at Plymouth*, ed. Henry Martin Dexter (Boston: John Kimball Wiggin, 1865), 133.
2. For a discussion of these English and Wampanoag accounts, see David J. Silverman, *This Land is Their Land: The Wampanoag Indians, Plymouth Colony, and the Troubled History of Thanksgiving* (New York: Bloomsbury, 2019), 167–73. See also "Wampanoag on Thanksgiving," Many Hoops, accessed July 12, 2021, http://manyhoops.com/wampanoag-on-thanksgiving.html.
3. For a detailed description and up-to-date history of the myth of the First Thanksgiving's public life in the United States over the last two centuries, see James W. Baker, *Thanksgiving: The Biography of an American Holiday* (Lebanon: University of New Hampshire Press, 2009).
4. In the twentieth century, perhaps the most significant of these critics was Wamsutta Frank James, a Wampanoag activist who established the National

Day of Mourning on the 350th anniversary of the First Thanksgiving. For a transcription of James's famous Thanksgiving Day speech at Plymouth Rock, see Frank James, "National Day of Mourning," in Siobhan Senier, ed., *Dawnland Voices: An Anthology of Indigenous Writing from New England* (Lincoln: University of Nebraska Press, 2014), 455–58. For a recent scholarly account of James's life and legacy, as well as a synthesis of the many voices who have critiqued Thanksgiving as a ritual of settler colonialism and white possession, see Silverman, *This Land is Their Land.* Other critiques of the Thanksgiving also holiday abound. For a classic, critical perspective on the holiday from a cultural anthropologist, see Janet Siskind, "The Invention of Thanksgiving: A Ritual of American Nationality," *Critique of Anthropology* 12, no. 2 (1992): 167–91.

5. See Ronald Reagan, "Proclamation 5577: American Indian Week, November 24, 1986," in *Public Papers of the Presidents of the United States: Ronald Reagan, 1986* (Washington, DC: Government Printing Office), 1586; and US Congress, Senate, *To Authorize and Request the President to Proclaim the Week of November 23, 1986, to November 30, 1986, as "American Indian Week,"* Senate Joint Resolution 390, 99th Congress, October 14, 1986.
6. The disciplinary historical literature on the agricultural and dietary practices of precolonial Native New England is broad. For an introduction, see Virginia DeJohn Anderson, *Creatures of Empire: How Domestic Animals Transformed Early America* (Oxford: Oxford University Press, 2004); M. K. Bennett, "The Food Economy of the New England Indians, 1605–75," *Journal of Political Economy* 63, no. 5 (1955): 369–97; and William Cronon, *Changes in the Land: Indians, Colonists and the Ecology of New England* (New York: Hill & Wang, 1983).
7. See Mark Fiege, "Satan in the Land: Nature, the Supernatural, and Disorder in Colonial New England," in *The Republic of Nature* (Seattle: University of Washington Press, 2012), 23–56.
8. On the one hand, it is anachronistic to use phrases like *agroforesty* to describe Native practices of transforming and managing woodlands into perennial sites for food production. Also, from a historical point of view, it is also necessary to note that when such terms have been used in the past it was often to mark Native agricultural practices as "primitive," and therefore comprehensible to the settler-colonial state charged with dispossessing Native landownership. On the other hand, though, some Native communities in the twenty-first century have embraced phrases like *agroforesty* as appropriate shorthand for describing the value of traditional practices, with the intention of charting out a future oriented toward food sovereignty and greater ecological sustainability. For example, the Tuscarora Food Forest, a collaboration between the Tuscarora Nation and the agroforestry program at Cornell University, is a project aimed toward restoring the historical forest of nut trees that help sustained Tuscarora communities in past centuries. See Sam Bosco and Brad Thomas, "The Skàru:rę Food Forest," *Forage!* (Society of Ethnobiology), July 30, 2019, accessed November 19, 2021, https://ethnobiology.org/forage/blog/skarur-food-forest.

   Context is paramount in determining appropriateness, and I have selected to use *agroforesty* here because I think it helps a broad audience appreciate the enormous generational investment of Native expertise in creating and managing American forests. Evidence of this expertise abounds in the forests of North America, but it often goes unseen, and teaching the public how to recognize the legacy of Native forest modifications is an important task in unsettling colonial expectations. One good example of this work in practice is the joint effort of the Comanche Nation and the Texas Historic Trees Coalition to locate and recognize Comanche marker trees throughout the state, which were often grown to indicate low water crossings and other significant sites throughout the bottomland forests of the southern plains and prairies. See Steve Houser, Linda Pelon, and Jimmy W. Arterberry, *Comanche Marker Trees of Texas* (College Station: Texas A&M University Press, 2016).

9. See Richard H. Grove, *Green Imperialism: Colonial Expansion, Tropical Island Edens and the Origins of Environmentalism, 1600–1860* (Cambridge: Cambridge University Press, 2010).
10. See Charles V. Cogbill, John Burk and G. Motzkin, "The Forests of Presettlement New England, USA: Spatial and Compositional Patterns Based on Town Proprietor Surveys," *Journal of Biogeography* 29, no. 10/11 (2002): 1279–1304.
11. Marc D. Abrams and Gregory J. Nowacki, "Native Americans as Active and Passive Promoters of Mast and Fruit Trees in the Eastern USA," *The Holocene* 18, no. 7 (2008): 1123–37.
12. Thomas Bonnicksen, *Ancient Forests: From the Ice Age to the Age of Discovery* (New York: Wiley, 2000), 15.
13. See Fiege, "Satan in the Land."
14. See Cronon, *Changes in the Land*; and Anderson, *Creatures of Empire*.
15. See Kelly Wisecup, ed., *"Good News from New England," by Edward Winslow: A Scholarly Edition* (Amherst: University of Massachusetts Press, 2014).
16. See Rebecca Earle, *The Body of the Conquistador: Food, Race and the Colonial Experience in Spanish America, 1492–1700* (Cambridge: Cambridge University Press).
17. John Gerarde, *The Herball or Generall Historie of Plantes* (London: John Norton, 1597), 77.
18. See Ian Miller, "Feeding in the Workhouse: The Institutional and Ideological Functions of Food in Britain," *Journal of British Studies* 52, no. 4 (2013): 940–62.
19. For critical discussions of the archaeological evidence bearing on the geographic distribution of corn cultivation in New England, see David Demeritt, "Agriculture, Climate, and Cultural Adaptation in the Prehistoric Northeast," *Archaeology of Eastern North America* 19 (1991): 183–202; and Elizabeth S. Chilton " 'Towns They Have None': Diverse Subsistence and Settlement Strategies in Native New England," in *Northeast Subsistence-Settlement Change: A.D. 700–1300*, New York State Museum Bulletin 496, eds. John P. Hart and Christina B. Rieth (Albany: University of the State of New York, 2002), 289–300.
20. See Peter A. Thomas, "Contrastive Subsistence Strategies and Land Use as Factors for Understanding Indian-White Relations in New England," *Ethnohistory* 23, no. 1 (1976): 1–18, 8–9.
21. On moose tongues as a delicacy and trade good, see John Josselyn, *An Account of Two Voyages to England* (London: Printed for Giles Widdows,

1673), 129; and Thomas Wickman, " 'Winters Embittered with Hardships': Severe Cold, Wabanaki Power, and English Adjustments, 1690–1710," *William and Mary Quarterly* 72, no. 1 (2015): 57–98, 70–71. For a general discussion of this early maritime trade with European fisherman, see Peter A. Pope, *Fish into Wine: The Newfoundland Plantation in the Seventeenth Century* (Chapel Hill: University of North Carolina Press, 2004). And, for a discussion of the role of food as a medium of exchange, see Michael LaCombe, *Political Gastronomy: Food and Authority in the English Atlantic World* (Philadelphia: University of Pennsylvania Press, 2012), 172.

22. Roger Williams, *A Key into the Language of America* (Boston: Applewood Books, 1997 [1643]), 95, 97.
23. See Josselyn, *Account of Two Voyages*, 54.
24. One of the earliest colonial descriptions of succotash, or *Manusquessêdash*, comes from Williams, *A Key into the Language of America*, 10–12.
25. For a discussion of *nocake*, see "Creative Farmers of the Northeast: A New View of Indian Maize Horticulture," *North American Archaeologist* 15, no. 3 (1994): 235–52, 243.
26. See T. H. Hoskins and Paul Sesup, "An Indian on Indian Corn," *Garden and Forest* no. 8 (1895): 23.
27. This was certainly the case in southwestern North America, where O'odham farmers still cultivate a specific variety called sixty-day corn. See Gary Paul Nabhan, *Enduring Seeds: Native American Agriculture and Wild Plant Cultivation* (Tucson: University of Arizona Press, 2016), 52–53; and Amadeo M. Rea, *At the Desert's Green Edge: An Ethnobotany of the Gila River Pima* (Tucson: University of Arizona Press, 2016), 348.
28. Samuel de Champlain, *Voyages of Samuel de Champlain, 1604–1618*, trans. William Lawson Grant (New York: Scribner's, 1907), 71.
29. See Dimmick, "Creative Farmers of the Northeast," 242.
30. William Bradford and Edward Winslow, *Mourt's Relation or Journal of the Plantation at Plymouth*, ed. Henry Martyn Dexter (Boston: J. K. Wiggin, 1865 [1622]), 21.
31. For general descriptions of wooden bowls and other utensils and cookware, see Linda Murray Berzok, *American Indian* Food (Westport, CT: Greenwood Press, 2005), 99. Wood from maple trees was commonly utilized for this purpose throughout North America. For instance, early French ethnography mentioned the use of maple bowls as far west as the Osage country. See William Least-Heat Moon and James K. Wallace, eds. and trans., *An Osage Journey to Europe, 1827–1830: Three French Accounts* (Norman: University of Oklahoma Press, 2013), 43. For discussions of pottage and its English and Native American roots, see Trudy Eden, *The Early American Table: Food and Society in the New World* (Dekalb: Northern Illinois University Press, 2008); Laurel Thatcher Ulrich, *Goodwives: Image and Reality in the Lives of Women in Northern New England, 1650–1750* (New York: Vintage Books, 1982), 20; and Jennifer Jensen Wallach, *How America Eats: A Social History of U.S. Food and Culture* (Washington, DC: Rowman & Littlefield), 14.
32. Anderson, *Creatures of Empire*, 213.
33. Bennett, "Food Economy of the New England Indians," 394.

34. For a description of these practices, see Neal Salisbury, *Manitou and Providence: Indians, Europeans, and the Making of New England, 1500–1643* (New York: Oxford University Press, 1984), 31.
35. Daniel Gookin, *Historical Collections of the Indians of New England* (Boston: Apollo Press, 1792 [1674]), 190–91.
36. This is a figure that the historian and demographer Merrill K. Bennett estimated in 1955, in Bennett, "Food Economy of the New England Indians," 377.
37. For a detailed discussion of the Pilgrims' arrival to Cape Cod, see Nathaniel Philbrick, *Mayflower: A Story of Courage, Community, and War* (New York: Viking, 2006), 80.
38. See Thomas, "Understanding Indian-White Relations," 5.
39. See Henry M. Burt, *The First Century of the History of Springfield*, vol. 1 (Springfield, MA: Henry M. Burt, 1898), 156–60.
40. See Michael L. Fickes, " 'They Could Not Endure That Yoke': The Captivity of Pequot Women and Children after the War of 1637," *New England Quarterly* 73, no. 1 (March 2000): 58–81.
41. For detailed discussions of the historical memory of these atrocities and of Native survivance in New England, see Jean M. O'Brien, *First and Lasting: Writing Indians Out of Existence in New England* (Minneapolis: University of Minnesota Press, 2010); and Christine M. DeLucia, *Memory Lands: King Philip's War and the Place of Violence in the Northeast* (New Haven: Yale University Press, 2018). See also the essays in Colin G. Calloway, ed., *After King Philip's War: Presence and Persistence in Indian New England* (Hanover, NH: University Press of New England, 1997).
42. See LaCombe, *Political Gastronomy*, 152.
43. See LaCombe, *Political Gastronomy*, 167.
44. For a discussion of Uncas and Miantonomi, see LaCombe, *Political Gastronomy*, 144–45.
45. See Paul Pasquaretta, *Gambling and Survival in Native North America* (Tucson: University of Arizona Press, 2003), 34.
46. Two good starting points for considering the linkages between colonial views of the New England landscape and the colonial sexualization of women are Carolyn Merchant, *Ecological Revolutions: Nature, Gender, and Science in New England* (Chapel Hill: University of North Carolina Press, 1989); and Joyce Chaplin, *Subject Matter: Technology, the Body, and Science on the Anglo-American Frontier, 1500–1676* (Cambridge, MA: Harvard University Press, 2001).
47. William Morrell, "Morrell's Poem on New-England," in *Collections of the Massachusetts Historical Society*, 1st ser., vol. 1 (Boston: 1792), 135.
48. William Wood, *Wood's New-England's Prospect* (Boston: John Wilson and Son, 1865), 105.
49. James M. Volo and Dorothy Denneen Voto, *Family Life in 17th and 18th Century America* (Westport, CT: Greenwood Publishing, 2006), 40.
50. These statistics and their estimations are detailed in Daniel Scott Smith, "The Demographic History of Colonial New England," *Journal of Economic History* 32, no. 1 (1972): 165–83.
51. Ulrich, *Good Wives*, 20.

52. Sandra Oliver, *Food in Colonial and Federal America* (Westport, CT: Greenwood Publishing, 2005), 6.
53. Wood, *New-England's Prospect*, 35.
54. See Julian B. Fischer, Laura H. McArthur, and James B. Petersen, "Continuity and Change in the Food Habits of the Seventeenth-Century English Colonists in Plymouth and Massachusetts Bay," *Ecology of Food and Nutrition* 36, no. 1 (1997): 65–93, 79.
55. Anderson, *Creatures of Empire*, 65.
56. See Anderson, *Creatures of Empire*, 241.
57. See Samuel Deane, *The New England Farmer*, 2nd ed. (Worcester, MA: Isaiah Thomas, 1797), 73.
58. See discussion and estimates in Elinor F. Oakes, "A Ticklish Business: Dairying in New England and Pennsylvania, 1750–1812," *Pennsylvania History: A Journal of Mid-Atlantic Studies* 47, no. 3 (1980): 195–212, 208.
59. James E. McWilliams, " 'Butter, Milk, and a Spare Rib': Women's Work and the Transatlantic Economic Transition in Seventeenth-Century Massachusetts," *New England Quarterly* 82, no. 1 (2009): 1–20, 17.
60. See Oakes, "A Ticklish Business," 199; and Edwin Morris Betts, *Thomas Jefferson's Farm Book* (Princeton: Princeton University Press, 1953).
61. Oliver, *Food in Colonial and Federal America*, 115.
62. James E. McWilliams, *A Revolution in Eating: How the Quest for Food Shaped America* (New York: Columbia University Press, 2005), 89.
63. This phrase, of course, comes from the work of environmental historian Alfred Crosby. See Alfred Crosby, *Ecological Imperialism: The Biological Expansion of Europe, 900–1900*, 2nd ed. (Cambridge: Cambridge University Press, 2004 [1989]).
64. J. Hammond Trumbull, ed., *The Public Records of the Colony of Connecticut*, vol. 2 (Hartford: F. A. Brown, 1850), 381.
65. Anderson, *Creatures of Empire*, 237.
66. See George Madison Bodge, *Soldiers in King Philip's War* (Boston: George Madison Bodge, 1891), 198.
67. See Massachusetts Council, "At a Council, Held at Charlestown, June the 20th, 1676" (Cambridge, MA: Samuel Green, 1676).
68. See Francis Jennings, *The Invasion of America: Indians, Colonialism, and the Cant of Conquest* (Chapel Hill: University of North Carolina Press, 2010 [1975]).
69. See Jenny Hale Pulsipher, *Subjects Unto the Same King: Indians, English, and the Contest for Authority in Colonial New England* (Philadelphia: University of Pennsylvania Press, 2005), 202.
70. See William DeLoss Love, *The Fast and Thanksgiving Days of New England* (Cambridge, MA: Riverside Press, 1895), 200.

Chapter 2

1. See Milton W. Hamilton, "Sir William Johnson: Interpreter of the Iroquois," *Ethnohistory* 10, no. 3 (1963): 270–86
2. Heather Hutton, "Narrating Sovereignty: The Covenant Chain in Intercultural Diplomacy," *Journal of Early American History* 9 (2019): 118–44, 141.

3. William J. Campbell, *Speculators in Empire: Iroquoia and the 1768 Treaty of Fort Stanwix* (Norman: University of Oklahoma Press, 2012), 141.
4. For a description of Haudenosaunee seating practices, see F. W. Waugh, *Iroquois Foods and Food Preparation* (Ottawa: Government Printing Bureau, 1916), 46–47.
5. Parker, *Iroquois Uses of Maize and Other Food Plants*, 54–55.
6. Parker, *Iroquois Uses of Maize and Other Food Plants*, 61.
7. See Lewis Henry Morgan, *Houses and House-life of the American Aborigines* (Washington, DC: US Government Printing Office, 1881), 99.
8. Out of the six nations of the Haudenosaunee, only the western Senecas had fought against the British during the French and Indian War. The British were wary of alienating the rest of the Haudenosaunee and quickly worked to reestablish peace with the Senecas in 1763, in part to persuade them to join forces with the British against the Ottawas, Shawnees, and other Algonquian peoples led by Pontiac. One year later, this British goal was realized in a treaty in which the Seneca agreed to reenter their relationship with the British. The Seneca agreed to allow the British to build a fort at Niagara, and the British agreed to exonerate the Seneca for earlier siding with the French.
9. See Daniel K. Richter, *Facing East from Indian Country: A Native History of Early America* (Cambridge, MA: Harvard University Press, 2001). See also Daniel K. Richter and James H. Merrell, eds., *Beyond the Covenant Chain: The Iroquois and their Neighbors in Indian North America, 1600–1800* (Syracuse: Syracuse University Press, 1987).
10. See Hutton, "Narrating Sovereignty."
11. See T'hohahoken Michael Doxtater, "Tutelo Heights Short-Term 'Two Row' Lessons Central to Long-Term Mediation in the Grand River Valley," *Wicazo Sa Review* 26, no. 1 (2011): 43–65.
12. Thomas Wessel, "Agriculture and Iroquois Hegemony in New York, 1610–1779," *Maryland Historian* 1 (1970): 93–104, 97.
13. Daniel K. Richter, "War and Culture: The Iroquois Experience," *William and Mary Quarterly* 40, no. 4 (October 1983): 528–59, 534.
14. For a detailed consideration of cannibalism in colonial representations of seventeenth- and eighteenth-century North America, see Rachel B. Herrman, ed., *To Feast on Us as Their Prey: Cannibalism and the Early Modern Atlantic* (Fayetteville: University of Arkansas Press, 2019).
15. Erik R. Seeman, *The Huron-Wendat Feast of the Dead: Indian-European Encounters in Early North America* (Baltimore: Johns Hopkins University Press, 2011), 4.
16. Seeman, *The Huron-Wendat Feast of the Dead*, 9, 12.
17. Seeman, *The Huron-Wendat Feast of the Dead*, 15.
18. See Jane Mt. Pleasant, "The Paradox of Plows and Productivity: An Agronomic Comparison of Cereal Grain Production under Iroquois Hoe Culture and European Plow Culture in the Seventeenth and Eighteenth Centuries," *Agricultural History* 85, no. 2 (Fall 2011): 460–92; and Jane Mt. Pleasant and Robert F. Burt, "Estimating Productivity of Traditional Iroquoian Cropping Systems from Field Experiments and Historical Literature," *Journal of Ethnobiology* 30 (Spring/Summer 2010): 52–79.

19. See William A. Starna, George R. Hamell, and William L. Butts, "Northern Iroquoian Horticulture and Insect Infestation: A Cause for Village Removal," *Ethnohistory* 31, no. 3 (1984): 197–207.
20. Mt. Pleasant, "The Paradox of Plows and Productivity," 480.
21. See Brian Donahue, *The Great Meadow: Farmers and the Land in Colonial Concord* (New Haven: Yale University Press, 2004.
22. For a discussion of plow troughs in the northeast, see Tom Wessels, *Forest Forensics: A Field Guide to Reading the Forested Landscape* (Woodstock, VT: Countryman Press, 2010).
23. See Mt. Pleasant and Burt, "Traditional Iroquoian Cropping Systems."
24. John C. Kricher, "Weeds," *New York Times*, July 12, 1981, 4:21.
25. See Taylor Spence, "The Canada Thistle: The Pestilence of American Colonialism and the Emergence of an Exceptionalist Identity, 1783–1839," *Agricultural History* 90, no. 4 (2016): 511–44.
26. See Lance van Sittert, " 'The Seed Blows About in Every Breeze': Noxious Weed Eradication in the Cape Colony, 1860–1909," *Journal of Southern African Studies* 26, no. 4 (2000): 655–74.
27. For a sweeping history of no-till farming, see Rattan Lal, "Historical Development of No-Till Farming," in Rattan Lal, Peter R. Hobbs, Norman Uphoff, and David O. Hansen, eds., *Sustainable Agriculture and the International Rice-Wheat System* (New York: CRC Press, 2004).
28. For these population numbers, see Samuel Eliot Morison, *The Oxford History of the American People*, vol. 1, *Prehistory to 1789* (New York: Oxford University Press, 1927), 150.
29. See Daniel K. Richter, "Ordeals of the Longhouse: The Five Nations in Early American History," in Richter and Merrell, eds., *Beyond the Covenant Chain*, 11–27, 5, 19.
30. For a discussion of the Deganiwidah epic and its role in treaty-making traditions, see Robert A. Williams, *Linking Arms Together: American Indian Treaty Visions of Law and Peace, 1600–1800* (New York: Routledge, 1999), 57–59.
31. Richter, "Ordeals of the Longhouse," 16–17.
32. Richter, "Ordeals of the Longhouse," 21.
33. See Mary Druke Becker, "Linking Arms: The Structure of Iroquois Intertribal Diplomacy," in Richter and Merrell, eds., *Beyond the Covenant Chain*, 29–39.
34. Becker, "Linking Arms," 36.
35. See Waugh, *Iroquois Foods and Food Preparation*, 62.
36. Parker, *Iroquois Uses of Maize and Other Food Plants*, 74.
37. For a discussion of the Jesuits' negotiations of these burial demands, see Erik R. Seeman, *The Huron-Wendat Feast of the Dead: Indian-European Encounters in Early North America* (Baltimore: Johns Hopkins University Press, 2011).
38. See Michael Witgen, *An Infinity of Nations: How the Native New World Shaped Early North America* (Philadelphia: University of Pennsylvania Press, 2011), 31.
39. Richter, "Ordeals of the Longhouse," 15.

40. Michael Witgen, *An Infinity of Nations*, 19.
41. Becker, "Linking Arms," 36.
42. Witgen, *An Infinity of Nations*, 52.
43. James H. Merrell, *Into the American Woods: Negotiators on the Pennsylvania Frontier* (New York: W. W. Norton, 2000), 137.
44. See Paul A. W. Wallace, *Conrad Weiser, 1696–1760: Friend of Colonist and Mohawk* (1945).
45. See Fintan O'Toole, *White Savage: William Johnson and the Invention of America* (New York: Farrar, Straus and Giroux, 2005).
46. Merrell, *Into the American Woods*, 129.
47. Merrell, *Into the American Woods*, 137–38.
48. Merrell, *Into the American Woods*, 141.
49. General George Washington to Major-General John Sullivan, May 31, 1779, in *Letters and Papers of Major-General John Sullivan*, vol. 3, ed. Otis G. Hammond (Concord, NH: 1939), 48–49.
50. See Mt. Pleasant, "The Paradox of Plows and Productivity," 485.
51. See Manuscript Journal of Lieutenant Obadiah Gore, vol. 22, Sparks Collection, Harvard University Library. Cited in Thomas Wessel, "Agriculture and Iroquois Hegemony in New York, 1610–1779," *Maryland Historian* 1 (1970): 93–104, 101.
52. See Thomas Wessel, "Agriculture and Iroquois Hegemony," 101.
53. See Mary Jemison, *A Narrative of the Life of Mrs. Mary Jemison* (Ann Arbor: University of Michigan Press, 1967 [1824]), 69.

Chapter 3

1. R. Alfred Vick, "Cherokee Adaptation to the Landscape of the West and Overcoming the Loss of Culturally Significant Plants," *American Indian Quarterly* 35, no. 3 (2011): 395–417, 399.
2. Thomas Jefferson, *Notes on the State of Virginia* (Philadelphia: Prichard and Hall, 1787), 220.
3. George Washington, "Talk to the Cherokee Nation, August 29, 1796," in *The Writings of George Washington*, vol. 35, ed. John C. Fitzpatrick (Washington, DC: Government Printing Office, 1940), 193.
4. George Washington, "Letter to James Duane, September 7, 1783," in Fitzpatrick, ed., *Writings of Washington*, 27:140.
5. Andrew Jackson, "Second Annual Message [to Congress], December 6, 1830," in *A Compilation of the Messages and Papers of the Presidents, 1789–1897*, vol. 2, ed. James D. Richardson (Washington, DC: Government Printing Office, 1900), 500–529, 520–21. For more discussion of Thomas Jefferson's, George Washington's, and Andrew Jackson's statements on Indians living in the "hunter state," as well as how this framing has shaped subsequent scholarship on early American history, see James Merrell, "Second Thoughts on Colonial Historians and American Indians," *William and Mary Quarterly* 69, no. 3 (2012): 451–512.
6. Although it cannot be confirmed, this individual was likely William Wirt, who used the same nom de plume in travel writing related to the Cherokee and the American South prior to assuming the post of US attorney general, a position he held over three presidential terms. See "Thomas Jefferson to

William Wirt, 5 August 1815," in *The Papers of Thomas Jefferson*, vol. 8, ed. J. Jefferson Looney (Princeton: Princeton University Press, 2011), 641–46.

7. "Reflections on the Institutions of the Cherokee Indians, from Observations Made during a Recent Visit to That Tribe: In a Letter from a Gentleman of Virginia, to Robert Walsh, Jun.—June 1st, 1817," *Analectic Magazine* 12 (1818): 36–56, 45.
8. "Institutions of the Cherokee Indians," 39.
9. See Theda Perdue, *Cherokee Women: Gender and Culture Change, 1700–1835* (Lincoln: University of Nebraska Press, 1998), 121.
10. Cyrus Kingsbury Journal, February 13, 1817, Papers of the American Board of Commissioners for Foreign Missions, Houghton Library, Harvard University, Cambridge, MA. Cited in Perdue, *Cherokee Women*, 19.
11. See Gary C. Goodwin, *Cherokees in Transition: A Study of Changing Culture and Environment prior to 1775* (Chicago: University of Chicago Department of Geography, 1977), 51–55.
12. See Raymond Fogelson, "On the 'Petticoat Government' of the Eighteenth-Century Cherokees," in *Personality and the Cultural Construction of Society: Papers in Honor of Melford E. Spiro*, eds. David K. Jordan and Marc J. Schwartz (Tuscaloosa: University of Alabama Press, 1990), 174. Also see Perdue, *Cherokee Women*, 18.
13. James Adair, *Adair's History of the American Indians*, ed. Samuel Cole Williams (Johnson City, TN: Watauga Press, 1930), 436. Quoted in Perdue, *Cherokee Women*, 20.
14. Benjamin Hawkins, Journal, December 4, 1796, in *Letters of Benjamin Hawkins, 1796–1806*, Georgia Historical Society Collections 9 (Savannah: Georgia Historical Society, 1916), 24.
15. Samuel Cole Williams, ed., "Journey of the Moravians to the Cherokee and Cumberland Countries (1799)," *Early Travels in the Tennessee Country, 1540–1800* (Johnson City, TN: Watauga Press, 1928), 479.
16. Perdue, *Cherokee Women*, 23.
17. See Perdue, *Cherokee Women*, 25.
18. See Tom Hatley, "Cherokee Women Farmers Hold Their Ground," in *Appalachian Frontiers: Settlement, Society, and Development in the Pre-Industrial Era*, ed. Robert D. Mitchell (Lexington: University of Kentucky Press, 1991), 37–51.
19. Perdue, *Cherokee Women*, 80.
20. For quotation, see Barbara Graymont, *The Iroquois in the American Revolution* (Syracuse: Syracuse University Press, 1972), 213. The historian James Merrell remarked that during the Revolutionary War the Cherokees "lost twenty thousand bushels of corn to one invading army and fifty thousand more to another." See James Merrell, "Second Thoughts on Colonial Historians and American Indians," *William and Mary Quarterly* 69, no. 3 (2012): 451–512, 471.
21. See Tom Hatley, *The Dividing Paths: Cherokees and South Carolinians through the Era of Revolution* (New York: Oxford University Press, 1995), 139.
22. See Hawkins, Journal, March 30, 1797, in *Letters of Benjamin Hawkins*, 112.
23. John Norton, *The Journal of Major John Norton*, ed. Carl F. Klinck and James J. Talman (Toronto: Champlain Society, 1970), 142.

24. See William McLoughlin, *Cherokee Renascence in the New Republic* (Princeton: Princeton University Press, 1986); Tom Hatley, *The Dividing Paths*; and Tyler Boulware, *Deconstructing the Cherokee Nation: Town, Region, and Nation among Eighteenth-Century Cherokees* (Gainesville: University Press of Florida, 2011).
25. Tyler Boulware, "The Effect of the Seven Years' War on the Cherokee Nation," *Early American Studies: An Interdisciplinary Journal* 5, no. 2 (Fall 2007): 395–426, 398.
26. For a discussion of wood ashes in Cherokee cooking, see Mary U. Chiltoskey, *Cherokee Cooklore*, eds. Mary Ulmer and Samuel E. Beck (Greenville, OH: Coachwhip Publications, 2014 [1951]), 45.
27. Chiltoskey, *Cherokee Cooklore*, 32.
28. John Wyche's contributions to seed saving are discussed in Kim J. Young, *Ethnobotany* (New York: Chelsea House, 2007), 29; and in the *Seed Savers Exchange 1986 Yearbook*. See "Dr. John Wyche," *Seedsmen Hall of Fame*, accessed June 14, 2021, http://www.saveseeds.org/biography/wyche_john/index.html.
29. William Woys Weaver, *Heirloom Vegetable Gardening: A Master Gardener's Guide to Planting, Seed Saving, and Cultural History* (Stillwater, MN: Voyageur Press, 2018 [1997]), 96–97.
30. Paul B. Hamel and Mary U. Chiltoskey, *Cherokee Plants: Their Uses—A 400-year History* (self-published, 1975), 18–19.
31. Sean Brock (@hseanbrock), "I'm dying to try this! I've been reading about this tradition for years. This is from a book on Cherokee cooking . . .," Twitter post, September 21, 2017, https://twitter.com/hseanbrock/status/910836231109595136.
32. Jenn Rice, "The Southern Chef Reviving a Centuries-Old Cherokee Recipe for Yellowjacket Soup," *Vice Magazine*, April 1, 2019, https://www.vice.com/en_us/article/8xyydk/yellow-jacket-wasp-soup.
33. See Francis Newton Thorpe, ed., "Charter of Georgia, 1732," in *The Federal and State Constitutions, Colonial Charters, and Other Organic Laws of the State, Territories, and Colonies Now Or Heretofore Forming the United States of America*, vol. 2 (Washington, DC: US Government Printing Office, 1909), 765–77.
34. For a recent scholarly treatment of the Yazoo lands sale, see Charles F. Hobson, *The Great Yazoo Lands Sale: The Case of* Fletcher v. Peck (Lawrence: University Press of Kansas, 2016).
35. See "The Articles of Agreement and Cession," April 24, 1802, United States Congress, House Select Committee Appointed to Consider Certain Treaties with the Creek and Cherokee Indians (7th, 1st session: 1801–1802).
36. See "Andrew Jackson to James Monroe, 4 March 1817," in *The Papers of Andrew Jackson*, vol. 4, *1816–1820*, eds. Harold D. Moser, David R. Hoth, and George H. Hoemann (Knoxville: University of Tennessee Press, 1994), 96.
37. See "An Act to Provide for an Exchange of Lands with the Indians Residing in Any of the States or Territories, and for Their Removal West of the River Mississippi," May 28, 1830, United States Congress. (21st, 1st session: 1830).
38. *Acts of the General Assembly of the State of Georgia*, issue 1 (Milledgeville: State of Georgia, 1827), 249.

39. See Marion Lena Starkey, *The Cherokee Nation* (New York: Alfred E. Knopf, 1946), 109.
40. See Sarah H. Hill, *Cherokee Removal: Forts Along the Georgia Trail of Tears* (Washington, DC: National Park Service and the Georgia Department of Natural Resources/Historic Preservation Division, 2005), 27.
41. For a reprint of Rebecca Neugin's narrative, see Grant Foreman, *Indian Removal: The Emigration of the Five Civilized Tribes of Indians* (Norman: University of Oklahoma Press, 1932), 302–3.
42. See Daniel Butrick, *The Journal of Reverend Daniel S. Butrick, May 19, 1838–April 1, 1839* (Park Hill, OK: Trail of Tears Association, Oklahoma Chapter, 1998), 2, 8.
43. See Theda Purdue and Michael D. Green, *The Cherokee and the Trail of Tears* (New York: Penguin, 2007); and Anthony F. C. Wallace, *The Long Bitter Trail: Andrew Jackson and the Indians* (New York: Hill & Wang, 1993).
44. See William McLoughlin, *After the Trail of Tears: The Cherokees' Struggle for Sovereignty, 1839–1880* (Chapel Hill: University of North Carolina Press, 1994), 69–71.
45. See Vick, "Cherokee Adaptation," 407.
46. For a scholarly discussion of the history of the Cross Timbers, see Richard V. Francaviglia, *The Cast Iron Forest: A Natural and Cultural History of the North American Cross Timbers* (Austin: University of Texas Press, 2000).
47. Theda Perdue and Michael Green, eds., *The Cherokee Removal: A Brief History with Documents*, 3rd ed. (New York: Bedford/St. Martin's, 2016), 12.
48. "Institutions of the Cherokee Indians," 46.
49. See Andrew Denson, *Monuments to Absence: Cherokee Removal and the Contest over Southern Memory* (Chapel Hill: University of North Carolina Press, 2017).

Chapter 4

1. For a discussion of *folk imperialism*, see Gray H. Whaley, *Oregon and the Collapse of Illahee: U.S. Empire and the Collapse of an Indigenous World, 1792–1859* (Chapel Hill: University of North Carolina Press, 2010). Perhaps the first use of *manifest destiny* in print comes from John L. O'Sullivan, "The Great Nation of Futurity," *United States Democratic Review* 6, no. 23 (1839): 426–30.
2. See, for instance, Pekka Hamalainnen, *The Comanche Empire* (New Haven: Yale University Press, 2008). For an excellent discussion of Blackfoot history in the eighteenth and nineteenth centuries, see Ryan Hall, *Beneath the Backbone of the World: Blackfoot People and the North American Borderlands, 1720–1877* (Chapel Hill: University of North Carolina Press, 2020).
3. For aggregate death and casualty data, see Greg Michno, *Encyclopedia of Indian Wars: Western Battles and Skirmishes, 1850–1890* (Missoula, MT: Mountain Press Publishing, 2003), 367.
4. For a detailed discussion on Civil War foraging raids and their use in the postwar American West, see Lisa Brady, *War Upon the Land: Military Strategy and the Transformation of Southern Landscapes during the American Civil War* (Athens: University of Georgia Press, 2012).

5. One of the classic statements on these nineteenth-century transformations is found in William Cronon, *Nature's Metropolis: Chicago and the Great West* (New York: W. W. Norton, 1991). For discussions specific to Montana and the Blackfeet, see Michael D. Wise, *Producing Predators: Wolves, Work, and Conquest in the Northern Rockies* (Lincoln: University of Nebraska Press, 2016).
6. Inspector Thomas report, "Inspection of Blackfeet Agency and Charges against Agent Allen," October 10, 1885 (5017), in Bureau of Indian Affairs, *Reports of the Inspection of the Field Jurisdictions of the Office of Indian Affairs, 1873–1900*, reel 2.
7. Howard L. Harrod, *The Animals Came Dancing: Native American Sacred Ecology and Animal Kinship* (Tucson: University of Arizona Press, 2000).
8. Thomas E. Kehoe, "The Boarding School Bison Drive Site," *Plains Anthropologist* 12, no. 35 (1967): 1–165, 83.
9. See C. A. Reher and G. C. Frison, "The Vore Site, 48CK302, a Stratified Buffalo Jump in the Wyoming Black Hills," *Plains Anthropologist* 25 (1980): 46; and B. O. K. Reeves, "Bison Killing in the Southwestern Alberta Rockies," *Plains Anthropologist* 23 (1978): 151–74.
10. Russel Lawrence Barsh and Chantelle Marlor, "Driving Bison and Blackfoot Science," *Human Ecology* 31, no. 4 (2003): 571–93, 578.
11. See Donal Carbaugh, " 'Just Listen': 'Listening' and Landscape Among the Blackfeet," *Western Journal of Communication* 63, no. 3 (Summer 1999): 250–70.
12. For a discussion of the Blackfoot concept of natural alliances, see Betty Bastien, *Blackfoot Ways of Knowing: The Worldview of the Siksikaitsitapi* (Calgary: University of Calgary Press, 2004).
13. Clark Wissler to Franz Boas, May 12, 1905, Wissler Correspondence, Accession Records, Donor Clark Wissler, 1903, Department of Anthropology Archives, American Museum of Natural History, New York, NY.
14. See Rosalyn R. LaPier, *Invisible Reality: Storytellers, Storytakers, and the Supernatural World of the Blackfeet* (Lincoln: University of Nebraska Press, 2017), 77, 137.
15. For a discussion of these wolf-costume practices, see Barsh and Marlor, "Driving Bison and Blackfeet Science," 585–86.
16. See Maria Nieves Zedeño, Jesse A. M. Ballenger, and John R. Murray, "Landscape Engineering and Organizational Complexity among Late Prehistoric Bison Hunters of the Northwestern Plains," *Current Anthropology* 55, no. 1 (February 2014): 23–58, 31.
17. See Jonathan Driver, "Comments," in Zedeño, Ballenger, and Murray, "Landscape Engineering and Organizational Complexity," 44–45.
18. For a discussion of these band sizes, see LaPier, *Invisible Reality*, xviii.
19. George Colpitts, *Pemmican Empire: Food, Trade, and the Last Bison Hunts in the North American Plains, 1780–1882* (Cambridge: Cambridge University Press, 2014), 1.
20. See Colpitts, *Pemmican Empire*; as well as Claiborne Skinner, "The Sinews of Empire: The Voyageurs and the Carrying Trade of the Pays D'en Haut. 1681–1754" (PhD diss., University of Illinois at Chicago, 1991).
21. See Three Calf, interviewed by John Ewers, translated by Reuben Black Boy, November 8, 1943, "Making Pemmican," Series xiv, Box 16, John C. Ewers

Papers, National Anthropological Archives, National Museum of Natural History, Smithsonian Institution, Washington, DC. Cited in LaPier, *Invisible Reality*, 54.

22. See Noelie Vialles, *Animal to Edible*, trans. J. A. Underwood (Cambridge: Cambridge University Press, 1994).
23. For a full discussion of the history of Blackfeet meat-making in the late nineteenth century, see Michael D. Wise, "Colonial Beef and the Blackfeet Reservation Slaughterhouse," *Radical History Review* 110 (2011): 59–82.
24. See Henry M. Rice, "Pemmican [reprint]," *Minnesota Archaeologist* 40, no. 2 (1981): 96–100, 96. Cited in Colpitts, *Pemmican Empire*, 1.
25. For a full discussion, see LaPier, *Invisible Reality*, 53.
26. LaPier, *Invisible Reality*, 57.
27. See Meriwether Lewis, "Botanical Collections: Winter 1804–1805," Codex R, *Journals of the Lewis and Clark Expedition*, ed. Gary Moulton, accessed June 17, 2021, https://lewisandclarkjournals.unl.edu/item/lc.jrn.1804-1805.winter.part3#lc.jrn.1804-1805.winter.part3.02.
28. Joseph C. Winter, *Tobacco Use by Native North Americans: Sacred Smoke and Silent Killer* (Norman: University of Oklahoma Press, 2000), 183.
29. David Thompson, *The Writings of David Thompson*, ed. William Moreau (Toronto: Champlain Society, 2009), 1:215. Cited in Elizabeth Fenn, *Encounters at the Heart of the World: A History of the Mandan People* (New York: Hill & Wang, 2014), 231.
30. LaPier, *Invisible Reality*, 75.
31. White Calf, interview by George Bird Grinnell, October 25, 1897, Grinnell Diary, 1897, #327, George Bird Grinnell Papers, Southwest Museum, Los Angeles, CA. Cited in LaPier, *Invisible Reality*, 52.
32. LaPier, *Invisible Reality*, 73.
33. LaPier, *Invisible Reality*, xxiv.
34. See Albert J. Zhang, Agnes M. Rimanod, Wilbert Fish, Srinivasa R. Mentreddy, and Suresh T. Mathews, "Serviceberry [*Amelanchier alnifolia* (Nutt.) *Nutt.* ex. *M. Roem* (Rosaceae)] Leaf Extract Inhibits Mammalian A-Glucosidase Activity and Suppresses Postprandial Glycemic Response in a Mouse Model of Diet-Induced Obesity and Hyperglycemia," *Journal of Ethnopharmacology* 143 (2012): 481–87; and Aurélie de Rus Jacquet, Mitali Arun Tambe, Sin Ying Ma, George P. McCabe, Jay Hansford C. Vest, Jean-Christophe Rochet, "Pikuni-Blackfeet Traditional Medicine: Neuroprotective Activities of Medicinal Plants Used to Treat Parkinson's Disease–Related Symptoms," *Journal of Ethnopharmacology* 206 (2017): 393–407.
35. See John C. Ewers, *The Blackfeet: Raiders on the Northwestern Plains* (Norman: University of Oklahoma Press, 1958), 206–7.
36. George Manypenny to Alfred Cumming, Isaac I. Stevens, and Joel Palmer, May 3, 1855. Cited simply as "Indian Office Records" from the National Archives in Ewers, *The Blackfeet*, 214.
37. This Culbertson quotation is also cited in Ewers, *The Blackfeet*, 214, and identified as coming from a letter, circa 1835, from Culbertson to Isaac Stevens in "Indian Office Records" at the National Archives.
38. Albert J. Partoll, ed., "The Blackfoot Indian Peace Council," *Frontier and Midland* 17, no. 3 (1937): 199–207, 202–3.

39. For a discussion of Nelson Story and his contracts with the Indian office, see John C. Russell, *Treasure State Tycoon: Nelson Story and the Making of Montana* (Helena: Montana Historical Society Press, 2019).
40. See Ewers, *The Blackfeet*, 230.
41. See David Nugent, "Property Relations, Production Relations, and Inequality: Anthropology, Political Economy, and the Blackfeet," *American Ethnologist* 20, no. 2 (1993): 336–62.
42. See Wise, "Colonial Beef and the Blackfeet Reservation Slaughterhouse," 69.
43. See, for instance, Stanley R. Davidson and Dale Tash, "Confederate Backwash in Montana Territory," *Montana: The Magazine of Western History* 17 (1967): 50–58.
44. Agent Churchill to the Commissioner of Indian Affairs, September 15, 1909, in Thomas R. Wessel Indian Claims Commission Research Papers, 1855–1879, Collection 2059, Box 2, Folder 4, Montana State University Special Collections, Bozeman, MT.
45. Oscar Lipps, Supervisor, "Report on the Education, Industrial, Economic, and Home Conditions, Blackfeet Reservation, Montana," October 20, 1913, in Thomas R. Wessel Research Papers, Box 4, Folder 1, 5.
46. For a full discussion of grazing leases and the politics of beef on the Blackfeet Reservation, see Michael D. Wise, "The Place That Feeds You: Allotment and the Struggle for Blackfeet Food Sovereignty," in *Food Across Borders*, eds. Matt Garcia, E. Melanie DuPuis, and Don Mitchell (New Brunswick: Rutgers University Press, 2017), 163–80, 169.
47. There is a deep and growing scholarly literature on the history of allotment and how different Native communities responded and adapted to the forced privatization of reservation landownership. See Peter Iverson, *When Indians Became Cowboys: Native Peoples and Cattle Ranching in the American West* (Norman: University of Oklahoma Press, 1994); David Chang, *The Color of the Land: Race, Nation, and the Politics of Landownership in Oklahoma, 1832–1929* (Chapel Hill: University of North Carolina Press, 2010); David Chang, "Enclosures of Land and Sovereignty: The Allotment of American Indian Lands," *Radical History Review* 109 (2011): 108–19; Emily Greenwald, *Reconfiguring the Reservation: The Nez Perces, Jicarilla Apaches, and the Dawes Act* (Lincoln: University of Nebraska Press, 2002); Melissa Meyer, *The White Earth Tragedy: Ethnicity and Dispossession at a Minnesota Anishinaabe Reservation, 1889–1920* (Lincoln: University of Nebraska Press, 1999); and Kristin Ruppel, *Unearthing Indian Land: Living with the Legacies of Allotment* (Tucson: University of Arizona Press, 2008).
48. See Thomas R. Wessel, "Political Assimilation on the Blackfeet Reservation, 1887–1934: A Study in Survival," in Douglas H. Ubelaker and Herman J. Viola, eds., *Plains Indian Studies: A Collection of Essays in Honor of John C. Ewers and Waldo R. Wedel*, Smithsonian Contributions to Anthropology 30 (Washington, DC: Smithsonian Institution Press, 1982), 59–72, 68.
49. See Robert Hamilton file, Records of the Carlisle Indian Industrial School, Record Group 75, Student Records 1879–1918, Series 1327, box 28, folder 1309, National Archives and Records Administration, Washington, DC.
50. See Wessel, "Political Assimilation," 61–62.
51. Wessel, "Political Assimilation," 63.

52. Wessel, "Political Assimilation," 63.
53. For a full discussion of the battle over the surplus unallotted lands sales, see Paul Rosier, *Rebirth of the Blackfeet Nation, 1912–1954* (Lincoln: University of Nebraska Press, 2001).
54. Wessel, "Political Assimilation," 64.
55. See Hamilton file, box 28, folder 1309, National Archives and Records Administration.
56. See Wessel, "Political Assimilation," 64.
57. Oscar Lipps, "Subsistence Farming on the Blackfeet Reservation; Memorandum for Mr. Cooley," in *Thomas Wessel Collection* Box 8, Folder 5. See also "The Five-Year Program on the Blackfeet Indian Reservation," *Indian Leader* 26 (1923): 3.

Chapter 5

1. For a detailed account of Banks's years in Pipestone, see Dennis Banks with Richard Erdoes, *Ojibwa Warrior: Dennis Banks and the Rise of the American Indian Movement* (Norman: University of Oklahoma Press, 2004), 24–31.
2. For a discussion of an example of these federal starvation tactics on the Blackfeet Reservation, see Thomas R. Wessel, "Political Assimilation on the Blackfeet Reservation, 1887–1934: A Study in Survival," in Douglas H. Ubelaker and Herman J. Viola, eds., *Plains Indian Studies: A Collection of Essays in Honor of John C. Ewers and Waldo R. Wedel*, Smithsonian Contributions to Anthropology 30 (Washington, DC: Smithsonian Institution Press, 1982), 59–72, especially 61.
3. Philip Deloria, *Indians in Unexpected Places* (Lawrence: University Press of Kansas, 2004), 28.
4. For a reprint of Pratt's 1892 speech where he delivered this famous quotation, see Richard H. Pratt, "The Advantages of Mingling Indians with Whites," in Francis Paul Prucha, ed., *Americanizing the American Indian: Writings by the "Friends of the Indian," 1880–1900* (Cambridge: Harvard University Press, 1973), 260–71.
5. For a critical edition of Pratt's autobiography, see Richard Henry Pratt, *Battlefield and Classroom: Four Decades with the American Indian, 1867–1904*, ed. Robert M. Utley (Norman: University of Oklahoma Press, 2004).
6. For a compilation of federal statistics on boarding school enrollment, see K. Tsianina Lomawaima, *They Called it Prairie Light: The Story of Chilocco Indian School* (Lincoln: University of Nebraska Press, 1994), 6.
7. For detailed discussions of the Oraibi incidents, see Margaret D. Jacobs, "A Battle for the Children: American Indian Child Removal in Arizona in the Era of Assimilation," *Journal of Arizona History* 45 (2004): 31–62, 35; and Harry C. James, *Pages from Hopi History* (Tucson: University of Arizona Press, 1974), 111.
8. See Brenda Child, *Boarding School Seasons: American Indian Families, 1900–1940* (Lincoln: University of Nebraska Press, 2000).
9. See Banks and Erdoes, *Ojibwe Warrior*, 17–18.
10. For a discussion of McNickle's experience, see Brenda Child, *Boarding School Seasons*, 5. McNickle himself also wrote a short story reflecting on the experience of boarding the train to the Indian school. See D'Arcy McNickle, "Train

Time," in D'Arcy McNickle, *The Hawk is Hungry and Other Stories*, ed. Birgit Hans (Tucson: University of Arizona Press, 1992), 47–54.

11. Child, *Boarding School Seasons*, 27.
12. See Lomawaima, *They Called it Prairie Light*, 77.
13. This quotation from the superintendent of Haskell comes from the Haskell school files located in Record Group 75 of the National Archives and Records Administration and is cited in Child, *Boarding Schools*, 35.
14. For more discussion about these Ponca girls, see Lomawaima, *They Called it Prairie Light*, 124.
15. Lomawaima, *They Called it Prairie Light*, 167.
16. More information on this account of brewing beer can be found in Lomawaima, *They Called it Prairie Light*, 140.
17. See Unidentified Author, "The Work of Our School Kitchen and Dining Room," in *Oklahoma Indian School Magazine* 1, no. 6 (1932): 19.
18. This Sylvanus Stall quotation on the "endurance" of Native women has been widely cited in critical feminist and Indigenous texts since appearing in Barbara Ehrenreich and Deirdre English, *For Her Own Good: Two Centuries of the Experts' Advice to Women* (New York: Random House, 2005 [1978]), 114. Ehrenreich and English identify the Stall passage as a quotation in Alice Lee Moqué, "The Mistakes of Mothers," *Proceedings of the National Congress of Mothers Second Annual Convention* (Washington, DC: 1898), 43.
19. See Cecil B. DeMille, *The Squaw Man* (Jesse Lasky Feature Play Company, 1914); and Deloria, *Indians in Unexpected Places*, 4.
20. For a discussion on the working out system, see Lomawaima, *They Called it Prairie Light*, 89.
21. See Letter to Mr. E. B. Merritt, commissioner of Indian Affairs, "Reply to Circular No. 2546, Dated February 2, 1929," in Thomas J. Walsh and John Edward Erickson Papers, 1910–1934, Library of Congress, Washington, DC, Box 58, unmarked folder.
22. For these quotations, see Lomawaima, *They Called it Prairie Light*, 56, 58–60.
23. See Lewis Meriam, ed., *The Problem of Indian Administration* (Washington, DC: Government Printing Office, 1928).
24. See Susan Hood, "Termination of the Klamath Indian Tribe of Oregon," *Ethnohistory* 19, no. 4 (1972): 379–92; and Peggy Chiu, "Stewards of their Lands: A Case Study of the Klamath Tribes, Oregon," The Trust for Public Land, 2018.
25. For introductions to the deep history of treaty rights in the context of disputes over fishing and hunting in the late twentieth century, see Andrew H. Fisher, "Defenders and Dissidents: Cooks Landing and the Fight to Define Tribal Sovereignty in the Red Power Era," *Comparative American Studies* 17, no. 2 (2020): 117–41; Vera Parham, " 'It was a Spearhead of Change': The Fish-Ins of the Pacific Northwest and the Boldt Decision, Shifting Native American Protest Identities in the 1960s and 1970s," *Native Studies Review* 22, no. 1/2 (2013): 1–26; and Patty Loew, "Hidden Transcripts in the Chippewa Treaty Rights Struggle: A Twice Told Story of Race, Resistance, and the Politics of Power," *American Indian Quarterly* 21, no. 4 (1997): 713–28.
26. Gerald R. Ford, July 16, 1976, "Remarks at a Meeting with American Indian

Leaders," in *Public Papers of the Presidents of the United States, 1976–77* (Washington, DC: Government Printing Office, 1979), 1937.

27. See Henry H. Kaldenbaugh, "Statement of Dr. Henry H. Kaldenbaugh, USPHS, HIS, Rosebud S. Dak.," in United States Senate, *Supplementary Food Programs*, part 3 of *Federal Food Programs—1973: Hearings Before the Select Committee on Nutrition and Human Needs of the United States Senate, Ninety-Third Congress, First Session* (Washington, DC: Government Printing Office, 1973), 318.
28. Food and Nutrition Service, United States Department of Agriculture, *Report to the Select Committee on Nutrition and Human Needs, United States Senate, by the Comptroller General of the United States: Administration and Effectiveness of Family Food Programs on Selected Indian Reservations in New Mexico and South Dakota*, A-51604 (Washington, DC: Government Printing Office, 1973), 23.
29. See Victor Connelly to Earl L. Butz, March 7, 1974, "Re Blackfeet Tribal Commodity Program," in United States Senate, *Commodity Distribution and Food Stamp Programs: Hearings Before the Subcommittee on Agricultural Research and General Legislation of the Committee on Agriculture and Forestry United States Senate Ninety-Third Congress Second Session on S. 2871 and S. 3235, March 27 and 28, 1974* (Washington, DC: Government Printing Office, 1974), 74–75.
30. See, for instance, Louis Eskeets, "Statement of Louis Eskeets, Representative, Navajo Tribe, Window Rock, Ariz.," in United States Senate, *Food Stamps: Hearing Before the Subcommittee on Nutrition of the Committee on Agriculture, Nutrition, and Forestry, United States Senate, Ninety-Fifth Congress, First Session* (Washington, DC: Government Printing Office, 1977), 9–13.
31. Jeanne Volts, "Overcoming Food Stamp Reservations: Havasupai Were Using Commodity Distribution," *Los Angeles Times*, December 21, 1972.
32. See Melvin White Eagle, "Statement of Melvin White Eagle, Chairman, Standing Rock Sioux Tribe, Fort Yates, N. Dak., and Chairman, United Tribes of North Dakota," in *Commodity Distribution and Food Stamp Programs: Hearings* (Washington, DC: Government Printing Office, 1974), 152–54.
33. See Louis Eskeets, "Statement of Louis Eskeets," in *Food Stamps: Hearing*, 12–13.
34. See Charles E. Trimble, "Statement of Charles E. Trimble, Executive Director, National Congress of American Indians," in United States Senate, *Commodity Distribution and Food Stamp Programs: Hearings*, 83–87.
35. See Lorelei DeCora Means, "Statement of Lorelei Means, Community Associate, Food Resources Program, North Central Regional Office, American Friends Service Committee, Porcupine, S. Dak.," in *Commodity Distribution and Food Stamp Programs: Hearings*, 64–67.
36. See United States Senate, *Supplementary Food Programs*.
37. Jean Mayer, "Diet of Indians Needs Upgrading," *Washington Post*, February 8, 1973.
38. See Reuben Snake Papers, National Museum of the American Indian, Archives, Suitland, Maryland, Box 1, folder 2.
39. Ford, "Remarks at a Meeting with American Indian Leaders," July 16, 1976.

Epilogue

1. See "Indian Leader from Federal Dam Tries Business World," *Brainerd Dispatch*, August 16, 2000; and "Native Activist Gets into Food Business," *Deseret News*, August 15, 2000.
2. For more consideration of the history of these dichotomies of production, see Michael D. Wise, *Producing Predators: Wolves, Work, and Conquest in the Northern Rockies* (Lincoln: University of Nebraska Press, 2016).
3. Sean Sherman and Beth Dooley, *The Sioux Chef's Indigenous Kitchen* (Minneapolis: University of Minnesota Press, 2017), 2.
4. Sherman and Dooley, *Sioux Chef's Indigenous Kitchen*, 82.
5. Sherman and Dooley, *Sioux Chef's Indigenous Kitchen*, 122.
6. Sherman and Dooley, *Sioux Chef's Indigenous Kitchen*, 2, 77.
7. Sherman and Dooley, *Sioux Chef's Indigenous Kitchen*, 3–4.

BIBLIOGRAPHY

Abrams, Marc D., and Gregory J. Nowacki. "Native Americans as Active and Passive Promoters of Mast and Fruit Trees in the Eastern USA." *The Holocene* 18, no. 7 (2008): 1123–37.

Adair, James. *Adair's History of the American Indians*, edited by Samuel Cole Williams. Johnson City: Watauga Press, 1930.

Alfred, Taiaiake. "Sovereignty." In *A Companion to American Indian History*, edited by Philip Deloria and Neil Salisbury, 460–74. Malden, MA: Blackwell Publishing, 2002.

Anderson, M. Kat. *Tending the Wild: Native American Knowledge and the Management of California's Natural Resources*. Berkeley: University of California Press, 2005.

Anderson, Virginia DeJohn. *Creatures of Empire: How Domestic Animals Transformed Early America*. Oxford: Oxford University Press, 2006.

Baker, James W. *Thanksgiving: The Biography of an American Holiday*. Lebanon: University of New Hampshire Press, 2009.

Banks, Dennis, with Richard Erdoes. *Ojibwa Warrior: Dennis Banks and the Rise of the American Indian Movement*. Norman: University of Oklahoma Press, 2004.

Barker, Joanne, ed. *Sovereignty Matters*. Lincoln: University of Nebraska Press, 2005.

Barsh, Russel Lawrence, and Chantelle Marlor. "Driving Bison and Blackfoot Science." *Human Ecology* 31, no. 4 (2003): 571–93.

Basso, Keith. *Wisdom Sits in Places: Landscape and Language Among the Western Apache*. Albuquerque: University of New Mexico Press, 1996.

Bastien, Betty. *Blackfoot Ways of Knowing: The Worldview of the Siksikaitsitapi*. Calgary: University of Calgary Press, 2004.

Bennett, M. K. "The Food Economy of the New England Indians, 1605–75." *Journal of Political Economy* 63, no. 5 (1955): 369–97.

Berzok, Linda Murray. *American Indian Food*. Westport, CT: Greenwood Press, 2005.

Betts, Edwin Morris. *Thomas Jefferson's Farm Book*. Princeton: Princeton University Press, 1953.

Bodge, George Madison. *Soldiers in King Philip's War*. Boston: George Madison Bodge, 1891.

Bonnicksen, Thomas. *America's Ancient Forests: From the Ice Age to the Age of Discovery*. New York: Wiley, 2000.

Boulware, Tyler. *Deconstructing the Cherokee Nation: Town, Region, and Nation among Eighteenth-Century Cherokees*. Gainesville: University Press of Florida, 2011.

Boulware, Tyler. "The Effect of the Seven Years' War on the Cherokee Nation." *Early American Studies: An Interdisciplinary Journal* 5, no. 2 (Fall 2007): 395–426.

Bradford, William. *Of Plimoth Plantation*. Boston: Wright and Potter Printing, 1898.

Brady, Lisa. *War Upon the Land: Military Strategy and the Transformation of Southern Landscapes during the American Civil War*. Athens: University of Georgia Press, 2012.

Bruyneel, Kevin. *The Third Space of Sovereignty: The Postcolonial Politics of U.S.-Indigenous Relations*. Minneapolis: University of Minnesota Press, 2007.

Burroughs, Raymond Darwin. *The Natural History of the Lewis and Clark Expedition*. East Lansing: Michigan State University Press, 1995 [1961].

Burt, Henry M. *The First Century of the History of Springfield*. Vol. 1. Springfield, MA: Henry M. Burt, 1898.

Butrick, Daniel. *The Journal of Reverend Daniel S. Butrick, May 19, 1838–April 1, 1839*. Park Hill, OK: Trail of Tears Association, Oklahoma Chapter, 1998.

Cahill, Cathleen D. *Federal Fathers and Mothers: A Social History of the United States Indian Service, 1869–1933*. Chapel Hill: University of North Carolina Press, 2011.

Calloway, Colin G., ed. *After King Philip's War: Presence and Persistence in Indian New England*. Hanover, NH: University Press of New England, 1997.

Campbell, David C. "The Pick-Sloan Program: A Case of Bureaucratic Economic Power." *Journal of Economic Issues* 18, no. 2 (1984): 449–56.

Campbell, William J. *Speculators in Empire: Iroquoia and the 1768 Treaty of Fort Stanwix*. Norman: University of Oklahoma Press, 2012.

Carbaugh, Donal. " 'Just Listen': 'Listening' and Landscape Among the Blackfeet." *Western Journal of Communication* 63, no. 3 (1999): 250–70.

Cattelino, Jessica. "The Double Bind of American Indian Need-Based Sovereignty." *Cultural Anthropology* 25, no. 2 (2010): 235–62.

Chakrabarty, Dipesh. *Provincializing Europe: Postcolonial Thought and Historical Difference*. Princeton: Princeton University Press, 2000.

Champlain, Samuel de. *Voyages of Samuel de Champlain, 1604–1618*. Translated by William Lawson Grant. New York: Scribner's, 1907.

Chang, David. "Enclosures of Land and Sovereignty: The Allotment of American Indian Lands." *Radical History Review* 109 (2011): 108–19.

Chang, David. *The Color of the Land: Race, Nation, and the Politics of Landownership in Oklahoma, 1832–1929*. Chapel Hill: University of North Carolina Press, 2010.

Chaplin, Joyce. *Subject Matter: Technology, the Body, and Science on the Anglo-American Frontier, 1500–1676*. Cambridge, MA: Harvard University Press, 2001.

Child, Brenda. *Boarding School Seasons: American Indian Families, 1900–1940*. Lincoln: University of Nebraska Press, 2000.

Chilocco Indian School. "The Work of Our School Kitchen and Dining Room." *Oklahoma Indian School Magazine* 1, no. 6 (1932).

Chilton, Elizabeth S. " 'Towns They Have None': Diverse Subsistence and Settlement Strategies in Native New England." In *Northeast Subsistence-Settlement Change: A.D. 700–1300*, New York State Museum Bulletin 496, edited by John P. Hart and Christina B. Rieth, 289–300. Albany: University of the State of New York, 2002.

Chiltoskey, Mary U. *Cherokee Cooklore*. Edited by Mary Ulmer and Samuel E. Beck. Greenville, OH: Coachwhip Publications, 2014 [1951].

Chiu, Peggy. "Stewards of their Lands: A Case Study of the Klamath Tribes, Oregon." The Trust for Public Land, 2018.
Cogbill, Charles V., John Burk, and G. Motzkin. "The Forests of Presettlement New England, USA: Spatial and Compositional Patterns Based on Town proprietor Surveys." *Journal of Biogeography* 29, no. 10/11 (2002): 1279–304.
Colpitts, George. *Pemmican Empire: Food, Trade, and the Last Bison Hunts in the North American Plains, 1780–1882*. Cambridge: Cambridge University Press, 2014.
Connelly, Victor. "Re Blackfeet Tribal Commodity Program." In United States Senate, *Commodity Distribution and Food Stamp Programs: Hearings*, 73–75.
Cronon, William. *Changes in the Land: Indians, Colonists and the Ecology of New England*. New York: Hill & Wang, 1983.
Cronon, William. *Nature's Metropolis: Chicago and the Great West*. New York: W. W. Norton, 1991.
Crosby, Alfred. *Ecological Imperialism: The Biological Expansion of Europe, 900–1900*. 2nd edition. Cambridge: Cambridge University Press, 2004 [1989].
Davidson, Stanley R., and Dale Tash. "Confederate Backwash in Montana Territory." *Montana: The Magazine of Western History* 17 (1967): 50–58.
Davis, Mike. *Late Victorian Holocausts: El Niño Famines and the Making of the Third World*. London: Verso, 2001.
Deane, Samuel. *The New England Farmer*. 2nd edition. Worcester, MA: Isaiah Thomas, 1797.
Deloria, Philip J. *Indians in Unexpected Places*. Lawrence: University Press of Kansas, 2004.
DeLucia, Christine M. *Memory Lands: King Philip's War and the Place of Violence in the Northeast*. New Haven: Yale University Press, 2018.
Demeritt, David. "Agriculture, Climate, and Cultural Adaptation in the Prehistoric Northeast." *Archaeology of Eastern North America* 19 (1991): 183–202.
Denson, Andrew. *Monuments to Absence: Cherokee Removal and the Contest over Southern Memory*. Chapel Hill: University of North Carolina Press, 2017.
Dimmick, Frederika. "Creative Farmers of the Northeast: A New View of Indian Maize Horticulture." *North American Archaeologist* 15, no. 3 (1994): 235–52.
Donahue, Brian. *The Great Meadow: Farmers and the Land in Colonial Concord*. New Haven: Yale University Press, 2004.
Doxtater, T'hohahoken Michael. "Tutelo Heights Short-Term 'Two Row' Lessons Central to Long-Term Mediation in the Grand River Valley." *Wicazo Sa Review* 26, no. 1 (2011): 43–65.
Earle, Rebecca. *The Body of the Conquistador: Food, Race and the Colonial Experience in Spanish America, 1492–1700*. Cambridge: Cambridge University Press, 2012.
Eden, Trudy. *The Early American Table: Food and Society in the New World*. Dekalb: Northern Illinois University Press, 2008.
Ehrenreich, Barbara, and Deirdre English. *For Her Own Good: Two Centuries of the Experts' Advice to Women*. New York: Random House, 2005 [1978].
Eskeets, Louis. "Statement of Louis Eskeets, Representative, Navajo Tribe, Window Rock, Ariz." In United States Senate, *Food Stamps: Hearing*, 9–13. Washington, DC: Government Printing Office, 1977.

Ewers, John C. *The Blackfeet: Raiders on the Northwestern Plains*. Norman: University of Oklahoma Press, 1958.

Fenn, Elizabeth. *Encounters at the Heart of the World: A History of the Mandan People*. New York: Hill & Wang, 2014.

Fickes, Michael L. " 'They Could Not Endure That Yoke': The Captivity of Pequot Women and Children after the War of 1637." *New England Quarterly* 73, no. 1 (2000): 58–81.

Fiege, Mark. "Satan in the Land: Nature, the Supernatural, and Disorder in Colonial New England." In *The Republic of Nature*, 23–56. Seattle: University of Washington Press, 2012.

Fischer, Julian B., Laura H. McArthur, and James B. Petersen. "Continuity and Change in the Food Habits of the Seventeenth-Century English Colonists in Plymouth and Massachusetts Bay." *Ecology of Food and Nutrition* 36, no. 1 (1997): 65–93.

Fisher, Andrew H. "Defenders and Dissidents: Cooks Landing and the Fight to Define Tribal Sovereignty in the Red Power Era." *Comparative American Studies* 17, no. 2 (2020): 117–41.

Fogelson, Raymond. "On the 'Petticoat Government' of the Eighteenth-Century Cherokees." In *Personality and the Cultural Construction of Society: Papers in Honor of Melford E. Spiro*, edited by David K. Jordan and Marc J. Schwartz. Tuscaloosa: University of Alabama Press, 1990.

Ford, Gerald R. "Remarks at a Meeting with American Indian Leaders, July 16, 1976." In *Public Papers of the Presidents of the United States, 1976–77*, 1937. Washington, DC: Government Printing Office, 1979.

Foreman, Grant. *Indian Removal: The Emigration of the Five Civilized Tribes of Indians*. Norman: University of Oklahoma Press, 1932.

Foucault, Michel. *The History of Sexuality, Volume 1: An Introduction*, translated by Robert Hurley. New York: Pantheon Books, 1978.

Francaviglia, Richard V. *The Cast Iron Forest: A Natural and Cultural History of the North American Cross Timbers*. Austin: University of Texas Press, 2000.

Georgia General Assembly. *Acts of the General Assembly of the State of Georgia*. Volume 1. Milledgeville: State of Georgia, 1827.

Gerarde, John. *The Herball or Generall Historie of Plantes*. London: John Norton, 1597.

Gilman, Carolyn, and Mary Jane Schneider. *The Way to Independence: Memories of a Hidatsa Indian Family, 1840–1920*. St. Paul: Minnesota Historical Society Press, 1987.

Goodley, Dan. "Dis/entangling Critical Disability Studies." *Disability & Society* 28, no. 5 (2013): 631–44.

Goodwin, Gary C. *Cherokees in Transition: A Study of Changing Culture and Environment prior to 1775*. Chicago: University of Chicago Department of Geography, 1977.

Gookin, Daniel. *Historical Collections of the Indians of New England*. Boston: Apollo Press, 1792 [1674].

Graymont, Barbara. *The Iroquois in the American Revolution*. Syracuse: Syracuse University Press, 1972.

Greenwald, Emily. *Reconfiguring the Reservation: The Nez Perces, Jicarilla Apaches, and the Dawes Act*. Lincoln: University of Nebraska Press, 2002.

Grove, Richard H. *Green Imperialism: Colonial Expansion, Tropical Island Edens and the Origins of Environmentalism, 1600–1860*. Cambridge: Cambridge University Press, 2010.

Hall, Ryan. *Beneath the Backbone of the World: Blackfoot People and the North American Borderlands, 1720–1877*. Chapel Hill: University of North Carolina Press, 2020.

Hamalainnen, Pekka. *The Comanche Empire*. New Haven: Yale University Press, 2008.

Hamel, Paul B., and Mary U. Chiltoskey. *Cherokee Plants: Their Uses—A 400-year History*. Self-published, 1975.

Hamilton, Milton W. "Sir William Johnson: Interpreter of the Iroquois." *Ethnohistory* 10, no. 3 (1963): 270–86.

Harris, Cheryl I. "Whiteness as Property." *Harvard Law Review* 106, no. 8 (1993): 1707–91.

Harrod, Howard L. *The Animals Came Dancing: Native American Sacred Ecology and Animal Kinship*. Tucson: University of Arizona Press, 2000.

Hatley, Tom. "Cherokee Women Farmers Hold Their Ground." In *Appalachian Frontiers: Settlement, Society, and Development in the Pre-Industrial Era*, edited by Robert D. Mitchel, 37–51. Lexington: University of Kentucky Press, 1991.

Hatley, Tom. *The Dividing Paths: Cherokees and South Carolinians through the Era of Revolution*. Oxford: Oxford University Press, 1995.

Hay, Douglas. "Poaching and the Game Laws on Cannock Chase." In *Albion's Fatal Tree: Crime and Society in Eighteenth-Century England*, edited by Douglas Hay, Peter Linebaugh, John G. Rule, E. P. Thompson, and Calvin Winslow, 189–254. New York: Pantheon, 1975.

Hawkins, Benjamin. *Letters of Benjamin Hawkins, 1796–1806*. Georgia Historical Society Collections 9. Savannah: Georgia Historical Society, 1916.

Heat-Moon, William Least, and James K. Wallace, eds. and trans. *An Osage Journey to Europe, 1827–1830: Three French Accounts*. Norman: University of Oklahoma Press, 2013.

Herrmann, Rachel B. *No Useless Mouth: Waging War and Fighting Hunger in the American Revolution*. Ithaca: Cornell University Press, 2019.

Herrmann, Rachel B., ed. *To Feast on Us as Their Prey: Cannibalism and the Early Modern Atlantic*. Fayetteville: University of Arkansas Press, 2019.

Higgins, John. *Raymond Williams: Literature, Marxism and Cultural Materialism*. New York: Taylor & Francis, 2013.

Hill, Sarah H. *Cherokee Removal: Forts Along the Georgia Trail of Tears*. Washington, DC: National Park Service and the Georgia Department of Natural Resources/Historic Preservation Division, 2005.

Hobson, Charles F. *The Great Yazoo Lands Sale: The Case of* Fletcher v. Peck. Lawrence: University Press of Kansas, 2016.

Hood, Susan. "Termination of the Klamath Indian Tribe of Oregon." *Ethnohistory* 19, no. 4 (1972): 379–92.

Hoskins, T. H., and Paul Sesup. "An Indian on Indian Corn." *Garden and Forest* no. 8 (1895).

Houser, Steve, Linda Pelon, and Jimmy W. Arterberry. *Comanche Marker Trees of Texas*. College Station: Texas A&M University Press, 2016.

Hutton, Heather. "Narrating Sovereignty: The Covenant Chain in Intercultural Diplomacy." *Journal of Early American History* 9 (2019): 118–44.

Ingold, Timothy. *The Perception of the Environment: Essays in Livelihood, Dwelling, and Skill.* New York: Routledge, 2000.

Iverson, Peter. *When Indians Became Cowboys: Native Peoples and Cattle Ranching in the American West.* Norman: University of Oklahoma Press, 1994.

Jackson, Andrew. Andrew Jackson to James Monroe, 4 March 1817. In *The Papers of Andrew Jackson*. Vol. 4, 1816–1820, edited by Harold D. Moser, David R. Hoth, and George H. Hoemann. Knoxville: University of Tennessee Press, 1994.

Jackson, Andrew. "Second Annual Message [to Congress], December 6, 1830." In *A Compilation of the Messages and Papers of the Presidents, 1789–1897*. Vol. 2, edited James D. Richardson, 500–529. Washington, DC: Government Printing Office, 1900.

Jacobs, Margaret D. "A Battle for the Children: American Indian Child Removal in Arizona in the Era of Assimilation." *Journal of Arizona History* 45 (2004): 31–62.

Jacoby, Karl. *Crimes Against Nature: Squatters, Poachers, Thieves, and the Hidden History of American Conservation*. Berkeley: University of California Press, 2001.

Jacquet, Aurélie de Rus, Mitali Arun Tambe, Sin Ying Ma, George P. McCabe, Jay Hansford C. Vest, and Jean-Christophe Rochet. "Pikuni-Blackfeet Traditional Medicine: Neuroprotective Activities of Medicinal Plants Used to Treat Parkinson's Disease–Related Symptoms." *Journal of Ethnopharmacology* 206 (2017): 393–407.

James, Frank. "National Day of Mourning." In *Dawnland Voices: An Anthology of Indigenous Writing from New England*, edited by Siobhan Senier, 455–58. Lincoln: University of Nebraska Press, 2014.

James, Harry C. *Pages from Hopi History.* Tucson: University of Arizona Press, 1974.

Jefferson, Thomas. *Notes on the State of Virginia.* Boston: Lilly and Wait, 1832 [1787].

Jefferson, Thomas. Thomas Jefferson to William Wirt, 5 August 1815. In *The Papers of Thomas Jefferson*. Vol. 8, edited by J. Jefferson Looney, 641–46. Princeton: Princeton University Press, 2011.

Jemison, Mary. *A Narrative of the Life of Mrs. Mary Jemison.* Ann Arbor: University of Michigan Press, 1967 [1824].

Jennings, Francis. *The Invasion of America: Indians, Colonialism, and the Cant of Conquest*. Chapel Hill: University of North Carolina Press, 2010 [1975].

Jones, Karen R. *Epiphany in the Wilderness: Hunting, Nature, and Performance in the Nineteenth-Century American West*. Boulder: University Press of Colorado, 2016.

Josselyn, John. *An Account of Two Voyages to England*. London: Printed for Giles Widdows, 1673.

Kaldenbaugh, Henry H. "Statement of Dr. Henry H. Kaldenbaugh, USPHS, HIS, Rosebud, S. Dak." In United States Senate, *Supplementary Food Programs*, 318–19.

Kehoe, Thomas E. "The Boarding School Bison Drive Site." *Plains Anthropologist* 12, no. 35 (1967): 1–165.

Knoblauch, Frieda. *The Culture of Wilderness: Agriculture as Colonization in the American West*. Chapel Hill: University of North Carolina Press, 1996.

Kricher, John C. "Weeds." *New York Times*, July 12, 1981.
LaCombe, Michael. *Political Gastronomy: Food and Authority in the English Atlantic World*. Philadelphia: University of Pennsylvania Press, 2012.
Lal, Rattan. "Historical Development of No-Till Farming." In *Sustainable Agriculture and the International Rice-Wheat System*, edited by Rattan Lal, Peter R. Hobbs, Norman Uphoff, and David O. Hansen. New York: CRC Press, 2004.
LaPier, Rosalyn R. *Invisible Reality: Storytellers, Storytakers, and the Supernatural World of the Blackfeet*. Lincoln: University of Nebraska Press, 2017.
Lawson, Michael L. *Dammed Indians: The Pick-Sloan Plan and the Missouri River Sioux, 1944–1980*. Norman: University of Oklahoma Press, 1982.
Lawson, Michael L. *Dammed Indians Revisited: The Continuing History of the Pick-Sloan Plan and the Missouri River Sioux*. Pierre: South Dakota State Historical Society, 2009.
Lewis, Meriam, ed. *The Problem of Indian Administration*. Washington, DC: Government Printing Office, 1928.
Loew, Patty. "Hidden Transcripts in the Chippewa Treaty Rights Struggle: A Twice Told Story of Race, Resistance, and the Politics of Power." *American Indian Quarterly* 21, no. 4 (1997): 713–28.
Lomawaima, K. Tsianina. *They Called it Prairie Light: The Story of Chilocco Indian School*. Lincoln: University of Nebraska Press, 1994.
Love, William DeLoss. *The Fast and Thanksgiving Days of New England*. Cambridge, MA: Riverside Press, 1895.
Lowie, Robert H. *Robert H. Lowie, Ethnologist: A Personal Record*. Berkeley: University of California Press, 1959.
Many Hoops. "Wampanoag on Thanksgiving." Accessed July 12, 2021. http://manyhoops.com/wampanoag-on-thanksgiving.html.
Massachusetts Council. "At a Council, Held at Charlestown, June the 20th, 1676." Cambridge, MA: Samuel Green, 1676.
Mayer, Jean. "Diet of Indians Needs Upgrading." *Washington Post*, February 8, 1973.
McLoughlin, William. *After the Trail of Tears: The Cherokees' Struggle for Sovereignty, 1839–1880*. Chapel Hill: University of North Carolina Press, 1994.
McLoughlin, William. *Cherokee Renascence in the New Republic*. Princeton: Princeton University Press, 1986.
McNickle, D'Arcy. "Train Time." In D'Arcy McNickle, *The Hawk is Hungry and Other Stories*, edited by Birgit Hans, 47–54. Tucson: University of Arizona Press, 1992.
McWilliams, James E. *A Revolution in Eating: How the Quest for Food Shaped America*. New York: Columbia University Press, 2005.
McWilliams, James E. " 'Butter, Milk, and a Spare Rib': Women's Work and the Transatlantic Economic Transition in Seventeenth-Century Massachusetts." *New England Quarterly* 82, no. 1 (2009): 1–20.
Means, Lorelei DeCora. "Statement of Lorelei Means, Community Associate, Food Resources Program, North Central Regional Office, American Friends Service Committee, Porcupine, S. Dak." In United States Senate, *Commodity Distribution and Food Stamp Programs: Hearings*, 64–67.
Merchant, Carolyn. *Ecological Revolutions: Nature, Gender, and Science in New England*. Chapel Hill: University of North Carolina Press, 1989.

Merrell, James H. *Into the American Woods: Negotiators on the Pennsylvania Frontier.* New York: W. W. Norton, 2000.

Merrell, James H. "Second Thoughts on Colonial Historians and American Indians." *William and Mary Quarterly* 69, no. 3 (2012): 451–512.

Meyer, Melissa. *The White Earth Tragedy: Ethnicity and Dispossession at a Minnesota Anishinaabe Reservation, 1889–1920.* Lincoln: University of Nebraska Press, 1999.

Michno, Greg. *Encyclopedia of Indian Wars: Western Battles and Skirmishes, 1850–1890.* Missoula, MT: Mountain Press Publishing, 2003.

Mihesuah, Devon A. "Decolonizing our Diets by Recovering our Ancestors' Gardens." *American Indian Quarterly* 27, nos. 3–4 (2003): 807–39.

Mihesuah, Devon A. *Recovering our Ancestors' Gardens: Indigenous Recipes and Guide to Diet and Fitness.* 2nd edition. Lincoln: University of Nebraska Press, 2020 [2005].

Mihesuah, Devon A., and Elizabeth Hoover, eds. *Indigenous Food Sovereignty in the United States: Restoring Cultural Knowledge, Protecting Environments, and Regaining Health.* Norman: University of Oklahoma Press, 2019.

Milburn, Michael. "Indigenous Nutrition: Using Traditional Food Knowledge to Solve Contemporary Health Problems." *American Indian Quarterly* 26, nos. 3–4 (2004): 411–34.

Miller, Ian. "Feeding in the Workhouse: The Institutional and Ideological Functions of Food in Britain." *Journal of British Studies* 52, no. 4 (2013): 940–62.

Minnis, Paul E. *Famine Foods: Plants We Eat to Survive.* Tucson: University of Arizona Press, 2021.

Mitchell, Don. *The Lie of the Land: Migrant Workers and the California Landscape.* Minneapolis: University of Minnesota Press, 1996.

Moreton-Robinson, Aileen. *The White Possessive: Property, Power, and Indigenous Sovereignty.* Minneapolis: University of Minnesota Press, 2015.

Morgan, Lewis Henry. *House and House-life of the American Aborigines.* Washington, DC: US Government Printing Office, 1881.

Morison, Samuel Eliot. *The Oxford History of the American People.* Vol. 1, *Prehistory to 1789.* New York: Oxford University Press, 1927.

Morrell, William. "Morrell's Poem on New-England." In *Collections of the Massachusetts Historical Society*, 1st ser., vol. 1, 135. Boston: 1792.

Moulton, Gary, ed. *The Journals of the Lewis & Clark Expedition.* Accessed June 29, 2021. https://lewisandclarkjournals.unl.edu.

Mt. Pleasant, Jane. "The Paradox of Plows and Productivity: An Agronomic Comparison of Cereal Grain Production under Iroquois Hoe Culture and European Plow Culture in the Seventeenth and Eighteenth Centuries." *Agricultural History* 85, no. 2 (Fall 2011): 460–92

Mt. Pleasant, Jane, and Robert F. Burt. "Estimating Productivity of Traditional Iroquoian Cropping Systems from Field Experiments and Historical Literature." *Journal of Ethnobiology* 30 (Spring/Summer 2010): 52–79.

Murray, Wendi Field, María Nieves Zedeño, Kacy L. Hollenback, Calvin Grinnell, and Elgin Crows Breast. "The Remaking of Lake Sakakawea: Locating Cultural Viability in Negative Heritage on the Missouri River." *American Ethnologist* 38, no. 3 (2011): 468–83.

Nabhan, Gary Paul. *Enduring Seeds: Native American Agriculture and Wild Plant Cultivation*. Tucson: University of Arizona Press, 2016.

Nash, Margaret A. "Entangled Pasts: Land-Grant Colleges and American Indian Dispossession." *History of Education Quarterly* 59, no. 4 (2019): 437–67.

Norton, John. *The Journal of Major John Norton*, edited by Carl F. Klinck and James J. Talman. Toronto: Champlain Society, 1970.

Nugent, David. "Property Relations, Production Relations, and Inequality: Anthropology, Political Economy, and the Blackfeet," *American Ethnologist* 20, no. 2: 336–62.

O'Brien, Jean M. *Dispossession by Degrees: Indian Land and Identity in Natick, Massachusetts, 1650–1790*. Cambridge: University of Cambridge Press, 1997.

O'Brien, Jean M. *First and Lasting: Writing Indians Out of Existence in New England.* Minneapolis: University of Minnesota Press, 2010.

O'Sullivan, John L. "The Great Nation of Futurity." *United States Democratic Review* 6, no. 23 (1839): 426–30.

O'Toole, Fintan. *White Savage: William Johnson and the Invention of America*. New York: Farrar, Straus and Giroux, 2005.

Oakes, Elinor F. "A Ticklish Business: Dairying in New England and Pennsylvania, 1750–1812." *Pennsylvania History: A Journal of Mid-Atlantic Studies* 47, no. 3 (1980): 195–212.

Office of Indian Affairs. *Annual Report of the Commissioner of Indian Affairs, for the Year 1891*. Washington, DC: Government Printing Office, 1891.

Oliver, Sandra. *Food in Colonial and Federal America*. Westport, CT: Greenwood Publishing, 2005.

Organ, J. F., V. Geist, S. P. Mahoney, S. Williams, P. R. Krausman, G. R. Batcheller, T. A. Decker, R. Carmichael, P. Nanjappa, R. Regan, R. A. Medellin, R. Cantu, R. E. McCabe, S. Craven, G. M. Vecellio, and D. J. Decker. "The North American Model of Wildlife Conservation." *Wildlife Society Technical Review 12-04* (2012).

Parham, Vera. " 'It was a Spearhead of Change': The Fish-Ins of the Pacific Northwest and the Boldt Decision, Shifting Native American Protest Identities in the 1960s and 1970s." *Native Studies Review* 22, no. 1/2 (2013): 1–26.

Parker, Arthur C. *Iroquois Uses of Maize and Other Food Plants*. Albany: University of the State of New York, 1910.

Partoll, Albert J., ed. "The Blackfoot Indian Peace Council." *Frontier and Midland* 17, no. 3 (1937): 199–207.

Pasquaretta, Paul. *Gambling and Survival in Native North America*. Tucson: University of Arizona Press, 2003.

Perdue, Theda. *Cherokee Women: Gender and Culture Change, 1700–1835*. Lincoln: University of Nebraska Press, 1998.

Perdue, Theda, and Michael D. Green, *The Cherokee and the Trail of Tears*. New York: Penguin, 2007.

Perdue, Theda, and Michael D. Green, eds. *The Cherokee Removal: A Brief History with Documents*. 3rd edition. New York: Bedford/St. Martin's, 2016.

Philbrick, Nathaniel. *Mayflower: A Story of Courage, Community, and War*. New York: Viking, 2006.

Pope, Peter A. *Fish into Wine: The Newfoundland Plantation in the Seventeenth Century*. Chapel Hill: University of North Carolina Press, 2004.

Pratt, Richard Henry. *Battlefield and Classroom: Four Decades with the American Indian, 1867–1904*, edited by Robert M. Utley. Norman: University of Oklahoma Press, 2004.

Pratt, Richard Henry. "The Advantages of Mingling Indians with Whites." In *Americanizing the American Indian: Writings by the "Friends of the Indian," 1880–1900*, edited by Francis Paul Prucha, 260–71. Cambridge: Harvard University Press, 1973.

Pulsipher, Jenny Hale. *Subjects Unto the Same King: Indians, English, and the Contest for Authority in Colonial New England*. Philadelphia: University of Pennsylvania Press, 2005.

Rea, Amadeo M. *At the Desert's Green Edge: An Ethnobotany of the Gila River Pima*. Tucson: University of Arizona Press, 2016.

Reagan, Ronald. "Proclamation 5577: American Indian Week, November 24, 1986." In *Public Papers of the Presidents of the United States: Ronald Reagan, 1986*, 1586. Washington, DC: Government Printing Office.

Reeves, B. O. K. "Bison Killing in the Southwestern Alberta Rockies." *Plains Anthropologist* 23 (1978): 151–74.

Reher, C. A., and G. C. Frison. "The Vore Site, 48CK302, a Stratified Buffalo Jump in the Wyoming Black Hills." *Plains Anthropologist* 25 (1980).

Reisner, Marc. *Cadillac Desert: The American West and Its Disappearing Water*. New York: Penguin, 1986.

Rice, Henry M. "Pemmican [reprint]." *Minnesota Archaeologist* 40, no. 2 (1981): 96–100.

Richter, Daniel K. *Facing East from Indian Country: A Native History of Early America*. Cambridge, MA: Harvard University Press, 2001.

Richter, Daniel K. "War and Culture: The Iroquois Experience." *William and Mary Quarterly* 40, no. 4 (October 1983): 528–59.

Richter, Daniel K., and James H. Merrell, eds. *Beyond the Covenant Chain: The Iroquois and their Neighbors in Indian North America, 1600–1800*. Syracuse: Syracuse University Press, 1987

Rosier, Paul. *Rebirth of the Blackfeet Nation, 1912–1954*. Lincoln: University of Nebraska Press, 2001.

Ruppel, Kristin. *Unearthing Indian Land: Living with the Legacies of Allotment*. Tucson: University of Arizona Press, 2008.

Russell, John C. *Treasure State Tycoon: Nelson Story and the Making of Montana*. Helena: Montana Historical Society Press, 2019.

Salisbury, Neal. *Manitou and Providence: Indians, Europeans, and the Making of New England, 1500–1643*. New York: Oxford University Press, 1984.

Salmón, Enrique. *Eating the Landscape: American Indian Stories of Food, Identity, and Resilience*. Tucson: University of Arizona Press, 2012.

Saysewahum, Sylvia McAdam. *Nationhood Interrupted: Revitalizing nêhiyaw Legal Systems*. Vancouver: University of British Columbia Press, 2015.

Schneider, Fred. " 'Corn in the Crib is Like Money in the Bank': George F. Will and the Oscar H. Will and Company, 1917–1955." *North Dakota History* 76, nos. 1–2 (2010): 2–25.

Schneider, Fred. "Oscar H. Will: North Dakota's Pioneer Seedman." *North Dakota History* 68, no. 1 (2001): 2–19.

Seeman, Erik R. *The Huron-Wendat Feast of the Dead: Indian-European Encounters in Early North America*. Baltimore: Johns Hopkins University Press, 2011.

Sherman, Sean, and Beth Dooley. *The Sioux Chef's Indigenous Kitchen*. Minneapolis: University of Minnesota Press, 2017.

Silverman, David J. *This Land is Their Land: The Wampanoag Indians, Plymouth Colony, and the Troubled History of Thanksgiving*. New York: Bloomsbury, 2019.

Siskind, Janet. "The Invention of Thanksgiving: A Ritual of American Nationality." *Critique of Anthropology* 12, no. 2 (1992): 167–91.

Skinner, Claiborne. "The Sinews of Empire: The Voyageurs and the Carrying Trade of the Pays D'en Haut. 1681–1754." PhD diss., University of Illinois at Chicago, 1991.

Smalley, Andrea L. *Wild By Nature: North American Animals Confront Colonization*. Baltimore: Johns Hopkins University Press, 2017.

Smith, Daniel Scott. "The Demographic History of Colonial New England." *Journal of Economic History* 32, no. 1 (1972): 165–83.

Snake, Reuben. "Being Indian Is . . ." Reuben Snake Papers. National Museum of the American Indian Archives, Suitland, MD.

Spence, Mark David. *Dispossessing the Wilderness: Indian Removal and the Making of the National Parks*. Oxford: Oxford University Press, 1999.

Spence, Taylor. "The Canada Thistle: The Pestilence of American Colonialism and the Emergence of an Exceptionalist Identity, 1783–1839." *Agricultural History* 90, no. 4 (2016): 511–44.

Stark, Heidi Kiiwetinepinesiik. "Nenabhozo's Smart Berries: Rethinking Tribal Sovereignty and Accountability." *Michigan State Law Review* 339 (2013): 339–53.

Starkey, Marion Lena. *The Cherokee Nation*. New York: Alfred E. Knopf, 1946.

Starna, William A., George R. Hamell, and William L. Butts. "Northern Iroquoian Horticulture and Insect Infestation: A Cause for Village Removal." *Ethnohistory* 31, no. 3 (1984): 197–207.

Thomas, Peter A. "Contrastive Subsistence Strategies and Land Use as Factors for Understanding Indian-White Relations in New England." *Ethnohistory* 23, no. 1 (1976): 1–18.

Thompson, David. *The Writings of David Thompson*, edited by William Moreau. Toronto: Champlain Society, 2009.

Thompson, E. P. *Whigs and Hunters: The Origin of the Black Act*. New York: Pantheon, 1975.

Thorpe, Francis Newton, ed. "Charter of Georgia, 1732." In *The Federal and State Constitutions, Colonial Charters, and Other Organic Laws of the State, Territories, and Colonies Now or Heretofore Forming the United States of America*. Vol. 2, 765–77. Washington, DC: Government Printing Office, 1909.

Thrush, Coll. "Vancouver the Cannibal: Cuisine, Encounter, and the Dilemma of Difference on the Northwest Coast, 1774–1808." *Ethnohistory* 58, no. 1 (2011): 1–35.

Treuer, David. *The Heartbeat of Wounded Knee: Native America from 1890 to the Present*. New York: Penguin, 2019.

Trimble, Charles E. "Statement of Charles E. Trimble, Executive Director, National Congress of American Indians." In United States Senate, *Commodity Distribution and Food Stamp Programs: Hearings*, 83–87.

Trumbull, J. Hammond, ed. *The Public Records of the Colony of Connecticut*. Vol. 2. Hartford: F. A. Brown, 1850.

Ulrich, Laurel Thatcher. *Good Wives: Image and Reality in the Lives of Women in Northern New England, 1650–1750*. New York: Alfred A. Knopf, 1982.

Unidentified author. "Indian Leader from Federal Dam Tries Business World." *Brainerd Dispatch*. August 16, 2000.

Unidentified author. "Inspection of Blackfeet Agency and Charges against Agent Allen," October 10, 1885 (5017). In Bureau of Indian Affairs, *Reports of the Inspection of the Field Jurisdictions of the Office of Indian Affairs, 1873–1900*, Reel 2.

Unidentified author. "Native Activist Gets into Food Business. *Deseret News*. August 15, 2000.

Unidentified author. Reply to Circular No. 2546, February 2, 1929. In Thomas J. Walsh and John Edward Erickson Papers, 1910–1934. Library of Congress, Washington, DC.

Unidentified author. Robert Hamilton student file. Records of the Carlisle Indian Industrial School. Record Group 75, Student Records 1879–1918, Series 1327. National Archives and Records Administration, Washington, DC.

United States Department of Agriculture, Food and Nutrition Service. *Report to the Select Committee on Nutrition and Human Needs, United States Senate, by the Comptroller General of the United States: Administration and Effectiveness of Family Food Programs on Selected Indian Reservations in New Mexico and South Dakota*. A-51604. Washington, DC: Government Printing Office, 1973.

United States Senate. *Commodity Distribution and Food Stamp Programs: Hearings Before the Subcommittee on Agricultural Research and General Legislation of the Committee on Agriculture and Forestry, United States Senate, Ninety-Third Congress, Second Session, on S. 2871 and S. 3235*. Washington, DC: Government Printing Office, 1974.

United States Senate. *Food Stamps: Hearing Before the Subcommittee on Nutrition of the Committee on Agriculture, Nutrition, and Forestry, United States Senate, Ninety-Fifth Congress, First Session.* Washington, DC: Government Printing Office, 1977.

United States Senate. *Supplementary Food Programs*. Part 3 of *Federal Food Programs—1973: Hearings Before the Select Committee on Nutrition and Human Needs of the United States Senate, Ninety-Third Congress, First Session.* Washington, DC: Government Printing Office, 1973.

Van Sittert, Lance. " 'The Seed Blows About in Every Breeze': Noxious Weed Eradication in the Cape Colony, 1860–1909." *Journal of Southern African Studies* 26, no. 4 (2000): 655–74.

Vialles, Noelie. *Animal to Edible*, translated by J. A. Underwood. Cambridge: Cambridge University Press, 1994.

Vick, R. Alfred. "Cherokee Adaptation to the Landscape of the West and Overcoming the Loss of Culturally Significant Plants." *American Indian Quarterly* 35, no. 3 (2011): 395–417.

Vizenor, Gerald. "Firewater Labels and Methodologies." *American Indian Quarterly* 7, no. 4 (1983): 25–36.

Volo, James M., and Dorothy Denneen Voto. *Family Life in 17th and 18th Century America*. Westport, CT: Greenwood Publishing, 2006.
Volts, Jeanne. "Overcoming Food Stamp Reservations: Havasupai Were Using Commodity Distribution." *Los Angeles Times*, December 21, 1972.
Wallace, Anthony F. C. *The Long Bitter Trail: Andrew Jackson and the Indians*. New York: Hill & Wang, 1993.
Wallace, Paul A. W. *Conrad Weiser, 1696–1760: Friend of Colonist and Mohawk*. 1945.
Wallach, Jennifer Jensen. *How America Eats: A Social History of U.S. Food and Culture*. Washington, DC: Rowman & Littlefield, 2013.
Warren, Louis. *The Hunter's Game: Poachers and Conservationists in Twentieth-Century America*. New Haven: Yale University Press, 1999.
Washington, George. George Washington to James Duane, September 7, 1783. In *The Writings of George Washington*, Vol. 27, edited by John C. Fitzpatrick, 140. Washington, DC: Government Printing Office, 1940.
Washington, George. George Washington to Major-General John Sullivan, May 31, 1779. In *Letters and Papers of Major-General John Sullivan*, Vol. 3, edited by Otis G. Hammond, 48–49. Concord, NH: 1939.
Washington, George. "Talk to the Cherokee Nation, August 29, 1796." In *The Writings of George Washington*, Vol. 35, edited by John C. Fitzpatrick, 193. Washington, DC: Government Printing Office, 1940.
Waugh, F. W. *Iroquois Foods and Food Preparation*. Ottawa: Government Printing Bureau, 1916.
Weaver, William Woys. *Heirloom Vegetable Gardening: A Master Gardener's Guide to Planting, Seed Saving, and Cultural History*. Stillwater, MN: Voyageur Press, 2018 [1997].
Wessel Research Papers. Montana State University Special Collections.
Wessel, Thomas R. "Agriculture and Iroquois Hegemony in New York, 1610–1779." *Maryland Historian* 1 (1970): 93–104.
Wessel, Thomas R. "Political Assimilation on the Blackfeet Reservation, 1887–1934: A Study in Survival." In *Plains Indian Studies: A Collection of Essays in Honor of John C. Ewers and Waldo R. Wedel*, edited by Douglas H. Ubelaker and Herman J. Viola, 59–72. Smithsonian Contributions to Anthropology 30. Washington, DC: Smithsonian Institution Press, 1982.
Wessels, Tom. *Forest Forensics: A Field Guide to Reading the Forested Landscape*. Woodstock, VT: Countryman Press, 2010.
Whaley, Gray H. *Oregon and the Collapse of Illahee: U.S. Empire and the Collapse of an Indigenous World, 1792–1859*. Chapel Hill: University of North Carolina Press, 2010.
White, Kyle Powys. "Food Sovereignty, Justice, and Indigenous Peoples: An Essay on Settler Colonialism and Collective Continuance." In *The Oxford Handbook of Food Ethics*, edited by Anne Barnhill, Tyler Doggett, and Mark Budolfson, 345–66. Oxford: Oxford University Press, 2018.
White, Richard. *The Organic Machine: The Remaking of the Columbia River*. New York: Hill & Wang, 1996.
White Eagle, Melvin. "Statement of Melvin White Eagle, Chairman, Standing Rock Sioux Tribe, Fort Yates, N. Dak., and Chairman, United Tribes of North

Dakota." In United States Senate, *Commodity Distribution and Food Stamp Programs: Hearings*, 152–54.

Wickman, Thomas. " 'Winters Embittered with Hardships': Severe Cold, Wabanaki Power, and English Adjustments, 1690–1710." *William and Mary Quarterly* 72, no. 1 (2015): 57–98.

Willerslev, Rane. *Soul Hunters: Hunting, Animism, and Personhood Among the Siberian Yukaghirs*. Berkeley: University of California Press, 2007.

Williams, Raymond, and Michael Orrom. *Preface to Film*. London: Film Drama Limited, 1954.

Williams, Robert A. *Linking Arms Together: American Indian Treaty Visions of Law and Peace, 1600–1800*. New York: Routledge, 1999.

Williams, Roger. *A Key into the Language of America*. Boston: Applewood Books, 1997 [1643].

Williams, Samuel Cole, ed. "Journey of the Moravians to the Cherokee and Cumberland Countries (1799)." In *Early Travels in the Tennessee Country, 1540–1800*. Johnson City, TN: Watauga Press, 1928.

Wilson, Gilbert L., and Waheenee, *Native American Gardening: Buffalobird-Woman's Guide to Traditional Methods*. Mineola, NY: Dover Publications, 2005.

Wilson, Gilbert L. "Agriculture of the Hidatsa Indians: An Indian Interpretation." In *Studies in the Social Sciences*, no. 9. Minneapolis: University of Minnesota, 1917.

Wilson, Gilbert L. *Buffalo Bird Woman's Garden: The Classic Account of Hidatsa American Indian Gardening Techniques*. St. Paul: Minnesota Historical Society Press, 1987.

Wilson, Gilbert L. "The Horse and the Dog in Hidatsa Culture." In Anthropological Papers of the American Museum of Natural History, vol. 15, edited by Clark Wissler, 125–312. New York: American Museum Press, 1924.

Wilson, Gilbert L. *Waheenee: An Indian Girl's Story*. Lincoln: University of Nebraska Press, 1981.

Winslow, Edwin, and William Bradford. *Mourt's Relation or Journal of the Plantation at Plymouth*, edited by Henry Martin Dexter. Boston: John Kimball Wiggin, 1865.

Winter, Joseph C. *Tobacco Use by Native North Americans: Sacred Smoke and Silent Killer*. Norman: University of Oklahoma Press, 2000.

[Wirt, William?]. "Reflections on the Institutions of the Cherokee Indians, from Observations Made during a Recent Visit to That Tribe: In a Letter from a Gentleman of Virginia, to Robert Walsh, Jun.—June 1st, 1817," *Analectic Magazine* 12 (1818): 36–56.

Wise, Michael D. "Colonial Beef and the Blackfeet Reservation Slaughterhouse, 1879–1895." *Radical History Review* 110 (2011): 59–82.

Wise, Michael D. "Meat." In *The Routledge History of American Foodways*, edited by Michael D. Wise and Jennifer Jensen Wallach, 97–112. New York: Routledge, 2016.

Wise, Michael D. *Producing Predators: Wolves, Work, and Conquest in the Northern Rockies*. Lincoln: University of Nebraska Press, 2016.

Wise, Michael D. "The Place That Feeds You: Allotment and the Struggle for Blackfeet Food Sovereignty." In *Food Across Borders*, edited by Matt Garcia, E. Melanie DuPuis, and Don Mitchell, 163–80. New Brunswick: Rutgers University Press, 2017.

Wisecup, Kelly, ed. "*Good News from New England*," *by Edward Winslow: A Scholarly Edition*. Amherst: University of Massachusetts Press, 2014.

Wolf, Eric R. *Europe and the People Without History*. Berkeley: University of California Press, 1982.

Wood, William. *Wood's New-England's Prospect*. Boston: John Wilson and Son, 1865.

Young, Kim J. *Ethnobotany*. New York: Chelsea House, 2007.

Zedeño, Maria Nieves, Jesse A. M. Ballenger, and John R. Murray. "Landscape Engineering and Organizational Complexity among Late Prehistoric Bison Hunters of the Northwestern Plains." *Current Anthropology* 55, no. 1 (2014): 23–58.

Zhang, Albert J., Agnes M. Rimanod, Wilbert Fish, Srinivasa R. Mentreddy, and Suresh T. Mathews. "Serviceberry [*Amelanchier alnifolia* (Nutt.) *Nutt.* ex. *M. Roem* (Rosaceae)] Leaf Extract Inhibits Mammalian A-Glucosidase Activity and Suppresses Postprandial Glycemic Response in a Mouse Model of Diet-Induced Obesity and Hyperglycemia." *Journal of Ethnopharmacology* 143 (2012): 481–87.

INDEX